The Politics of
Waking Up

D1616081

PER
SPEC
TIVA

Introducing Perspectiva Press

Soul food for expert generalists

Perspectiva seeks to understand the relationship between systems, souls and society in a time of crisis, and to develop methods, grounded in an applied philosophy of education, to help us meet the challenges of our time.

As part of this broader endeavour, Perspectiva Press will specialise in short books with occasional longer works. These books will be well-presented and distinctive. Their purpose is to shape and share thinking that helps to:

- create a community of expert generalists with skills of synthesis and epistemic agility
- envisage a world beyond consumerism, and pathways for how we might get there
- support sociological imagination in a dynamic ecological and technological context
- cultivate spiritual sensibility; clarifying how it manifests and why it matters
- encourage a more complex and systemic understanding of the world
- commit to going beyond critique, by developing vision and method
- indicate how we can do pluralism better; epistemic, cultural, political, spiritual
- clarify what it means to become the change we want to see in the world
- develop the authority of people doing important work aligned with Perspectiva

It is unusual for a charity like Perspectiva to become a publisher, even a small one, but we value books as dignified cultural artefacts with their own kind of analogue power, and we believe ideas travel further and connect more deeply when they are rooted in the mandate of a publication designed to last for years, not merely moments. We also see a gap in the market for books that specialise in the kinds of integrative and imaginative sensibilities that speak to the challenges of our time.

Already published:

The World We Create: From god to market   *Tomas Björkman*
An entrepreneur offers an historical perspective on achieving a more meaningful and sustainable world

To be published in 2021:

Unlearn: A compass for radical transformation   *Hanno Burmester*
A compass for societal transformation, arising from the personal testimony of coming out in the shadow of Nazi Germany

The Entangled Activist: Learning to recognise the master's tools   *Anthea Lawson*
A seasoned campaigner on how your sense of agency changes when you realise 'getting the bastards' is not working

Collective Wisdom in the West: Beyond the shadows of the enlightenment   *Liam Kavanagh*
A cognitive scientist and contemplative on the nature of 'collective wisdom' and what we need to do to get there

Dispatches from a Time Between Worlds: Crisis and emergence in metamodernity   *Authors include Jonathan Rowson (ed), Layman Pascal (ed), Zak Stein, Bonnitta Roy, Daniel Görtz, Lene Rachel Andersen, Sarah Stein Lubrano, Minna Salami, John Vervaeke and Christopher Mastropietro, Tom Murray, Mark Vernon and Jonathan Jong, Siva Thambisetty, Jeremy Johnson, Brent Cooper*
An anthology of metamodern scholars and writers on our world-historical context and pathways to cultural renaissance

'The *Politics of Waking Up* invites us into a deeply personal conversation about how we can transform the world today to create a thriving society and planet. Indra Adnan's fractal approach to politics is a promising response to the fragmentation, polarization, despair, and disconnect that many people are feeling. This is democracy for the future, and it involves all of us, right here and right now. As Indra puts it, "wanting is not enough: it needs organization." The book is full of real-world examples of our potential for quantum social change, and it wakes us all to what is possible.'
Karen O'Brien, Professor of Human Geography, University of Oslo, Nobel Peace laureate with Intergovernmental Panel on Climate Change in 2007

'Laying important groundwork for the political transformation we need … Indra Adnan offers a penetrating analysis on the structural pathology of our current political system, which serves as a launching pad to explore the profound sociopolitical transformation beginning to take shape across the world. The book reorients us to a fundamentally different outlook on power dynamics, putting human agency and community at the heart of politics. With inspirational and illustrative examples from around the globe, Adnan introduces us to powerful new concepts such as fractal scaling, CANs (Citizen Action Networks, aka Community Agency Networks), and innovative forms of group decision-making which, taken together, provide the tools for "occupying the future" with a regenerative, life-affirming vision.'
Jeremy Lent, Author of The Patterning Instinct: A Cultural History of Humanity's Search for Meaning and Requiem of the Human Soul

'A passionately informed book that opens your eyes to a brave new world. Indra Adnan's beautifully crafted radical manifesto provides hope for our troubled earth and broken politics with illuminating intensity. Of interest to all who are looking for a blueprint for our future. A hugely important addition to the current literature on social change, enabling us to reimagine and co-create the world we want to live in.'
Marina Cantacuzino, Founder, The Forgiveness Project

'Powerful, provocative, brave and compassionate – *The Politics of Waking Up* is packed with cutting-edge ideas for how we can transform our politics, our relationships and ourselves, all while recognising that in the end this is one single endeavour. Drawing on her experience as both a psychotherapist and a political campaigner, Indra Adnan is perfectly placed to set out a new agenda that understands and acts on the feedback loops between our states of mind and the state of our communities and the world.'
Alex Evans, Author The Myth Gap, *Founder of Larger Us*

'It is incredibly important that clear thinking emerges now to guide us through the maelstrom – *The Politics of Waking Up* does just that.'
Peter Macfadyen, First Independent Mayor of Frome

'Even we who work for a radical transformation of human politics are challenged to emerge from a host of obsolete habits and presumptions. While brilliant men do "sensemaking" to abstract new principles and strategies to redesign governance, they miss that our current predicament is not a problem that can ever be "figured out". So the most enlightened seem mostly ineffectual and irrelevant. We're blessed that a wise woman is coming to our aid in these pages, inviting us into relationship and listening deeply for our deepest needs and aspirations. *The Politics of Waking Up* is not just brilliant and disarming, it's genuinely different. Instead of merely affirming hope, Indra Adnan provides it. She breaks genuinely new ground by sharing the living, embodied process of a new post-patriarchal political paradigm, the radical soft power of coming together humanly, to take care of our shared cosmolocal lives and future.'
Terry Patten, author and founder of A New Republic of the Heart and co-author of Integral Life Practice

'I picked this book up on Saturday morning and couldn't put it down again. I loved it. I read it in one sitting and by Saturday night my head was spinning with ideas and inspirations.'
Phil Teer, co-founder of St Luke's creative agency, author of The Coming Age of Imagination

'The world it is at a tipping point – emotionally, economically and ecologically. At any moment everything could so easily go deadly wrong. We try to tell ourselves and our kids that there will be a happy ending to the present crises. But do we honestly believe it? Do we feel it? Or is the truth rather that many of us have difficulties even imagining a better, more meaningful and brighter future. Indra Adnan's new book will help us all believe in the possibility of that happy ending. It is an astonishing and deeply moving political vision as well as a concrete road map to a better, more meaningful, deeply democratic, equal and awake society with just the right daring dance between mind, soul and body. Between I, we and the world. Adnan's book is a heady cocktail containing a wonderful mix of Buddhism, feminism and anarchism. And what's not to like about that? In short: I was blown away after reading this book. You will be too.'
Uffe Elbæk, founder of Kaospilot (School for Creative Leadership and Meaningful Entrepreeurship), co-founder of Alternativet and Independent Green political parties, Denmark

'What a book! It integrates everything so well: science, spirituality, conceptual frameworks, what's going on on the ground. It's a deeply compassionate account of who we are and what we need, and what we could be. Relationships with those who share our common values, and those that don't, who share a common humanity: that's how to change things. This hopeful and timely book shows how each of us who is working for change locally is building something bigger, something fractal that is beginning to transform the world order. This decade needs the kind of integral and connected thinking that this book so eloquently articulates. A reasoned and compassionate call to hope, and to action.'
Margaret Mulowska, co-founder Trust the People

The Politics of Waking Up

Power and possibility in the fractal age

Indra Adnan

Perspectiva Press, London, UK

systems-souls-society.com

First published in 2021

ISBN (pbk) 978-1-9998368-4-9
ISBN (POD) 978-1-914568-01-5
ISBN (ebk) 978-1-9998368-8-7

Illustrations Christopher Burrows

Cover design Studio Sutherl&

Typeset in Baskerville and Akzidenz Grotesk by www.ShakspeareEditorial.org

For Connor/RegenA

Contents

Introduction   1

Ada!   1

Reimagining power; The case for an Alternative; Conflict transformation; Integral philosophy; Expanding the feminine; The shocking soft power of story; Emotional needs and resources; The party is over; The Alternative UK; A new politics kicking off

1 Acute Challenges, Keenly Felt   21

What is waking up?   24

Before and after the World Wide Web; Movements popping up across the globe; Covid the accelerator; Black lives mattering; Humanity gets self-conscious

What are we waking up from?   31

What are we waking up to?   33

Desire and attraction; Gaming and harnessing our attention; Infinite fragmentation

Can we get on with our lives?   38

Look and you will find; New signs of response-ability; Patterns and fractals

Upgrading ourselves   42

Internal and external technologies; Autonomy, agency and futurism; The whole human system

2 Where is the Human Agency in Party Politics?   46

The story of powerlessness   47
Reconnecting I–We–World; Realms as lenses; Insights from quantum physics

The legacy of disconnect   52

Paying attention to the future   54

3 The Story of 'I'   55

3.1 Why we are hooked on our self-destruction   55
The illusion of freedom; Never enough attention or control; Legacy of Mad Men

3.2 Our inner Russian doll   62
When Maslow is misleading; Integral operating systems; Women seeing differently; Internal and external diversity

3.3 Being more than the self   70
Through death to becoming; A spiritual journey in public; The existential challenge of Burning Man; A virtual self: what happened during Covid

4 The Story of 'We'   79

4.1 Our failure to come together till now   79
Multiple forms of agency; Herding cats is old school; New forms of 'we' appear in virtual spaces; The era of the non-state actor points at people power

4.2 Everyone has a story   89
You can't just make it up; Pattern-matching and emotional authenticity; Tribes are glued together by myth; Soft power wraps hard power; Sci-fi is not doing its job

4.3 Relationship as the rebel act   97
No one is immune to success; An economy built on disconnection; Relationship hacks the system

4.4 Feminising the future   103
Where can we find the conscious feminine?; When masculine culture destroys men; Networks, emotional literacy, relational structures; Feminine leadership saving lives

5 Where is the World?   113

5.1 What planet are you living on?   113
Globaliser, Earthling or Worldist?; The ambition of cosmolocalism; Organising co-evolves; Hashtag global emotions

5.2 A new global architecture   123
Scaffolding for the new system arising; A skeleton of global governance; Fractals spontaneously scaling; How each one of us takes part

6 From the Map to the Territory   130

6.1 The story of Alternativet DK and The Alternative UK   130
What is the politics of all this?; Uffe Elbæk and the politics of human agency; Why and how The Alternative UK was born

6.2 Containers, constitutes, platforms   142
Getting traction; Co-labs: experimenting with collaboration; A fourth-sector platform shaping up

6.3 Citizen/community action/agency networks: CANs   148
Meeting our emotional needs; Principles, values, affordances; Feminisation of culture and form; Indigenous design and development

7 The New Socio-Politics   155

7.1 Freedom and Independents   155
Flatpackers make democracy look easy; A friendly kind of anarchism; A rising tide of Independents; Forging parallel power; But what about Me?

7.2 Cosmolocalism and the next economies   167
What is a living?; The Three Horizons; The blind men and the elephant; Covid opens eyes everywhere; Our chance to Bounce Beyond

7.3 The feel of it all   180

Goodbye airless rooms, manels and a fixation on the past; Festivals prefiguring, theatre incubating, music liberating, dance embodying; Living the larger life

8. Now What? The Future Arising   185

Being and intending; Integrity and truth-force; Creating the conditions for response-ability; How to get from here to there; The quantum social change now possible

9 Backwards and Forwards   195

The Mother of all challenges; Back to Telawa; Forward from Telawa; As of now; Hold your nerve

Afterworlds   208

Endnotes   213

Acknowledgements   232

Index   237

Figures

Figure 3.1 Maslow's hierarchy of needs　　　　　*63*

Figure 3.2 Ken Wilber's AQAL (all quadrants all levels)
incorporating Don Beck's spiral dynamics　　　　*66*

Introduction

Ada!

TELAWA: A small village in Central Java under military rule in mid-eighties Indonesia.

In this clearing in the forest, water was an hour's walk away and the land had been barren for a decade. The army was delivering food once a week: an improvement on earlier years for which the people were grateful. In a country that was 93 per cent Muslim, the village practice was still guided by Adat: local indigenous wisdom.[1] They were content though apathetic: the young people in particular were torn between leaving and looking after their elders.

I was a rookie journalist rediscovering my roots in Indonesia, where my father was born and raised. I had recently started spending time with a group of Buddhist 'anarchists' in a retreat in the mountains of Bandung, a major university town just outside Jakarta – led by a man called Senosoenoto, a family friend. I'd heard stories of social upheaval: how members of the super-privileged classes were joining in with the marginalised, particularly Chinese, immigrants, to study lessons from Japanese Buddhism about overcoming poverty and social transformation. When I heard that they had been invited by the Chief of Telawa to share their stories, I was keen to tag along.

On our arrival, everyone gathered to listen to a talk by Senosoenoto that I couldn't understand – my Indonesian was still very sketchy. Even so, I was mesmerised by the rhythm of the words, frequently interspersed with the phrase Ada. When he said it, everyone paid attention, including me. Despite my inability to grasp what I sensed were deep, challenging lessons, I was strangely moved and uplifted.

In conversation afterwards, I heard that Ada translated roughly to 'it's there'. Senosoenoto used it as a pattern of speech connecting the negative to the affirmative. Such as: you think there are no resources for you, there are. Or: you think you have no power, you do. When I try to recall it all these years later, I realise it was not a series of questions to which he had the answer; it was more like a drawing of the landscape of our minds. He described thoughts arising, responses coming – but not in the more familiar ruminative way, where questions escalate to fear. Instead, he was telling a wider story of abundance, where our sense of helplessness was being allowed to diminish in the face of our infinite resourcefulness.

After the lecture, they chanted together, then made a circle in which they exchanged their experiences of life, young and old. The children were hesitant, the elders philosophical. They talked about what the future might hold, mostly as if it wasn't in their hands. Before leaving, the leader of our pack invited them to study and chant together regularly and made himself available should they want to meet again.

Returning by invitation to Telawa six months later, we found some remarkable improvements. The villagers had found a way to bring water to the village. There were strips of land ploughed and already showing the green shoots of crops growing. A road had been built connecting one side of the village to the other. More homes had been constructed, allowing young couples to set up their own homes close to their parents.

The Buddhists offered another study lecture, with the same gentle storytelling. Again, they chanted and opened the circle for sharing at the end. This time, the energy was high – villagers jumped up to give their account of how they had started something new since we'd last visited. In particular, I noticed the young people speaking up with confidence about connections they had made to people outside the village. When we asked them what had changed, they couldn't be sure – other than that they had been inspired by our visit to meet regularly, study and chant together, exchange experiences and talk about the future.

In several of the reports I heard the word Ada, 'it's there': it moved like a flame constantly catching between them. I felt I was witnessing magic.

Over the next few months I spent much more time with the Buddhists and felt myself transformed by my interactions with them. I read relevant books and pondered philosophical questions about what poverty is, why the world is in the state it is in, how to overcome anger and greed. The more I reflected, the better I understood Ada – it's there: we already have the answers, the resources, the capacities, if we wake up to them. I felt I was waking up in their presence, but my questions kept coming.

I resisted joining their organisation (Nichiren Shoshu Indonesia[2]) or even chanting with them, staying doggedly with my journalistic stance, filing my reports for Condé Nast back home on this extraordinary social-political-economic phenomenon. How they were bringing communities together in remote parts of Indonesia (which has 13,000 islands), starting new businesses, telling a new story about social cohesion. But when my sister announced she was getting married in London and I should return home, I suddenly decided to jump in and sign up. In the days before I left Indonesia,

I received a mandala to chant to, becoming a fully fledged member of what I later understood was a global Buddhist movement.

While I then felt like I was giving in to something, if willingly, I now understand how important that act of immersion into the practice of NS Buddhism was, as an answer to my questions about how change happens. It would never be enough to witness and comment on both the daily challenges and extraordinary experiences of others, while holding onto my own agenda for change. I needed to take part in the action. It was like seeing the benefits of exercise without ever getting off the couch or becoming a therapist without being in therapy. My own issues, and all the things I cared about, would never be addressed if I didn't subject myself as well. As a therapist, not engaging would leave me with unconscious biases which in turn would affect the way I listened to clients. As a social agent of any kind, I had to be part of the experiments I was observing to really understand their power.

Until that last day in Indonesia, I had been holding myself separate, keeping myself safe. Not only from disappointment – afraid that nothing is ever as good as it looks from the outside – but from the inevitable challenge of becoming responsible for the story of change I had been amplifying. Even as I jumped into my new practices, I hadn't fully understood that becoming response-able *was* the personal revolution that has to occur before the social revolution becomes possible.

Reimagining power

What happened next for me was a series of journeys on the route to understanding what power is and where our agency lies as human beings on this ailing planet. I forayed into the worlds of conflict, hard and soft power and eventually politics, where I joined the management board of a political think tank and even stood to be an MP. I am writing this book now because, during the Covid crisis, many of the pieces of a puzzle I've been working out all my life now newly present themselves as a workable assemblage: a picture of human agency that works for the health of the planet, via the health of communities not unlike those in Telawa. Thanks to the arrival of the internet in the 1990s and the steep learning curve we have all been on since then, we can for the first time share solutions at a global scale. What looked like magic 30 years ago is now possible to understand as a set of perfect conditions coming together, to produce an unexpected outcome.

On The Alternative UK platform that I started with my partner Pat Kane in 2017, we have been working on these shifts. We are building a new axis for a politics that is fit for the 21st century – the reconnection of citizens to planet via what we call waking cosmolocal communities: I to We to World. It's a peoples' politics that can get us out of the mess we are in.

We embarked on this journey as a direct result of the murder of British Labour Party MP Jo Cox on 16 June 2016, one week before the British referendum on our membership of the European Union. At that moment I was on the island of Bornholm taking part in Folkmodet – an annual festival of politics off the coast of Denmark in which voters mingle easily with politicians to discuss the issues of the day. I was there as a guest of Alternativet, a new political party started by global entrepreneur Uffe Elbæk that had become the fastest-growing party in Denmark – and was having the time of my life.

The energy, creativity and joy of the Alternativet crew was unlike anything I had ever experienced until then in British politics. My own involvement with the progressive left, including being a board member of the think tank Compass[3] and even standing to be an MP for the Labour Party, had left me disconnected from my psycho-social-spiritual past. Now here was a story about rich human potential, diverse participation and the urgent needs of the planet which appealed strongly to young people and the newly politicised engine of Alternativet. The political programme had been crowdsourced through political laboratories, open to everyone, all over the country. It was refreshingly different from the dry, deeply divisive politics that I knew.

Some months before my Denmark visit, I had published a Compass paper titled 'Is the Party Over?' In this I criticised the structure, culture and dullness of political life that accounted for only 2 per cent of the UK electorate becoming members.[4] More importantly, our first past the post system – awarding the seat to the winner in each constituency, even when the proportion of their vote is significantly below 50 per cent – had created a propensity for overly simplified, oppositional messaging.[5] Left versus Right, rich versus poor, them versus us. This was never more so than in the Brexit Referendum, where Leave versus Remain had become a dangerous hotbed of crude rhetoric. Leavers were being pilloried as xenophobic and deluded for their dream of 'taking back control' of the future. Remainers were branded 'enemies of the people' for trying to stop them.

When I heard that Jo Cox, a long-term campaigner for national unity, had been shot and stabbed in the streets of her constituency for wanting to Remain, I felt a sudden and deep certainty that UK party politics was irremediably broken: we needed an alternative. Over the 24 hours that followed, colleagues as well as total strangers who knew that I was a visitor from the UK shared their grief for Jo and fears for the referendum. The seriousness of the events caused me to reflect on what I had learned since my time in Telawa – about complex human emotion, the power of narrative, the hijacking of our psyches by consumerism and our collective inability to transcend our differences within the outdated power hierarchies we occupy. At the same time, I was thoughtful about how the birth of the internet had changed everything, the acceleration of connection, the access to knowledge.

There was a direct link to be made between the people waking up to their own resources and society's collective power that would add up to a better political structure. Alternativet were plugging into that source and, while it was early days for their own journey into the huge task of changing politics forever, I knew they were on the right track. Before I left Bornholm, I had made a commitment to Uffe and his team that I would start an Alternative political platform in the UK.

The case for an Alternative

In the seven months between making that commitment and launching on 1 March 2017, I had to take stock deeply. What was the basis of my claim that something genuinely new was possible? My partner Pat Kane and I had been part of the progressive Left all of our political lives; Pat was first and foremost a committed Independence activist in Scotland. Yet when we stepped out of the party-political conversation, we both had a great sense of human potential that was being wasted by the current socio-economic-political system.

My own background and eligibility for political entrepreneurship was eclectic. After Telawa I spent ten years in the crucible of the lay Buddhist organisation Soka Gakkai International (SGI) — loosely translated as Movement for the Creation of Value through Culture, Education and Peace. At the heart was the teaching of engi — inseparability or oneness — which described the relationship between self and environment, or past, present and future. Value, from that perspective, is always relative to the worldview and the moment in which it is being generated.

The SGI-UK General Director Richard Causton was a social visionary and a second father to me, taking me under his wing and encouraging my world-changing ambition. He was also an ex-brigadier major and ran the organisation with precision. I was part of the building and running of a global movement from the ground up. I joined individuals doing 'their internal human revolution' — wrestling the ego, releasing inner power — while generating the architecture that took small neighbourhood groups (in districts and chapters) up to national and international level. It was quite a magnificent structure, consisting of small local circles which were overseen by ever larger circles, each with four leaders — adult and youth, male and female — in a global system of care and guidance.

SGI was at once a think tank, a publishing house, a daily newspaper, an education system and, in Japan, a political party called Komeito, which has been in coalition government for the past eight years.[6]

While each country had its own networks, founder and President of the SGI, Daisaku Ikeda, was in constant dialogue with global public figures such as philosopher Arnold Toynbee, economist Hazel Henderson and Russian President Mikhail Gorbachev.[7] When I initiated Conflict and Peace Forums in the early nineties, a think-and-do-tank in the field of conflict transformation, I therefore had direct access to these key figures and many more, whom we invited to London to give talks or training.

Conflict transformation

Of all of Ikeda's dialogue partners, the 'father of peace studies' Johan Galtung made the deepest impression on me, becoming a mentor until this day.[8] His core teaching was that there is a profound difference between conflict resolution and conflict transformation. Simply put, conflict resolution imagines conflict as arising between two parties who negotiate the peace in a zero-sum format. The gain of one is the loss of the other, and compromise is necessary while often sowing the seeds of the next conflict.

Conflict transformation, on the other hand, always views conflict as implying multiple parties. It recognises the role of structural and cultural violence; it expects causes to be complex and entangled, and effects difficult to manage. Transformation occurs through the facilitated participation of all the parties in reimagining a future they can all buy into, one in which the conflict falls away because there is an improved outcome for all. This lesson is invaluable for the kind of community organising we now see as necessary to overcome the party-political divides in our country.

Galtung also introduced me to Peace Journalism: an exploration into how the media promotes certain agendas while convincing readers – and even itself – that it is simply reporting the facts. Together with Sky anchorman Jake Lynch and reporter Annabelle McGoldrick,[9] we ran a series of residential courses involving journalists from the BBC, all the broadsheet papers (*Guardian*, *Times*, *Telegraph*) and occasionally some of the red-tops (*Mirror*, *Sun*). It was the time of the Kosovo war and a tricky period in which to be calling out the establishment's war agenda, but we went ahead.[10]

From Galtung I not only learned how to see the agenda behind the facts that news media offers, but also how to state my own agenda up front. Fake news, from this perspective, is only an escalation of the hidden (or even unconscious) agendas we've come to associate with the mainstream press. Without a more conscious news media operating with the stated agenda of human and planetary flourishing, we are unlikely to lift ourselves out of the confusion of constantly reacting to events as if the future is not in our hands.

In those years I visited Japan seven times; working with 12 million members over 186 countries, I learned invaluable lessons about global movements. On the one hand, I experienced the thrill of gathering large numbers and the joy of being part of something genuinely diverse. Our global meetings were like the Olympics, complete with flags and carefully arranged cultural exchanges. My ex-husband wrote a song for the movement and overnight it was translated into 20 languages and taught in communities worldwide – each of whom had a choir who recorded the song and played it back on video within days.[11]

On the other hand, I saw close up how an overly centralised system can stifle the creativity of participants, as well as make excessive demands on their time. Always obliging them to pay attention to the national and international movement, often at the expense of developing strong, mutual relationships within their own community – or sometimes even within their own family. When that happens, the shared values, practices and rules of engagement become bubble-like, separating the members psychologically from the wider society.

I grappled for many years with the tension between the inside and outside of the SGI – not least because being part of such a strong group fulfilled so many needs and accelerated my own development, including the capacity for response-ability. In that sense, it was natural that I would eventually move away from the core operations of the movement – as many do – to pay more attention to the world beyond the bubble. Ultimately, the true gift to a big agenda is the growing autonomy and self-organising of all the elements – everyone's ability to take care of themselves and each other in diverse communities facing the future together.

Integral philosophy

As I was moving out of the orbit of the SGI I was beginning to learn from Ken Wilber and the Integral community about the different forms of agency available to us, each of which will make a different kind of demand on the group.[12] For example, those who have little control over their lives make their needs known by shouting out. Those who can see and relate to others, but are living in a state of scarcity, might be very strategic. While it appeared in pockets, there was not enough of what Integrals call 'teal' agency in the SGI: the ability to lead without controlling others.

Together with Integral practitioner Matthew Kalman, I hosted the London Integral Circle, which met monthly for ten years, bridging the 1990s and 00s. We hosted any Integral stars while they were in town – including Susanne Cook-Greuter, Terry Patten and John Rowan. Several of our regular group visited Boulder, Colorado, where Wilber hosted them. Here I learned some of my key political lessons, namely how our circumstances and history shape our styles of agency. It was in this period that I began to see that the main goal of politics should not be to manipulate or nudge behaviour to suit government agendas – that would only have minimal effects, as our capacities for agency are so diverse. Instead, politics should focus on creating the conditions for people to bring out the best of their innate capabilities so they can then set the agenda themselves.

I was now spending so much time among people whose idea of agency had nothing to do with spiritual practice, and this prompted me to return to university for a master's degree in politics. It was time to learn the language of government.

Expanding the feminine

All the while I was focused on the national and global sphere, something else was reshaping my world entirely on the most personal level: I got pregnant. While my husband and I were thrilled by the news, I felt a profound loss of control over my life, with no sense of what being a mother would mean.[13] My own mother had lost a husband, a son (my older brother by ten years) and six of her seven siblings to cancer before I was out of my teens. I barely remember the confident woman she once was before she dropped into a lifetime of depression. My mother's losses propelled me into a solitary journey of searching for meaning and agency. When I found out that I was expecting a boy, I suddenly saw the opportunity I had to re-engage some of that story for my family. All of my sisters had boys first and I later found out that each of them had inwardly taken on that same task: to stay close to their sons and get them past the age of 21.

What I hadn't expected was that bringing up a boy, latterly as a single mum, was to become my most constant source of joy. It would change how I saw everything. I hadn't grown up as a feminist: I was my father's tomboy and did my best to play the son, eschewing the women's movement and showing little interest in the fight for equality. Yet as I watched my boy growing, socialising and finding his way in the world, I came face to face with sex and gender issues. Mostly it was a joyful revelation: having been brought up with three sisters, I revelled in discovering my son's different ways of behaving and socialising. I noticed how difficult it was for him to stand up for his masculinity and so I surprised myself when, after my husband and I split up, I sent him to an all-boys school. I wanted him to have access to a masculine register. I also did things like take on the role of football team manager so that I could try to understand what he would be facing later in life.

Deep down, all the while I was being a mother, I was beginning to understand how many of the problems in public life were caused by the lack of women in positions of leadership. At first I saw that there was a lack of emotional literacy and I noticed the high reactivity between men when they are threatened or lose status. Later I could see how much we were missing out in the design of our services, by not understanding relationship and the power of connectivity. Eventually I came to believe that the gender debate offers a unique opportunity for a conversation between men and women: a conversation that begins to move everything beyond the binary, without losing the diversity.

To me, it was good for everyone – especially boys – to face a shifting power landscape in which the world expected them to be less dominant than their fathers were before them. As it is, the many sons of single mothers might be a force for change in themselves: mine is now teaching me how gender balance works in a regenerative culture.

Yet the fundamental challenge remains, nowhere more so than in the corridors of power. I had to delay finishing my politics degree for a year to give birth. I consequently didn't play the prominent part in the election of Tony Blair's New Labour to government that, as a journalist well connected to members of the inner sanctum, I might otherwise have played. For example, many of my university classmates stepped right into special advisory roles while I was on sore nipples and nappies.

Much later, in 2013, together with Lee Chalmers I would co-found The Downing Street Project to get more women into positions of leadership.[14] Later still I would be writing actively on the feminisation of politics.[15] But at the time, once I got over missing the party on election night, I knew I had the bigger prize. Indeed, all that I experienced in those early mothering years that taught me about community, networks and what it takes to raise a human being have become the vital lessons for a new politics. When New Labour began to show all the signs of being embedded in the old politics, I was already ahead of the game.

In that period, I shifted my work patterns into a more portfolio style, distributing my attention to a number of different projects and stepping back from the front line of Conflict and Peace Forums. I started to work under the brand name of Poiesis, meaning the activity of bringing something into being that didn't exist before as if it were a work of art. An act of poiesis seemed an appropriate frame for integrating the raising of a child with the emergence of a new politics as we moved towards the end of the 20th century and into the 21st.

The shocking soft power of story

For the digital natives reading this, it will be difficult to imagine what a period of acceleration the 1990s and 00s were for those who could remember living without the internet and World Wide Web. From sitting in front of our computers responding to internal emails sent by colleagues, we were now sitting in front of a portal to the entire world. It was suddenly up to us to go and mine its riches – we could become proactive. Networks were not gifted, but forged. Facebook became the platform upon which everyone performed: not only watching their newly acquired friends (poached from other friends of friends) but also watching themselves succeed or fail in the world of reputation.

It was in this heady atmosphere that I started to pay more attention to the work of Joseph Nye and what he called soft power. Serving as an advisor to Bill Clinton in the post-Vietnam war era, Nye claimed that while the USA might have lost the war in Indochina, it would always remain globally dominant because of the lasting *attraction* of the American Dream. People would always want to be in a relationship with the home of freedom and democracy and through this bond, America would always have influence over their behaviour.

Conjuring with this notion I could see how Hollywood and Disneyland had become the vehicles of soft power, as Nye described it. At the same time, in a more abstract way, he was also pointing at the power of narrative itself: how to reshape others' views of the world through storytelling. Wasn't this, to some extent, what the Buddhist lecturer was doing in Telawa – telling the villagers a new story of possibility that profoundly shaped their actions?

Despite no longer being in the Buddhist environment, I was beginning to find a new language for the effects I had experienced first-hand in Indonesia. The magic was becoming a bit easier to grasp. Later I initiated the Soft Power Network and began to meet practitioners of Nye's ideas – including Nye himself – with an open exploration of how an understanding of soft power would change the way we look at agency.

For six years I wrote regularly for *The Guardian* on this topic.[16] And through my relationship with Wilton Park (where the Foreign Office holds its conferences) worked as a soft power consultant in Brazil, Finland and Mexico. Memorably, I was invited twice to NATO HQ in Brussels to give a talk on the changing face of soft power: both times I was heckled for being uncompromising about the failure of NATO to tell a good story about their mission to protect. My first book *Soft Power Agenda* describes all of these explorations into geopolitical life.[17]

Emotional needs and resources

By the time my son was in secondary school, I was working not only as a soft power advisor and columnist, but also in the world of conflict transformation, which included writing about social cohesion and reimagining public services.[18] Yet there was a piece missing, namely a non-spiritual language for the inner world that could explain why humans flourish (or fail to).

My search for this missing piece led me to study Human Givens psycho-social therapy for two years, eventually taking on clients from my home office. It taught me about essential emotional needs and the resources we have to meet those needs. I understood how our brains operate through pattern-matching, taking short cuts through linear cognitive processes by seeing similarities between past and present events, which makes us able to respond faster to stimuli. I learned about how trauma works to shut our capacities down, forcing us into fight or flight responses many times in a day. And how our dreaming brain can both free us of emotional clutter at night, as well as trap us into trances of unconscious obedience during the day. In short, I learned much of what I was still missing in my general understanding of human agency.

At first, I celebrated this clear map of emotional drives and resources. It explained so much about why our society was dysfunctional, and why so many people get into trouble while trying and failing to get their needs met in a balanced way. But slowly the penny dropped: it dawned on me that the vast majority of people are ritually addicted to consumerism through the abuse of exactly this knowledge about human emotions. Through the 'soft power' of advertising, we have been persuaded that we can get status, belonging, meaning and purpose – all vital for our survival within our emotional system – through buying a pair of trainers, or a handbag. The strength of that addiction is what has kept us on the hamster wheel, working day and night to buy the things we believe we need to take part in society. I was familiar with the anti-capitalist critiques of consumerism. However, Human Givens provided me with a better understanding of the psychology of desire that made us so vulnerable.

Once I really grasped the ingenuity – the creative brilliance – upon which this mass hypnosis depends, I almost lost all hope of beating the system. The possibility of re-orienting our behaviour around relationships and community as the healthier resource for getting our emotional needs met seemed nearly impossible.

Then I observed that I was now fully awake to that manipulation and had new choices. In that sense I am just part of a wave of people waking up the system that manipulates them. Did the average winner of the ad industry's biggest prize, the DA&D awards, understand the link between his (probably his) cool ad and the destruction of the planet in the 1970s? Probably not. And advertising itself is waking up to its responsibilities as the growth in ethical marketing shows.[19]

More importantly, what to do with all this waking-up-ness? It's one thing to resist buying something the moment you have an emotional call. But what is the bigger picture of people taking back control of their lives and wanting to choose a different economic system? Where do they get to make that decision, if all the official parties themselves are part of it?

The party is over

My son was getting older, freeing my time. So I stepped up my activity in the party-political sphere, joining the management board of Compass and standing unsuccessfully to be a Member of Parliament in 2015. Together with Neal Lawson, I wrote a paper called 'New Times: How A Politics of Networks and Relationships Can Deliver A Good Society', but I had strong doubts that the current political system was up to it.[20] When David Miliband started the Movement for Change back in 2014, I had been excited by the application of Saul Alinsky's community resilience ethos.[21] But just like Jeremy Corbyn's Momentum group, no matter how much energy you release from within your own party members, it fails the broader community if it can't cross the party-political divide.

Still, I suddenly saw many promising signs of socio-political initiatives that deliberately eschewed the old party politics in order to open up new ground. People and projects were taking on ideas such as integral practice, soft power, conflict transformation, the role of the feminine, the importance of community, solutions-based journalism, emotional needs and cosmolocalism.[22]

Our heuristic model of I–We–World helped me to map out these initiatives. On exploring individual internal development (the I-realm), I found (and admired) organisations such as Perspectiva and the Alter Ego networks, calling for a new politics that arose from the complexity of what it means to be human.[23, 24] They were less homo economicus, and more complex 'bio-psycho-social-spiritual' entities – shaped by multiple operating systems. On the social front (the We-realm), movements like Transition Towns were offering a whole new framework for the move towards sustainable living.[25] Flatpack Democracy encouraged citizens to stand as independents to give the people full participation in decision-making. On the global front (the World-realm), I learned about The Good Country Index that measures the value created by nations for each other and describes the dual mandate for national politicians, requiring them to be as responsible for the world as for their own country.[26] Dark Matter Labs discover and design institutional infrastructure for the tech revolution and climate breakdown. They inspired me, as did London Futurists who constantly rocked my reality with information about technology already poised to change our lives exponentially.[27] I easily resonated with all these exciting spaces and collectives and became involved in them.

Adding them together, the backbone of a new political axis that linked the flourishing of a complex human to the flourishing of the planet began to emerge. A framework shaped by I–We–World.

The Alternative UK

So when Pat and I sat down to get serious, we started with imagining the power of these networks to create the foundations of The Alternative UK. Pat is a musician and lead singer in the band Hue and Cry, and is still making albums with his brother Greg since their top ten hits in the mid-eighties. Concurrently Pat has worked successfully as a writer and journalist and in 1999 he became co-founder of *The Sunday Herald.* In the early 2000s he left the newspaper industry to write a book called *The Play Ethic: A Manifesto for a Different Way of Living in 2004.* Pat was also lead curator of NESTA's (National Endowment for Media, Technology and the Arts) annual Future Fest for three years and continues to consult there, as well as for the recently announced Festival UK2022.

Between us all we were bringing a very rich context, and an awareness of the conditions within which a new politics could arise, even if we could not see yet what form that might take. We could sense a collective yearning for something new. But equally there was a lot of resistance to our attempts. New initiatives like ours often got off the ground in defiance of the current system, and that autonomy is of course precious. But the term 'politics' cannot help but suggest all the dysfunctionality of party politics, and many want to maintain a wide berth.

Even so, there was enough willingness from these friends and peers to come together, get to know each other a bit better and begin a conversation. In the room at that first meeting in 2016 were Peter and Annabelle Macfadyen (Transition Towns and Flatpack Democracy), Indy Johar (Dark Matter Labs), David Wood (London Futurists), Simon Anholt (Good Country Project), Jonathan Rowson (Perspectiva), Danii Evans (One Taste), Pat Kane (The Play Ethic) and me. To me it felt like a fractal – a pattern of relationships that might lie at the heart of a transformed socio-economic-political system: but it was early days.[28]

While there was plenty of hesitation, there was also plenty of intrigue – enough for each group to agree to speak on our platform for the launch on 1 March 2017, together with Uffe Elbæk and Rasmus Nordqvist, who flew over from Denmark. Serendipitously, we chose the Impact Hub at King's Cross, not knowing that Uffe's name was inscribed there as one of the founders. On the night, we invited Chickenshed Theatre to provide some shocking political drama, and Danii to curate movement and soul. We were packed out and had to turn people away due to fire regulations.

We discussed stimulating, nourishing topics: the brokenness of politics and the way communities hold relationships between people that can incubate creativity and agency; the impoverished idea of the human at the heart of our system; the whole human we know exists; the powerlessness of people with no opportunity to participate; the ingenuity of Flatpack's local political practice and the power of festivals; the crisis of our environment; the good country that takes its responsibility for the planet as seriously as its responsibility to its people; mental health and depression; the soul of the people and their desire to 'dance'.

When Uffe Elbæk spoke of the journey of Alternativet – its six values, and how the promise to hold at its core the connection between the health of the people and the health of the planet had made it the fastest-growing party in Denmark – we too felt the possibility of a new politics coming into view.

Ada. It's there.

Since that day, the best way to describe what we do is as follows: we curate, assemble and amplify those elements which might constitute a new and better socio-political-economic system. Only 2 per cent of the UK (2–5 per cent of the European) electorate is a member of a political party, which is quite astounding. That doesn't mean 98 per cent of people have no political affiliation, but rather that very few people think it's worth the time or money to get involved directly. More importantly, the political conversation the media is feeding off is narrow and overly determined. Our job has been to see what is emerging more broadly, engage those bringing the innovation, drive collaboration between them and share the outcomes.

This takes shape concretely as four actions:

1. Produce The Daily Alternative, a daily news-and-views service that tells 'a new story of us'

2. Convene the new socio-economic system, drive collaboration between actors

3. Initiate cosmolocal Citizen Action Networks on the ground

4. Design and co-create a parallel local-to-global governance system that can work *in partnership* with the state (councils, municipalities, government).

The third, in particular, is a Labour of Love:[29] CANs (standing for Citizen Action Networks, or Community Agency Networks) bring the fully diverse population of an area into relationship with each other and connect them to the new, wider system that is appearing. CANs are not flat, small and modest entities: they are miniature systems that ambitiously download all the best prototypes and learnings from the global commons to their communities, generating a new economy from the ground up. This includes traditional paying jobs – but more than that, new forms of living.

A new politics kicking off

Apart from those we are building, CANs are appearing everywhere in slightly different emanations, from the Trust the People network of community transformers to Future Leeds or Cooperation Jackson in Mississippi. We believe that CANs are the natural containers of people politics; they are fractals of a new socio-economic system and the units of democracy for the future. We need new architecture to further connect different CANs to each other, carrying their decision-making power further and wider, upwards and outwards to the world.

I expect readers of this book to come from the sectors who feel they are consciously shaping present society. Some of you will be part of the new system already, some of you will be ready to take part in the building of it, some of you might be sceptical to the ideas presented here.

Here is my hope: that those readers who experience the new politics when they walk into a local meeting of their CAN for the first time will experience something like I did in Telawa. I hope that they will be curious, ready to engage, that they will eat and sing together, listen to inspirational talks, have the chance to express their thoughts and listen deeply to others. As a result, I hope they walk out of that place ready to start building a future they can look forward to.

In the following chapters, I'm going to look deep into the magic and its components. What do we need to know about human beings that makes us vulnerable to manipulation? What resources do we already have to take control of our lives? What are the many ways that power works and how do we get access and agency? Do we have the power to influence the world and, if so, how do we organise?

Each chapter begins with evoking sonder – the momentarily overwhelming realisation that every person has a story of their own to tell.[30] A few lines of dialogue locate where public problems intersect with our private lives and where the human revolution begins.

1 Acute Challenges, Keenly Felt

He's so frail. I look at him behind the glass, braving a smile as his carer seems impatient to move on. He's telling me to be careful out there, wear my mask and don't go to any wild parties. But he doesn't know the half of it. Soon as I've done my duty here, I'm meeting the crew and we're off to do our stint outside the police station. It's Day 4 of the Rebellion and I'm on the rota, making sure the arrestees know their rights as they get slammed behind bars. If I don't catch them when they get out the vans, they could disappear for two years.

Why should we care about your climate crisis? Why should we cry about the future for your children? Or the health of your elders as we come out on the streets today? Our ancestors died in slavery to your American Dream. Our people face imminent death every day from the moment they are born. Our families are weak from poor food and bad housing. Our sons obliged to die in your colonising armies or shot in the back while jogging in the street.

She took a deep breath but was close to losing it. Could he not hear himself? She was almost embarrassed for him as he had obviously not clocked she was his senior, not his junior. Scale this, scale that. When was he going to get up to speed with the new ways of doing things?

I N THIS age of multiple crises, we have recently moved into a period of acute challenges, keenly felt. Only a few years ago we knew that environmental breakdown, social polarisation and mental health epidemics were all threatening. This past year of Covid, forest fires and uprisings everywhere have brought the emergency up close and personal, right into our faces – especially to those parts of the world where people were previously more sheltered.

Not only are those on the front line of climate change abandoning their homes for safety elsewhere, risking their lives in small boats to cross the seas to safer territory, but even in the safe havens themselves, whole counties have caught fire, razing previously flourishing towns and villages to the ground. As the pandemic wreaks havoc upon the consumer societies that gave rise to it, economies are crashing. Global confidence in the old ways of doing everything is disappearing. Yet even as that story dominates our daily news, something else is stirring. Not as a response, but as a rapidly emerging new way of looking at life that could change everything.

You'll know the story of the frog in a pan full of water, slowly coming to boiling point. The frog has just understood the increasing heat could cook her. But she's lost her spring: where did it go? As she watches the cook smirking, her anger is rising. Although her legs are sluggish after being lulled into inaction for too long, her head is above water and she's spotted the other frogs waking up to their predicament. Some are panicked and squawking, but some are already looking around – like her – for allies. Can we topple the pan? Can we climb on each other's backs? Can we reach the sous-chef? Or: if we close our eyes, will it soon be over?

For anyone engaged in socio-economic-political discourse, the new movements for change – Black Lives Matter, Extinction Rebellion, School Strikes, many, many versions of Pride – are good signs that people in groups, scattered across the globe, are waking up. First and foremost, they are waking up to who they are, why their lives are the way they are, how they could be. Together they see the historic and current urgency to transform our societies – but they are also coming to know their own power to make a difference.

Yet even in the midst of those groups, few believe that what they are currently doing will be enough to trigger the changes we need. We know that most of our societies are still in the grip of the 'old order' – a story of power that disenfranchises 99 per cent of the people on the planet. A story so insidious that the 99 per cent have bought into the idea of their own powerlessness. To use another human-over-nature story, we are like the elephant trained to stay tethered to a sapling long after it has the power to tear that tree from its roots.

This book is the new story about what is possible. About the power we always had but are only now slowly waking up to. It's also about the task of transforming that power from something apparently scattered, amorphous, into something we can rely on to serve us. We are only years away from a level of environmental degradation that we can no longer halt or put into reverse and social injustice threatens to destabilise global society. Unless we manage, each of us, to master our own doubts, to find our own spring and work together with commitment to get out of this predicament, we might be approaching a place of no return.

What is waking up?

For those who remember Y2K, our move into the 21st century was darkened by a major possibility that all the software and technology running our societies – from local businesses to national governments and international networks – could suddenly come to a halt at 12.01 on 1 January 2000. The implications were massive – so much so that extremely sensible people had prepared for Armageddon-like effects, stockpiling food and water and learning about how to get the national power grid working again.

More than anything, this possibility caused a moment of wide reflection about how dependent we had all become on our tech. How this steady flow of 0s and 1s was not only organising our core resources but, maybe more importantly, maintaining our connection with each other throughout the World Wide Web. If the 20th century would be best remembered for the hard power accumulated, the suffering generated, by two World Wars and a rampant global economy, the last ten years of that century had completely transformed our idea of the future with the birth of the internet.

Before then, the majority of people – even in the most developed of countries – had relied upon vertical structures of authority to give them access to information about what was going on in their world. Newspapers, educational establishments, organisational hierarchies: unless we were told by entities with more resources than us, we knew nothing. And what we were told was expressed via the framework, in the language and values, of the bosses.

Before and after the World Wide Web

Suddenly anyone with an internet connection was able to go in search of new sources of material for their interests, making direct connections with people they would otherwise have never expected to meet. At first it was simply a portal to the wider world that we could gaze at by visiting simple explanatory websites of all kinds – like window shopping. But very soon those new sites began to actively engage with their visitors and try to anticipate what would make them stay longer.

Others observing their interaction would open new sites to expand the points of interest they were uncovering and offer more.

In many ways it was like witnessing the growth of a giant marketplace which started by selling a few basic tools but ended up selling everything, and in so doing, became the main meeting place for the people of a town where everyone could find out what was going on across the community with all the news and gossip too. Except, on the World Wide Web you could do that without leaving home and your marketplace was increasingly the whole world.

As the internet grew, everyone started to get access to much of the same information that the executive class had always had, at the same time. Often, different conclusions were drawn when presented with the same facts. Instead of saving those new insights for the pub or the mosque, we could instantly share our views with friends, then friends of friends. Social media users developed online personas, performing their opinions, seeing their impact on others. Over the course of a decade our experience of daily life – what we did with our time and our attention – changed dramatically.

Some of the information being shared more widely was to have profound and lasting effects on our minds and subsequent behaviour, comparable to the rites of passage any one of us experience as we grow up. We have lives before the internet – and lives after. With access to educational tools, more sources of global news and the sharing of research, there have been multiple series of social and political awakenings. We can watch the way that the Arab Spring evolved from a single shocking image in Tunisia shared by hundreds of thousands of viewers and led to the overthrow of President Hosni Mubarak in Egypt. Or we can see how online gaming spawned new ways for young people to relate to each other globally. Each one of them has spawned new streams of books and entrepreneurship of all kinds.

Of course, environmentalism, anti-globalisation, anti-nuclear, anti-racism and feminist movements (and more) had been building steadily over the 20th century. Yet, because the status quo takes time to change, these movements had not been successful enough in halting the acceleration of the growth economy, the increasing wealth gap and the subsequent polarisation of society, all of which were having a destructive effect on the planet. What changed with the internet – particularly with social media – was that we were no longer just learning the facts and figures of injustice for the marginalised. We were now immersed in the stories of their experiences. We were hearing first-hand not only from those who suffered but also from those who were committed to working closely with them. With their thoughts and feelings came a whole new kind of rationale for why we are in the state we are in.

As the decade wore on, anyone with broadband found that, online, they could unprecedentedly mobilise those who agreed with their opinions or passions. If movements were mostly the size and nature of marches and communes in the 20th century, by the early 21st century they could be as large and amorphous as a country (the online petition site Avaaz has over 50 million members) and more global than Adidas, operating in 55 countries (the Occupy movement spanned 951 cities across 82 countries).

But even so, these protests are not as large nor have as great a global reach as McDonald's. Its 34,000 restaurants in 118 countries and territories serve more than 69 million people every day worldwide. Still peddling its recipe for a dying planet – intense beef factory farming, cheap addictive food with minimum nutrients, replacing locally produced food and business – the old ways are still winning. Nor are McDonald's as pervasive – or extractive – as the airline industry which, before Covid, facilitated over 1.46 billion flights per annum.[31] Despite our general awareness about the destructive effect of aviation on the planet, only the *rate of acceleration* has slowed a bit: the numbers have never dropped below their danger level as a consequence of our active, conscious choices.

Yet none of this is as impenetrable as a socio-political-legal-economic-cultural system that still cannot see the marginalised as fully human, resourceful, equal members of our society. Poor people are given money but in a manner that compromises respect and dignity. Members of the

BAME (Black, Asian and Minority Ethnic) community have gained more rights but little meaningful commitment from the establishment, so equality never occurs. The young and old are rarely seen − or heard from − by those in positions of power. The experience of the elders and the new perspective of the youngsters is almost entirely missing from the puzzle of how we get out of this mess. The divisive structures of this system condemn us to spending all our energy fighting each other. Like trying to lift the table we are standing on.

Movements popping up across the globe

Yet the waking-up process continues: like popcorn exploding in a pan, there's no stopping it once it starts. To look at just one example, in the International Panel on Climate Change report of 2018, the stark set of truths about the true state of our planet became the evidence Greta Thunberg needed to begin her school strike.[32] At first she was a lone figure, playing truant to sit with her banner in front of the Swedish parliament. But with the power of social media amplifying her remarkable integrity, and her ability to speak truth to power, Thunberg's simple action evolved into a global movement for change. Children the world over, often with their parents' help, began to skip school every week and take to the streets as Fridays for the Future.[33]

With perfect timing, amid that teenage uprising came Extinction Rebellion (XR).[34] Their waves of young and old were prepared to block the streets of capital cities around the world − risking, even embracing, imprisonment − to draw attention to our burning house of a planet. Using all the soft power tools of spectacle, narrative and relational organising, XR burst upon the scene in 2019. Their members chained and glued themselves to the doors of banks or trains about to depart and clung to the underside of trucks to block bridges. Using various methods of self-endangerment in order to save the future for everyone's children, they seized global attention.

But only briefly. XR's second and third uprisings had diminishing returns, as they increasingly became embroiled in the very system they were challenging, part of which was a media and politics that had deep expertise in suppressing change. But what XR nevertheless established was a keen sense that – for anyone listening – the next ten years were crucial.

For those of us who were hoping for a strong and mythical change, the 2020s loomed as the decade for saving the human race. Yet the celebrations were muted as we said goodbye to the 2010s. Watching the millions of pounds of polluting fireworks going off around the globe, our dilemma was clear. Even as the evidence is accumulating that we, as a global population of people, are waking up to the truths of our lives as never before, we are still – in our behaviour and commitments – very much part of and upholding the system that is killing us.

Covid the accelerator

When the coronavirus arrived (officially becoming a pandemic in March 2020) and sent whole populations into lockdown, we were suddenly all on the receiving end of a global intervention that no one owned up to starting and no one knew how to control.[35] But the result was that we were now, for the first time, discussing the same health risk across the globe.

As ever in our divided world, Covid is a tale of at least two vastly different experiences. On the one hand, it means extreme pressure and hardship for the poor and hardworking, whether workers on the front lines in hospitals and food shops who were thrust most directly into danger's way; or those poorly paid in failing industries, losing their livelihoods and trapped in inadequate accommodation, often with the mentally vulnerable; or those working in cities like Mumbai, who were sent back to their village homes, where there is little or no running water, to keep themselves free of infection.

On the other hand, the more privileged were now mostly working from home rather than in the office. They were obliged – through spending more time with their children, or on video communication channels like Zoom, or just staring out the window with nowhere to go – to pay more attention to issues they could ignore before.

Some were joining up the dots between the pandemic and all the other causes we have made – systemic injustices such as local and intra-national inequality, extractive growth economies, loss of biodiversity, abuse of animals and nature – so they could be fully engaged with the crises we are facing. Others were simply witnessing the plight of others, not knowing how to respond other than to step outside once a week to applaud health workers.[36] Others were drumming their fingers, wondering when they can get back to normal – although, according to the polls, they were in the minority.

That essential dichotomy and conundrum continues to this day: such divides are not easily bridged. But who can avoid noticing the different ways different governments have handled the crisis? The worst – among them the US and the UK – are mostly unable to manage the situation, displaying chaotic decision-making, allowing high death rates and collapsing their economies. The best (at least at the time of writing) – including New Zealand and Germany – minimise the impact of the infection on every count. Yet none know how, yet, to assure their populations that the future looks bright.[37]

Black lives mattering

On 25 May, three months into this intense period of global attentiveness, a 46-year-old Black American man called George Floyd was murdered by police officers while being arrested in open air, for allegedly using a counterfeit $20 note, in Minneapolis, Minnesota. Despite Floyd being handcuffed, white police officer Derek Chauvin was filmed kneeling on his neck for over eight minutes while Floyd repeatedly said, 'I can't breathe' and called for his mother. Three other police officers restrained Floyd and another held back onlookers who called for Chauvin to remove his knee. All four were subsequently jailed and are now facing trial for murder.

This was another episode in a history of Black Americans' deaths while in police custody, part of a much longer and broader history of assault and murders of unarmed Black people in public spaces. This in turn points back at decades and then centuries of injustice for Black people in predominantly white societies. It is not only the history of racial bias in police killings that criminal justice lawyers have exposed but also a much longer train of evidence going all the way back to the end of the slave trade in 1807. The use of long sentencing for minor crimes incarcerated so many of the Black community, impoverishing generations of Black families.[38]

This was not the first time such a brutal, unjust killing of a Black man had made global headlines. In 2012 African American teenager Trayvon Martin had been killed while out jogging by mixed-race security guard George Zimmerman. When he was acquitted, thousands of people took to the streets, giving birth to the term Black Lives Matter (BLM). Although there was little or no centralised organisation of the movement, BLM made the headlines again a year later, following the police killing of Michael Brown in Ferguson, Missouri. This popularised the Black consciousness term 'woke' to refer to someone aware of the ongoing effects of global colonisation.[39]

Floyd's death triggered massive protests all over America and then globally in over 60 countries, where people stood in solidarity with anti-racism of all kinds, venturing out despite the Covid crisis. It seemed apparent to me that people of all backgrounds were engaging not only with the protests but also with their own deeper understanding of their responsibility to it, creating new alignments between the environmental, justice and democracy movements.

Humanity gets self-conscious

For some, this is another aspect of the 'waking up' happening everywhere, in multiple domains. For others, these are disconnected, random occurrences that just happened to coincide. My own view is precisely that it's inevitable that there will be multiple perspectives.

What matters is what they have in common, as that will be crucial to our potential for making the kind of personal, social and global shifts that will benefit everyone, regardless of their beliefs and experiences.

Over the period between March and September 2020, due to government restrictions on movement, flights dropped from over two million per day to under 8,000. Pollution from cars dropped 53 per cent in London and similarly elsewhere.[40] People recorded their joy at rediscovering nature, time and relationships on their social media everywhere. At The Alternative we designed an app called Before&Now, which invited people to capture those moments for posterity. One user said, '[before] I skated over details in a rush to make broad brushstrokes which showed everyone that I was capable and participating. Now, I have taken pleasure in delving into boxes of memories. I have found time and energy to spend hours mindfully digging and weeding in the garden. And I have created a new network of old friends and a forum for us to share. New ways to teach and share. I have seized this moment.'

Yet how encouraging is this for our ability to move on from our crises? Together with a growing movement of people from across diverse movements and sectors of society, I'm confident that these are all signs of a return to our own resources for responding to crises. We are choosing to stand, at this time, for our growing human and social potential for making change. And for its acceleration.

What are we waking up from?

In the meantime, despite unprecedented numbers of mobilised people, we find ourselves hopelessly fragmented and fractured as a society – national, continental and global. We need clear, strong leadership at the international and national level, committed to responding to what is now emerging. But even people who broadly agree do not necessarily find it easy to collaborate successfully.

This is not simply a familiar, if escalated, reality – like a series of conflicts that only need resolving for everything to be better. Waking up includes grasping the complexity of life and the world we have created. The problems present themselves as systemic and wicked: they require unprecedented competencies and political will to resolve. One might observe that it is actually a time in our global socio-political history when we are especially incapable of showing strong leadership and coming together to take clear action.

There's a reason for this. We are struggling with the explosion of information – personal, social, global – that our network societies have brought to us. Our ability to shape and control, and also to be shaped and controlled, has been massively intensified. The human challenge to act is more enormous, precisely because we know so much more than we ever did.

Grasping for the first time that your inability to progress in life may be as much due to systemic issues – racism, sexism, class or caste – as to the personal failings laid at your door, generates more anger than freedom. Learning about the history of your kind – race, sex, class or caste – and how they have been disadvantaged to the point of being systemically abused, without the mainstream of society noticing or caring, generates as much dismay as liberation. Meeting others who are experiencing similar insights to share stories of realisation and mutual support releases as much grief as joy.

What is obvious to all those embarking on the journey for transformation is that there is no architecture for power, existing or adequate, that would help the people play their part in shaping the future. While democracy – governance by, with and for the people – is a fine notion, our voting systems do more to frustrate it than deliver it.

Party politics divides the people much more than it enables them. Of the six top economies in the world – the US, China, Japan, Germany, India and the UK – only Germany has a fully proportional system of elections (Japan has a mixed system). This means that the votes people cast are not divided up according to the parties they voted for, but distributed by a first past the post system in constituencies around the country. Even if the second party wins 49 per cent of the national vote in each case, the quirkiness of constituency seats means they can end up with no parliamentary power.

But even Germany's system has no formal provision for citizen action other than to vote for a party every four years. Which means choosing between manifestos drawn up by politicians with a minimum of participation from party members. When you remember that only 2–5 per cent (across Europe) of people are members of political parties, you begin to see how dire this situation is. And even if you are one of the small majorities whose party is in power, it is distressing to see how little really changes.

This is partly because the system calls for the opposition to discredit everything the government attempts to do. But it's also because most of our politicians are reliant on business and a compliant civil service to keep the economy growing. Suffice to say, they have led us to the edge of the cliff. If we go along with the IPCC report and the Paris Agreement, we have ten years to save ourselves, and no easy way to bring people together to even begin the task.

Where do the people even start to take concerted action if most of them are now trapped in lives that have so little social or political agency? Add to that the speed and immensity of the waking-up process, the force of which can easily rob us of our ability to even take that first step. Those who can are leading the movements. But there are far more who self-medicate with various distractions, unwilling to move forward into the darkness on a weak promise of eventual light.

What are we waking up to?

Most of us 'frogs' find ourselves in the constantly responsive, slowly warming waters known as the internet. The internet serves up a daily diet of surprises and innovations: in many ways it shows us that we live in incredibly exciting times. For the first time in history, any individual with access to broadband can see themselves as a participant in the public sphere. Whatever their age and formal competence, they can find an audience ready to engage and to amplify what would until only recently have been a private thought. That's a challenge to our identity and ego we have not been educated to manage.

Watching each other online has been enlightening. We simply didn't know before what we now know about human behaviour. We never understood what social animals we were. Observing our own energetic, often obsessive activity on social media, it's clear we really didn't know ourselves. All these new insights are occurring even within each of the communication bubbles that we inevitably frequent. The few times we stray out of our digital comfort zone into a completely different field of activity, we can barely process what we are reading – it's all so new.

Desire and attraction

To borrow the Chinese phrase wryly, a thousand – no, millions – of flowers are blooming. Each one offering a different perspective on life, a different way of expressing reality. People who once felt alienated from the mainstream of society are finding others like them to share time with, by means of platforms such as Facebook and Twitter.

Patterns that were previously visible only to those who study markets have become more obvious to all of us. For example, it turns out that we are not simply creatures with material needs, but that we are diverse bio-psycho-social-spiritual beings with complex emotional needs and desires. Those compulsions play out in the ways we gather, respond to events, make life-choices. The impact of being able to observe, articulate and discuss our needs and desires collectively, how they are being met either well or badly, is enlightening.[41]

But we're not all in it together like one big happy family opening our presents on Christmas morning. While some are simply enjoying the new communities they are building online, others are harnessing and gaming each other – playing one interest group off against another. After lifetimes of living in a capitalist culture, we instinctively look at each other as potential customers in order to bank any idea we might have to enhance our community.

Gaming and harnessing our attention

When they see people gathering, those with accumulated power see this as their opportunity to meet the crowds directly, answering their gaze with new messages that entrance. The internet's power is reduced to an expensive advertising hoarding to which you might give a fleeting glance as you are out shopping. Like kids looking for attention, we give ours away easily to anyone making promises. Especially when the promisers know what we really want – because we told them with all the choices we've made online.

In 2012 Facebook – and later, its acquisition Instagram – shifted its business model from being a friends' network with banner advertising, to being an active trader in social data.[42] All the information they had access to about who we talked with most, what we liked, how our mood changed in response to certain posts – evidence even our closest friends would be hard pressed to provide – became available to advertisers for a price.

Not for the first time, those who could pay took full advantage of being able to manipulate Facebook users' decisions. Not only to buy their products but for innumerable socio-political ends, including influencing voters. With 1.69 billion users (in 2020) Facebook has since been held accountable for swinging elections, generating massive conspiracy theories through fake news and inducing high levels of depression, particularly among the young.

In the run-up to the UK Referendum on the European Union, Cambridge Analytica – a data research company – identified the mindset of a very specific demographic (the three million people who never voted) as having a need to 'take back control' of their lives. Not 'taking control': that would suggest aggression. But taking *back* control – our right to what was once ours. Playing into that keenly felt need, with slogans and promises, was one of the reasons that Leave won. (Although the victors had no realistic plans to be able to deliver on that promise, as our continuing political breakdown is illustrating).

But Cambridge Analytica were not the first to use emotional tools, and the internet was not the first vehicle for propaganda. Before them, the advertising industry, the popular media – even our parents to some extent – played a similar role. Their persuasions turned us into consumers and hardworking cogs in the machine of our growth economy – something that both the political Left and Right have been committed to throughout the 21st century.

What's different today is that we are increasingly capable of observing our own manipulation and reflecting upon it. Our attempts to enlighten each other – or to call third parties out for poor behaviour – has become an international sport. The huge array of conspiracy theories may look idiotic to us now, but history will probably play that back at us as a generation who tried to wrestle their cognitive power back from the elite institutions without really knowing what to do with it.

Infinite fragmentation

However, that growing awareness has also led to the infinite fragmentation of previous social solidarities. Only 20 years ago, people could identify easily with such broad categories as class, religion, family or place. Today in the UK, Brexit has revealed how even families, let alone old demographic groupings such as age or race, can no longer agree, for a whole host of reasons. Too many people are finding themselves ploughing their own furrow; looking for the attention, energy and resources of others.

Our politics reflects this extreme fragmentation. Previously non-negotiable categories like Left and Right are coming into question, particularly outside of Westminster. New questions like Leave or Remain or, in the case of Scottish Independence, Yes or No, are dividing the previously aligned Progressives or Tories.

At the same time, our old national and global economic models have been failing spectacularly. In 2008 we experienced a complete global financial meltdown, with the collapse of banks and the stock market creating a 4 per cent drop in the global economy. But instead of redesigning our economic system to be more robust, resilient and generative, we chose to bounce back to the old ways.

Now history has served us another very hard ball, with the Covid crisis causing a 5.2 per cent drop in the global economy, leading to massive loss of jobs and security for millions.[43] But the extent to which we can bounce back this time has not yet become clear. There is a greater appetite for doing things differently this time – as evidenced by the deepening conflict between those for and against Green politics. But those with the will have not yet found the way.

Innumerable books, think tanks and experiments have pointed at increasingly feasible socio-economic alternatives. They call out the disconnection at the heart of a market economy. They show new mechanisms for reconnecting personal and social well-being to planetary health. But our political systems (and the media systems that amplify them) do not seem able to shift to these possibilities. While groups and even recognisable movements champion new and exciting ways of addressing our problems, the sad truth is that a majority of people will never know about them.

Can we get on with our lives?

The public space is ripe and ready for a new political idea. In the three years after Brexit over 90 new parties registered in the UK, hoping to step into the vacuum. This year alone, a further 30 have managed to register despite lockdown.[44] Many of them containing the words 'United' or 'Britain', demonstrating the clear need to come together and heal the polarisation.

Yet none have hit the nerve that the 'architect of Brexit' Nigel Farage and the UK Independence Party (UKIP) did in 1993 – by citing the desire for autonomy lying underneath the goal of coming together. Looking back now, if UKIP had been willing or able to follow up their harnessing of people's emotional need with a community strategy for action, they would have become a significant story of social development. But the culture of participation was absent.

So what if politics itself is really broken, meaning completely unfit for purpose in these wholly new times? Politicians and parties, largely caught up in old ideologies and binary dynamics, are stuck in a top-down agenda for controlling us – the people. With individual exceptions, they collectively lack the imagination to get us away from the past.

What is needed today is a completely new political idea that puts the need for human agency, rather than abstract ideology, at the heart of its project. This would be a political framework that meets the desire for coming together and healing in the process of 'taking back control' of our lives. It would connect people to a more sustainable, as well as a technologically enhanced, economy.

Look and you will find

If that sounds idealistic, then look carefully, because – in small ways – it is already happening. As my Uncle Seno said in Telawa, Ada: It's there.

Organisations and movements such as the Transition Network, the Permaculture movement, the peer-to-peer (P2P) network for a commons transition, or the long familiar cooperative movement now operating on open platforms, have systemically self-organised for resilience for more than a decade.[45] Offsprings have proliferated as their open-sourced software and resources allow the copying and adapting of basic models to suit different places and contexts.

The UK's Preston Model has been transforming the northern English city via a new form of localised economy.[46] That was in itself an imitation of what happened with community wealth-building in Cleveland, Ohio.[47] It has since been picked up and amplified in Cooperation Jackson, Mississippi.[48] Added to those are the Participatory Cities model in Barking and Dagenham.[49] Maybe also recall the policy and community innovation that occurred when Scotland formed its own parliament with a proportional system.

There are so many examples of new political forms that express a desire for action independent of big central government or the socio-economic system it upholds. This is a cry for agency to impact the futures of societies that people inhabit. These are not initiatives that settle for small ambitions: they are cosmolocal, connecting people to the best solutions available from all over the world. It's distinct from glocal – the term that describes keeping the global in mind while acting locally – in that the separation between the two realms diminishes as open-source global resources are used locally, whether those are technologies that allow relationship to develop while organising, or blueprints for soil regeneration, new currencies or food recipes.

Covid, shaking up everyone's assumptions, has only accelerated the linking of the very local to the very global in the most dramatic and physical way. As people share experiences, they are also sharing responses and solutions to problems. We are increasingly standing on our own patch, scouring the planet for equipment, protection, cures and good ideas.

New signs of response-ability

From a political perspective, you might be aware of the growth of citizen-led community initiatives such as Flatpack Democracy.[50] This fosters independent politicians, often in sufficient numbers to take over the local council and change the rules of engagement. Many others are experimenting with participatory budgeting and People's Assemblies. As described in the Introduction, The Alternative UK is developing Citizen Action Networks (CANs). These are capacious socio-technical structures that bring conflicted communities together, offering them creative spaces to become connected with the solutions already available.

What is crucial to this kind of modelling is that it does not offer detailed blueprints that are only successful elsewhere when rigidly followed. Instead they are prototypes arising from a pattern of values and organising principles to which people can relate emotionally as well as practically. To take a common example, the idea of a family may have started biologically, with a pattern of relationships that nurture and develop each member individually, within a shared identity. But familial *patterns of relationships* can be carried into organisations, clubs, initiatives of all kinds. We all know when the people we meet with – formally and informally – feel like family. It's in the design.

The Preston Model mentioned above is about community wealth-building. It describes how anchor institutions in any given town can invest inwards and procure locally, rather than sourcing all their services from around the globalised world. It's a simple switch that emphasises the importance of the community in wealth and building, rejuvenating local economies. It's an idea that is being copied all over the UK quickly, as it doesn't rely on a central body to scale it.

Other examples are those travelling under the headline of the 'well-being economy'. They repurpose business to create the conditions for human flourishing. This is often achieved by shifting the model from a single (profits only) to a triple (profit, people and planet) bottom line.[51] Examples include Elinor Ostrom's Commons model, Transition Towns and Permaculture, which all echo one another in pattern and principle by linking person to community to planet.[52] As organic systems – reflexive, iterative, process-orientated – they replicate natural and human organising, meeting emotional and physical needs. They feel less like hierarchical structures for towns and cities to fall into line with and more like an open field where different kinds of flowers bloom.

Patterns and fractals

Such patterns reflect what I call *fractal emergence* – rapid imitating and replicating, based on self-similarity rather than rigid structures.[53] They show what it could mean to be free to express authentically at the community level – both real and virtual.

In her enlightening book *You Matter More Than You Think*, Professor Karen O'Brien describes fractals thus:

> Fractals are self-similar patterns that repeat themselves at every scale. Examples in nature and mathematics include beehives, tree branches and river systems, Mandelbrot sets and Sierpinski triangles. Human and social fractals represent self-similar patterns that can be generated by individuals from moment to moment through conscious intent and agency. If our actions are consistent with values that apply to the whole, they will create new patterns that are replicated through language, stories, and meaning-making at all scales, such that each [part/ whole] reflects those qualities … Research on social tipping points suggests that action at a scale of between 10,000 and 100,000 people can have the greatest impact; however, from the perspective of quantum fractals, every person who takes actions based on universal values such as equity, dignity, compassion, and integrity affect all scales. This entangled [I/we] space represents a powerful 'sweet spot' for social change.[54]

Some of the smallest and brightest appeared during the first Covid lockdown as neighbourhood mutual-aid groups.[55] They sprung up spontaneously when local councils had neither the resources nor the relationships of trust with the people to be able to effectively care for the newly vulnerable. All over the country small groups like this reported the successful delivery of food and medicine, while also remarking on how people were enjoying meeting their neighbours for the first time. This was not the ticking of boxes and 15-minute allocations permitted to care workers, but a new kind of relational welfare that was generating new trust in the place in which they were living.

Are these new fractal possibilities – collectively – describing the new model that Buckminster Fuller once called for, making the old one obsolete? Maybe. However, if the new model stays within the current system it will have to suffer its fate like any other initiative – as a political football to be kicked back and forth between two parties and ideologies.

We need a new idea of politics, one that prioritises the importance of communities coming together outside of the division created by national-level parties. Without the possibility of energetic engagement by all the members of a shared community, we won't be able to evolve out of this very tight corner we find ourselves in.

Upgrading ourselves

Evolving out of tight political corners means moving into the broader culture of agency described above. But it also means offering citizens opportunities to upgrade their personal capacities. We need technology that gives everyone equal opportunity to be a community builder. We need learning clubs where anyone can learn the tools of self-mastery – physical, psycho-social, spiritual. Plus beautiful spaces in which people can meet, transform conflict and experience joy as well as grief.

Such Citizens Action Networks, occurring organically in neighbourhoods, towns, cities and regions, can also be seen as fractals of the bigger, more cohesive economic ecosystems of change described above.

Internal and external technologies

Only when this emerging connected and relational culture becomes established in a community can we add new forms of democratic self-governance that are capable of controlling their own decision-making. Important as ideas arising from the local citizens are, CANs won't just be based singularly on those. These local networks will also deliberate on cosmolocal solutions, pulled down from a growing global commons of shared ideas and designs that can halt the destruction of the planet.

The difficulty is that subtle decision-making tools are still rare. They tend towards binary Yes/No questions, or a list of tick boxes that ask you to state your preferences from an array of choices compiled by whoever designed the questionnaire, according to their agenda. Participants have no access to any information about who is taking part; they only see the results. Liquid democracy adds a new dimension by allowing voters to choose someone else – typically an expert – to make a decision on their behalf.[56] And the digital ledger known as blockchain adds new elements of security and transparency by making the registration details of every voter definitive and verifiable.[57]

Meantime, newer tools such as pol.is are becoming increasingly popular because they allow responses along a continuum – how much do you agree or disagree with this proposal?[58] The results tend to show much more convergence around the centre ground than our traditional divides would allow. It also enables participants to start a new question of their own that others can respond to. However, the complex results rely upon artificial intelligence to draw conclusions from all the input, and very few people understand how that 'black box' does its work. Audrey Tang, digital minister for Taiwan where pol.is is a central tool of government, says it works because the people trust each other and maybe that is a good prerequisite for introducing such a tool.[59] Whichever form is used, a rich, connected community should become capable of the different kinds of digital voting described above, clearly expressing its sovereignty.

Standing back, these kinds of self-similar, self-replicating patterns of individual human and community development, connected to the emerging planet-friendly new economies, add up to a possibility of rapid, fractal change.

Autonomy, agency and futurism

To accelerate that possibility, a fractal politics must shift the focus away from the vertical power of the state and look for the local and municipal energy that can connect human flourishing with planetary flourishing. This isn't simply achieved by the call for more and better jobs and housing – as the political Left might claim – but by embracing the more humanly complex psychological and relational needs that these new times have generated. We should build platforms that prioritise communities working together across old divides, liberating the energy of autonomy, agency and futurism.

But once that is tasted and felt by enough people, the power it generates cannot simply be handed over to the old system for the parties to divide and conquer. We need a benign and friendly version of the revolutionary practice called 'dual power' that can offer the people their own coherence and completion.[60] I propose a People's Parliament to replace the House of Lords to work in partnership with party politics at all levels, including the House of Commons. This would give the old forms of governance a broader political system within which the traditional state can slowly transform.

This kind of innovation points at an ambitious vision of power and voice, fit for tumultuous times that is far more natural and conducive to human flourishing than anything we have had until now. A new socio-political system that prioritises participation and co-creation from everyone would not only achieve new outcomes but also offer a sense of belonging, meaning, purpose and autonomy that people are craving. Without this, we cannot generate the hope that will make life worth living, and nor will we amass the energy to withstand the bumpy ride ahead.

In Telawa the generations had learned to live peacefully but passively. They were trapped by their shared dependency on the army's weekly deliveries, and little could change without a dramatic new input of diverse intelligences. When the teenagers and young adults woke up and began to add their voices to the mix – opening up multiple levels of new conversation around purpose, desire and the future – the dynamics changed radically: energy came back to the village.

The whole human system

Over the next chapters I'm going to dive deeper into why and how a new concept of the human being is the starting point for a new politics. I will then demonstrate how unlocking complex humans within the newly emerging systems is already re-making communities, both place-based and virtual. I will show how breakthrough tech can be better harnessed by integrated communities which, in turn, are increasingly the platforms for the cosmolocal collaboration the planet urgently needs in order to continue supporting the human race, among all forms of life on earth.

2 Where is the Human Agency in Party Politics?

Sitting on the bridge, they felt the warmth of each other's commitment. The sheer joy of being able to do something to register the dismay that had been building up for years. They knew the whole world would be watching as the police picked them off one by one, sometimes having to carry them to the van, chains and all. When politicians wouldn't halt the climate disaster, creating a spectacle was the only power they had.

Sometimes I yearn for the old days. When you could be a good parent by sending your kids to school, push them hard to do their homework and generally, just do as they're told. Now I'm lost. What did a lifetime of toeing the line do for me, or for any of us? We're ten years away from extinction, not even allowed to meet each other for a hug. Surely everything – everything – has to be questioned now? I sometimes think I should take them out of school: let them work it out for themselves – they'll probably do a better job. No, that's ridiculous: they'd never survive. They're too busy making friends and playing games.

Right at the heart of our triple crisis of lack of individual, social and planetary well-being is the question of agency. Who or what has the power to save us from human extinction? According to the scientists, governments could. But they prove to be in the grip of national and global dynamics they can't step out of.

According to popular narrative, God is either not listening or sitting in judgement.[61]

Everywhere, people are asking, what is my role in this? What difference does it make if I completely change my lifestyle to cut carbon, if no one else does?

The story of powerlessness

These questions resonate with a lifetime of learning about the relative powerlessness of individual human beings against forces they can't control. It's not only that the common people can't do much about socio-economic systems that are run by inaccessible elites; it's also that the evidence is broadly against us: history proves our human fallibility. We cannot control our outcomes goes the murmur. Control is an illusion.

At the same time, evidence to the contrary abounds. Entrepreneurs inventing practical solutions to age-old conundrums. Futurists using technology to leap forward into previously unimaginable capabilities. Psychologists revealing direct routes to permanent and sustainable well-being. Spiritualists offering the internal techniques that might found a Renaissance. Community organisers pointing again and again at how people transform through support and relationship. Art constantly offering alternative existential realities. The villagers of Telawa, springing to life.

Why do we not choose *these* stories above others? Even when we have the evidence that power is available to us, we still don't turn to it and use it.

There are good reasons for this. Firstly, while internally we might be able to grapple with 'being the change we wish to see', the constant message from the outside is that we won't be able to achieve these changes. Our culture too often upholds a story of self-defeat – one that our media amplifies readily. This isn't necessarily a conscious attempt to weaken us; bad news sells newspapers and it's a business for them. Capitalism thrives on instant reaction. Sensationalism fuels the power of attraction and no stories of pain or suffering are off-limits when it comes to clickbait.[62]

That may seem perverse on first hearing but, again, there is an explanation. Hearing what we most fear echoed in our environment may have an obvious downside of depressing us. But it has a stronger psychological secondary gain: it gives us an excuse to disown our responsibility for changing it. If everyone agrees that we are going to fail, then it's not anyone's fault. We feel that we can't possibly do anything about it. It lets us off the hook.

By contrast, being surrounded by positive news – and people who believe we can do something about the mess we are in if only we try harder – places a huge burden on us individually to rise to the challenge. The task feels overwhelming. Especially if we look around us and see no one there to help us face the mountain we must now climb.

Core to this continuing belief is the separation of individuals from their communities. As long as we look around ourselves and see those around us as our competitors, either for resources or for prizes, we will be confirmed in our helplessness. Only those with the conditions for developing confidence – parents with enough time and attention to give to their kids, good personal health, thick networks of support, access to learning – can rise above the story that everyone wants to beat you at the game of life.

Follow this trail further and we can see how much the story of competing individuals rests upon the notion that those who focus upon themselves are a different breed from those who focus on others. Individualists are selfish. Socialists are selfless. Yet it is the selfless who fail to make an impact in a competitive world. How can humanity win?

Those invested in community – 'localists' for example – are too often perceived as a challenge to globalists. Each considers the other a dangerous waste of time. When our jobs keep us busy night and day, leaving only tiny windows of time for our families, our disincentive to be part of our community is doubled. Yet without community, who are we?

All these contending stories in our head only serve to confuse and disarm: if we spend too much time trying to get to the bottom of where our agency lies, it feels as if the battle is already lost. Again, that is not accidental. All these stories of separation and disconnect are played out and amplified in our political discourse. Over decades, even centuries, this has kept the vulnerable unable to challenge the powerful. And the powerful unable to transform society in a way that benefits everyone.

Holding these anomalies as inevitable, political parties remain justified for pursuing their cause, each promising their voters the earth for success at the polls.

Reconnecting I–We–World

Yet if we stop to consider, there is no real reason these different aspects of our action and decision-making should clash. Outside of party politics and the public realm it mediates, the interests of a flourishing individual, the flourishing community and the flourishing planet – I, We and World – seem natural allies. As Buddhism taught me, these realms don't compete as domains within us: just different lenses with which to observe what's going on. Understanding myself is no obstacle to understanding you. On the contrary, practitioners come to see how their perception of themselves shapes their perception of others – they cannot be separated. Working on strengthening the self is directly related to working on the world – the human revolution that fuels the global revolution.

Socially engaged Buddhism – there are many schools – works from the point of view that lively communities of people become themselves the very conditions within which individuals can live good lives.[63] Global Buddhist movements also pay attention to how nations can act interdependently to safeguard the operations of local communities and the people within them. They are realms within realms which together become the substance of our consciousness.

Realms as lenses

This isn't to sell Buddhism as a practice. It's only to share the insights that Buddhism has offered to me, and that are available to anyone prepared to accept there may be different ways of looking at the apparent solidity, or rigidity, of a material world that is inevitably competitive. We don't have to overcome our separateness as much as let go of it, be free of it.

The work I do on myself – mindful observation of my own emotions and the story holding sway – gives me key insights into the world I'm observing, and vice versa. My vulnerability is its vulnerability, its vulnerability is my vulnerability. If that sounds narcissistic, consider that it might be the opposite of narcissism: something more like a dissolving of the ego, where your critique or appreciation of what emerges in your environment can become your agenda for self-development, your embodying of reality.

I'm not invoking a dream-like world here, a non-duality where the material self disappears. On the contrary: Buddhism offers an understanding of the human condition that accepts the keenly felt suffering and joy of everyday life as the terrain on which our Buddha nature walks. While we embody spirituality, we function day to day as people on the path to Buddhahood – Bodhisattvas – responding to the world actively on its own terms and being in service to mundane life. Yet we remain informed by the unconstrained, infinite possibilities of our non-material self. As the relationship between them is often described: 'two but not two'.

Insights from quantum physics

From another perspective entirely, quantum physics picks this shift up with its insight into wave–particle duality. Enlightenment physics described the two entities of wave and particle as entirely distinct. But following experiments in which the same entity could be perceived as behaving as both a particle and a wave – depending upon who was looking – scientists were obliged to let go of the distinction.

As Karen O'Brien describes in *You Matter More Than You Think*:

Rather than opening our mind to new ways of seeing and being in the world, we tend to retrofit new ideas into existing frameworks and describe them with familiar language. This may be the usual approach, but we live in a time that compels us to consider alternatives.

Quantum social science represents one possible alternative, and offers an entry point for generating deeper conversations about meaning and mattering in a changing climate. In physics, quantum theory has provided us with a new lens on the world, particularly at the atomic and subatomic scales, through concepts such as entanglement, complementarity, uncertainty and quantum leaps.[64]

This departure from the idea that truth can be universally observed is vital for our liberation from the failed present. If two people can describe the same phenomenon completely differently, the role of the observer changes dramatically: suddenly each of us has a role to play in our own truth-making and a responsibility to work with others to understand the bigger picture. Like the blind men and the elephant, in which each one can only feel one part of the animal before them, only the conversation between them will reveal the whole beast.

The legacy of disconnect

Keeping the realms of I, We and World separate is how work and play have come to occupy different territories. The needs of our personal world are seen as separate from our obligations to the one we share – the public space, where we serve others. Work gets financially rewarded and play generally costs money.

Over centuries this has become a virtuous circle: you have to work first, in order to play after. But it means that work is rarely playful – imaginative, creative, dynamic – and play is associated with spare time and triviality. This division allows those with power to instrumentalise the majority of people: making them parts of a working machine that delivers our collective right to play in spare time, 're-creation' for the grind. That, historically, the public space was designed by men is another reason that our socio-economic-political system lacks the emotion, connectedness and principles of care we associate with the private space.

Within that overall mindset, the complex internal lives of individuals become a separate issue from the job of delivering growth for society as a whole. The former becomes the purview of biology and psychology: those needing help to thrive are described as mentally ill. Women tend to pick up the slack at home, doing all the emotional labour of putting the pieces of disconnected individuals back together again at the end of the day.

Politics plays a particular role in this instrumentalisation of people. While politicians do the difficult job of representing the people in their constituencies – who they generally care about – they are upholding this distorted political system: one that renders this separation of the playful, responsive, private self from the functional, often mechanistic, public self as vital for economic growth. Humans become *homo economicus*: requiring only a job and tax credits in return for taking on the job of responsible citizenship. When they fail in their duteous labours, they are seen as deviant to a still prevailing 'work ethic'.[65]

As the failures of our economic systems become more and more obvious, this disconnect of realms at the heart of politics leads to ever greater pressure on people to increase their efficiency as machines. The behavioural sciences' nudge theory, according to which we are led by our limbic (early and animal) brains, constantly responding to small fears, always longing for comfort, can explain this. Nudging enjoys easy wins when our lives are so constrained and the external triggering of our most basic instincts is deployed to get predictable results for the economy.

Yet science has also taught us that humans became distinct from animals when our frontal cortex evolved.[66] At this stage, we developed the ability to observe our own thinking, create new forms of value and, above all, imagine new futures and act upon them. Of all the animals on this planet we are, in the words of The Alternative UK's Pat Kane, the 'radical animals: capable of creating new realities at will'.[67]

It's time to be creative. If we believe deep down that humans are capable of much more than this life of servitude to the growth economy which is killing our planet, then we need answers to key questions. Can it ever be right that humans are expected to live and work as parts of a machine, like hamsters on a wheel unable to stop long enough to be at rest and be creative? If no, then what is the alternative? Is it enough to relieve people of poor jobs without offering different forms of earning or ways to achieve? Or, to put it more succinctly, in a better world what is 'a living'?[68]

Paying attention to the future

To answer these questions we need to be able to shift our gaze from the current media sphere and develop a certain quality of focus. Brain science teaches us that whatever we give our attention to grows our sense of what the world is and what we experience as reality.[69] We are not like computers with the kind of operating systems that keep the contents safely stored in correct folders. For good or ill, the content we download is reflexive, making new sense of itself at every step, showing us back a world we are designing, often subconsciously.[70]

When we take all our information from the mainstream media, we live by it. If we are constantly giving our attention to a world in which we are powerless to change anything, that becomes our reality. At The Alternative UK one of our key commitments is to write a Daily Alternative – offering people constant real-world evidence that we are not a failed species: humans are ingenious.[71]

But given the pervasive effects of the mainstream media, it's clear that we have to re-train our focus, or remain vulnerable to the innumerable calls on our attention that keep us in thrall to the prevailing culture. When we see constant evidence of the fundamentally radical nature of human animals, all sorts of new things become possible.

In the next few chapters I'll look at how we can reclaim our whole selves at this crucial time. Only as whole selves will we be able to design and occupy a better 'operating system' for our communities and planet, bringing the domains of I, We and World together.

3 The Story of 'I'

3.1 Why we are hooked on our self-destruction

I can't describe it. But sometimes I'm out walking and I get 'the call'. I need something – can't be sure exactly what it is, but I know that feeling. Sometimes a can of Coke will do it. Not because I'm thirsty – a glass of water is better for that. And coffee is better for the buzz. But Coke gives me a fuzzier feeling: having enough money in my pocket for a can makes me feel free. Like I've got what it takes. Sometimes though, I find myself walking towards the bigger shops. I can usually find what I'm looking for – it's amazing the stuff on offer.

We sat, intent, listening to the politician. What the people want, he explained, is jobs. Security. Money in their pocket. We looked at each other then: all we needed was time, precious time. Later on, the kids asked, how did he find out what the people want? Did he ask you?

A T THIS moment of intense crisis, we could be forgiven for asking ourselves: how did it come to this? How could we possibly have let slip our concern for our very survival as a species? We have ignored the science that links climate breakdown directly to human behaviour – excessively consuming, extracting, flying, waste-producing.[72] Through sheer neglect we have allowed a disrupted biosphere to release global pandemics.[73] How could we have carried on, knowing what we knew?

It's easiest to blame our leaders. After all, they have the power and the resources to make meaningful changes. But increasingly, we look at each other. We shame whoever is doing less well than we are while trying to live up to Greta Thunberg's model of integrity.

And in our darker moments, we might even turn on ourselves. What am I being so defensive about? I agree with everything Extinction Rebellion is saying. So why do I keep copping out?

The illusion of freedom

None of this is unreasonable behaviour. But its angsty defeatism arises from the belief that we are fully capable human beings, free to act according to our will. We believe that any failure can be corrected simply by internally determining to do things differently. But the evidence is that we can't simply do this. Our internal motivational system – our programming if you like – is consistently creating outcomes for us. We now need to change those outcomes.

What is this programming? Is it deeply personal, or broadly cultural? Did someone design it on purpose to keep us all in thrall to the growth economy? Or is there a bigger evolutionary story at the core? More importantly, where can we find the agency to re-programme ourselves and our communities in sufficient numbers, to avert disaster?

When I first came across the Human Givens (HG) model of psycho-social therapy, it appeared deceptively simple. Founders Joe Griffin and Ivan Tyrell describe how we are born with 'given' – or evolutionarily adaptive – emotional needs. Together with our physical needs, these givens guide us on how to survive and thrive as social entities. They are:

- Security – safe territory and an environment which allows us to develop fully

- Attention (to give and receive it) – a form of nutrition

- Sense of autonomy and control – having the volition to make responsible choices

- Emotional intimacy – to know that at least one other person accepts us totally for who we are, 'warts and all'

- Feeling part of a wider community

- Privacy – opportunity to reflect and consolidate experience

- Sense of status within social groupings

- Sense of competence and achievement

- Meaning and purpose – which come from being stretched in what we do and think.[74]

As I explore more in the next chapter, from the HG perspective Maslow's hierarchy of needs is misleading. Emotional needs are not preferences, secondary to our physical needs. They are instead essential from birth, present so that we can create the conditions for our survival. We need to be seen, heard and counted in a community – or we die.

Never enough attention or control

While each of the givens is worth dwelling on at length, one or two stand out as acute drivers of our current crises. For example, the need for *autonomy/control* was politically harnessed as a rationale for Brexit. While we might recognise the need for control as an antidote to chaos, we have also learned how to distrust that call: we accuse each other of being control freaks, or any strong leadership as being over-controlling. In preparation for the referendum, director of Vote Leave Dominic Cummings used focus groups taken from the three million households that hadn't voted in the past two general elections and discovered that there was a strong sense of a past in which they had more control over their lives. That was when the campaign slogan shifted from the politically aggressive 'take control' to the personal and more poignant 'take back control' that appealed strongly to those missing voters.[75]

To forensically mine and manipulate the emotional lives of voters is not a new phenomenon, although the Labour Party has often chosen to reject that strategy as immoral.[76] Does that mean we should not be emotionally literate and articulate when we develop political vision? It was often my experience in the political discussions I took part in while active on the Left, that the emotional lives of our voters were forbidden territory. But that leaves politics with little access to the deep motivations of the people they serve. For example, where autonomy overlaps with the (forever debated) notion of freedom is regularly a strong political driver on the traditional right. Freedom is a clear emotional need, but society has not yet understood how to meet it with the necessary depth and complexity. This urgently needs to be the terrain upon which a strong democracy – and a new politics – is forged.[77]

Social media, for all its pros and cons, is an extraordinary vehicle for our desire to give and receive *attention* and *status*. Would Facebook, Twitter or Instagram have become the major industries they are now, if people were not crying out for ways to express themselves and be counted?

While we may have been shamed as children for being 'attention seekers', there is in truth no other way to download into our physiologies the information we need to thrive. Parents gazing into the eyes of their infants while feeding is programming them for empathy and connection. When members of a community meet in the street, giving each other the time of day, they are exchanging vital data for their social brains, forging bonds of trust.

At the same time, nature did not design us as dependents. Alongside 'given' needs, we are born with 'given' resources for getting those needs met. On the Human Givens Institute website, Griffin and Tyrell itemise these as:

- The ability to develop complex long-term memory, which enables us to add to our innate knowledge and learn

- The ability to build rapport, empathise and connect with others

- Imagination, which enables us to focus our attention away from our emotions, use language and problem solve more creatively and objectively

- Emotions and instincts

- A conscious, rational mind that can check out our emotions, question, analyse and plan

- The ability to 'know' – that is, understand the world unconsciously through metaphorical pattern-matching

- An observing self – that part of us that can step back, be more objective and be aware of itself as a unique centre of awareness, distinct from intellect, emotion and conditioning

- A dreaming brain that preserves the integrity of our genetic inheritance every night by metaphorically defusing expectations held in the autonomic arousal system because they were not acted out the previous day.[78]

But the time available for us to stream from our natural social environment has only got shorter over the years. In a media landscape of newspaper headlines, advertising and TV, we are constantly seduced by the spectacle of lifestyles we should aspire to. We turn away from the communities that might provide mutual nurturing and instead get on the hamster wheel. In stressful jobs, often with physical and mental constraints, it's hard to put our innate resources to work.

Even so, in the small gaps in our work schedules, our need for attention continues to drive us. We pore over posts, images and websites that give us the tiniest clues about the world. We shape our own comfort zones by liking and boosting others as we go. While society is increasingly fragmented, Facebook, Instagram and others have become the spaces in which we 'find the others' like ourselves, craving mutual appreciation. It's hard to pull ourselves away: their ever-cleverer algorithms and computations know this, and game it.[79]

Legacy of Mad Men

Added to this digital capture is the more clearly defined activity of the standard consumer economy. Even if citizens are becoming dimly aware of the psychology of emotional needs, the advertising industry has long been built on these insights. Being able to make the psychological connection between a pair of trainers and the need for belonging is a skill that business has been willing to pay for.

More insidious are connections like those between Coca-Cola – teaching the world to sing – and our need for meaning and purpose.[80] Deathly was the connection between smoking cigarettes and *achievement*, aimed in more recent years specifically at women and the Global South. The TV series *Mad Men* did much to explain, retrospectively, how we got hooked and who benefited. It made for chilling viewing.

Keeping us in the trance of trying to get our needs met is what has allowed the growth economy to prosper unchallenged. Precisely because no amount of buying stuff can satisfy those needs, we keep going back for more. The promise of fulfilment, met by only a fleeting moment of pleasure, is the very mechanism of addiction. This is what keeps us on the hamster wheel.[81]

This drag into the whirlpool of unmet needs has ever-escalating consequences: depression, frustration, anger – all the symptoms of a society instrumentalised by the demands of unrelenting growth.

But the worst impact has been on our loss of responsibility – which we could rephrase as our response-ability, our ability to respond – to what we see happening around us in real time. When Greta Thunberg asks why we do not act to save our world, the simple answer is because we can't. We're hooked on our *own* self-destruction.

3.2 Our inner Russian doll

She couldn't pin him down. All suit and tie during working hours. Then a mad rocker at the weekends. Generally, a very strategic type: carefully listening and planning the best way forward – whether in business, or even sorting out our weekends. But occasionally something would set him off and he'd just want his own way on everything. Politics was the worst thing: just like a child, insisting he's right.

My friends without kids don't get it. On the one hand I give them far too much of my time. Letting them go to different schools was the last straw – surely they should just all go to the same one? And then I let them go off with their friends on some hare-brained jaunt, not knowing from one day to the next where they are. But you've got to give them just enough care and freedom to help them grow up to be themselves, not just fall in line. If I had ten kids, I'd still treat them all differently – though there's no doubt they are all family.

I F HUMAN Givens goes some way towards explaining why our Western societies are so prone to addiction, what explains the further conundrum of our inability to see eye to eye?

Why is it that a room full of strangers would find it hard to calmly have a conversation about political issues – even when they all live in the same city, on the same streets? Even members of a family can find it hard to hear each other out on matters that exercise them, as if they talk across each other, rather than engage.

When Maslow is misleading

As I touched on in 3.1, the psychologist Abraham Maslow attributes our differences to a hierarchy of needs – the way we engage with reality is shaped by what we are hoping to achieve. At base, we need the material, physiological conditions to be able to survive and procreate: food, water, sleep, shelter and so on. But once these needs are met, we begin to develop ever more sophisticated needs – from security to love and belonging, self-esteem and eventually self-actualisation.

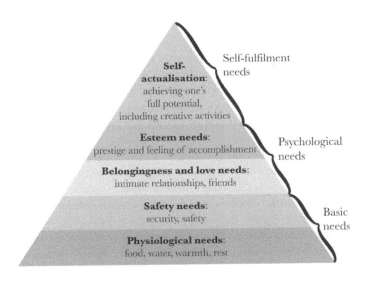

Figure 3.1 Maslow's hierarchy of needs

This idea of a hierarchy of needs is well reflected in our politics, which focuses on the base needs first – food, shelter, money – believing that our capacities to deliver the rest will follow on naturally. However, the Human Givens model would say that humans have all those needs in our sights from day one. Without being able to get our emotional need for self-esteem met in a balanced way, we can become overly dependent on social media. Without belonging we might become very lonely and alienated. Both of these are triggers for mental health problems such as depression or self-harm. Or they can be the cause for social unrest or criminal behaviour. Without designing our lifestyle so that all these needs are met, we cannot have a safe and secure society.

Although our capacity for developing to different levels of need is implied by Maslow, our politics is geared to meet us on that first level. We are, in the minds of our party-political culture, driven by material wants, characterised as homo economicus. Is this true? In my experience this is not true. Of all my professional engagements, two years on a project called Reimagining Social Work made this clear to me.[82] The call for self-actualisation can exist right alongside hunger and homelessness. Being seen and heard as a complex human matters at the same time as the need for a bed for the night. If the first gets met, it makes the second incrementally easier to achieve. I'm not suggesting that the government should prioritise workshops over foodbanks, but that we should never imagine that answering physical and material needs is enough to set people on the path to self-reliance.

A great example of this point is the difference between housing the homeless in temporary accommodation – an overnight hostel or a cheap hotel – and giving them a home to live in. While the first provides a physical berth, it does not offer the chance to create relationships with others, and onwards for creating roots and networks from which to begin building a new life. Homeless people can be trapped for years in the daily cycle of earning enough to stay out of the cold. Whereas in Finland, homelessness has almost disappeared because of a policy to house people as quickly as possible.[83]

Integral operating systems

Other models of lifelong human development run into similar problems – albeit with different consequences. Don Beck's Spiral Dynamics, for example, posits our different capacities for managing both our internal and external conditions as a colour-banded hierarchy.[84] We move up through the colours, towards ever higher forms of consciousness and capability.

The initial premise is logical – that there is a natural arc of development from birth to maturity. From that first total dependence of the newborn, we see a slowly developing sense of agency as we learn to interact with the forces around us, in order to get our needs met.

The first four levels Beck describes – first the mystical (purple), then the egocentric (red), moving towards a broader, foundation building impulse (blue), followed by strategic (orange) – are all experienced as victory-orientated, zero-sum sensibilities, with little mutual appreciation. In the same way that adolescents look down on infants, each new level makes us feel better equipped to deal with circumstances as we move towards our own sense of independence. The lower levels look at the rest of the world with distrust, sensing their own dependence on others.

The important shift occurs at 'green'. This is a stage of relativism, when suddenly all levels appear to have equal validity and any sense of direction or progress is lost. This is the bridge to what Beck describes as moving from first- to second-tier consciousness. It's the point at which humans can get an aerial view of the different stages of their lives.

After green, we come off the ladder of development and see ourselves as containing all the previous stages of development: we experience them as integrated, rather than merely conquered. The structure is more like a Russian doll than some kind of super-human overview. We stop judging others because we can now experience each level within us, but now with less attachment. That feeling of egotistically demanding to be heard, for example, can rise and fall away, rather than define and capture us.

Higher levels of development (associated with the colours yellow, then teal) map out this new consciousness, which is often described as post-egoic: a deepened, some might say spiritually informed, interdependence with the world around us. This leads eventually to an experience of reality where the inner and outer are entirely fused

– which Spiral Dynamics calls coral. Buddhists might describe this as the 'non-dual'.[85]

Integral philosopher Ken Wilber's genius was to apply all these levels to a vision of reality, mapped by a matrix of four quadrants.[86] The quadrant arises through two axes – vertically from individual to collective, horizontally from internal to external. These offer four lenses through which we can see the complexity of any human phenomenon. It's not just the view from the inner and outer world of the individual. But also, the inner and outer world of society – inner meaning that society's culture and values, outer indicating its structures and governance. Together they form an integrated picture of life at any given moment.

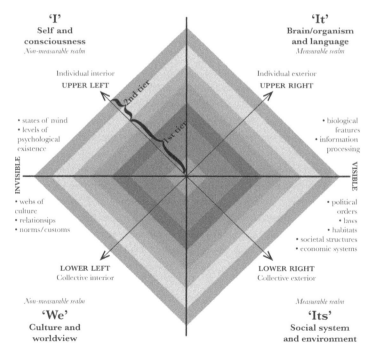

Figure 3.2 Ken Wilber's AQAL (all quadrants all levels) incorporating Don Beck's spiral dynamics

At first glance, all of this can seem elitist. Until you reach the second tier it can't help but look like people at higher stages of development looking down at the lower levels – a ladder of capacities. Yet in order to address the problems we face today, we must be able to talk about how we can *all* move to the next stage of human evolution, both personally and collectively. And in so doing, we will become more capable of transforming what we ourselves have created.

Women seeing differently

Maybe we need a different metaphor than the ladder to demonstrate the universality of the approach. And softer language. Perhaps something more like the rings of a tree – showing all the stages of growth as essential to the integrity of the tree, rather than as stages you leave behind?

With Matthew Mezey-Kalman, I hosted the London Integral Circle (LIC) for ten years, as the 20th century morphed into the 21st. It was an oasis in the desert for those involved in socio-politics who wanted a much more complex analysis of who we are individually as well as collectively and how that manifests in our private and public power structures. In 2005, the women in the group began to meet separately and in parallel. We were tired of studying Wilber's theory in meetings that were sometimes dry, competitive and overly cerebral. We wanted to explore integral theory's implications for our daily lives more actively – what Polish-American scientist and philosopher Alfred Korzybski would call distinguishing the map from the territory.[87] This women's integral group talked more about community, health, politics – all forms of what we called embodied learning.

Although the men set up their own group (to explore their feelings about this change), the dynamic was altered – and the LIC slowly stopped meeting. Yet the women came alive: excited to meet together and plot the future. The move to women's circles is a pattern that is being repeated elsewhere in similar groups and, in my experience, is as much about new ontologies – ways of seeing and being – as new cognitive capacities.

The challenge for future circles will be whether or not they can integrate these shifts well enough to contain the transformation of the whole space that is being asked for – typically by the women. This has major implications for the evolution of our society, as I explore in Chapter 4, the 'We' section.

Suffice to say, Wilber's theory remains hugely relevant to both 'the map' and to 'the territory' – whether in personal or in political development. Being able to see the diverse levels of agency in a room, a community or a nation points at a very different idea of the public realm than the one currently promoted by party politics. Although class divisions remain relevant, where they were once definitive they are now no longer adequate to describe what agency is and how it develops.

A full and rich journey of individual development could be completed quite early in life: young parents, for example, often display what Wilber or Laloux would describe as second-tier abilities in their relationship with their children, regardless of material resources or intellectual ambition. They can see when to lead directly and when to stand back and let independence develop through self-organising.

On the other hand, sophisticated executives, with infinite resources, can regularly display childlike egos when challenged – resorting to bullying to get their way. Those early-year frustrations don't necessarily disappear with age: they can re-assert themselves under pressure.

But if the conditions in which we live make us feel powerless, then we will be experiencing a 'first-tier' sense of frustration most of the time: looking down on those we feel are naïve, looking up at people who seem more capacious. Unable to call out seniors for their very junior behaviour.

Internal and external diversity

The important knowledge here is that human beings are diverse, not just because of manifest traits – colour, gender, age, etc – but also internally, due to their different experiences of agency. The integral development of our society would deliver not only more equality and new forms of power, but also new ontologies: evolved senses and experiences of being together. These are all factors that a broken politics cannot ignore any longer.

Politicians who claim to know 'what the people want' – without acknowledging that 'want' will always be a diverse mix of needs – do not have the capacity we require in leaders today. Creating the conditions for far more subtle political spaces to appear will be the key to our future development as a society.

The breakthrough to developmental literacy – including the many internal and external levels of human agency – is as important as the introduction of emotional literacy once was.

development

3.3 Being more than the self

To see this rise in the middle of lockdown is shocking in ways it's hard to express. The crowds gathering in towns and cities all over the world, not always masked and distanced, in solidarity with George Floyd and all the Black Lives that Matter too. That he died pleading to be allowed to Breathe made him an Everyman for this time. I can only call it a global spiritual awakening, the power of his death and what is happening now.

Turning on his computer was like, well, turning on. From the drab walls of his sad, useless, bedroom, he was suddenly in his own altered reality. Headphones on, he could conjure up his mates wherever they were, the best beats with mind-blowing images, properly immersive learning vids, stuff to buy. He could watch, without being watched, to his heart's content. And yeah, in the best games, he could actually be someone else, occupy another body and live another life. This was surely what freedom meant.

When I was 11 my brother died in a car crash. I remember praying all night to God that he would live: a desperate child bargaining with the ultimate power – I would have given anything to save him. When I got up in the early hours to see what was happening, I found my mother staring vacantly out the window: he had died two hours earlier and she had gone with him. In that moment I lost God. Despite a primary education shaped strongly by nuns with attitude, I was catapulted out of a universe in which Hail Marys made sense. No one was listening to the prayers of this child.

Through death to becoming

In hindsight I can see that that was only the start of my spiritual journey. In what a psychotherapist might describe as dissociative behaviour, I took my mind away from the scene of grief to some far place, so distant from this disabling loss that I could meet my brother there. As if I had escaped time and space.

I didn't have a name for it and heaven did not describe it. Just as God no longer described, for me, the force that determines our lives. Yet there was something more than nothing at all. Relating to this 'more than' life as we know it was what I began to think of as my spirituality.

During my teenage years my mother lost six of her seven siblings to cancer. My father's younger brother drowned in a freak accident in shallow waters. I watched my formerly glamorous, professional mother become a shadow of herself, existing only to keep house for her family and my father, unable to make it all right for us and turning away.

I began to construct my own – childish – belief system in which humans were entirely free to step out of the present and occupy reality from the perspective of the future, the past and the adjacent as if they were fused. I taught myself to look at the world through the eyes of friends – and strangers – who seemed happier than me, so I could subtly occupy their better fortune. I now see that I was trying to liberate myself from the limitations of the present. And I succeeded to a reasonable extent. I became self-sufficient, but I was crippled by an inability to explain myself to others. Like many adolescents, I dreamed of one day writing a book that made sense of this growing autonomy I was forging for myself.

But that book had already been written. I remember the first time I sat down with one of Senosoenoto's pupils – Iwan Sastrowardojo – in the gardens of the mountain retreat outside Bandung to get a quick download about Buddhism in preparation for my article. As soon as Iwan started talking I felt as if I had stepped into a deep blue ocean pulling me urgently into its depths but without any fear of drowning: an instant fathomless belonging. Every word he spoke was telling my life back to me in new metaphors that integrated and expanded my disconnected thoughts into a whole new organising system for my mind that seemed beyond my conscious ability to control.

This was not my rational brain clicking and whirring – I felt the effects of it long before I could understand the complex teachings he was sharing. When I look back at it now, it remains powerful proof that deep and meaningful change doesn't have to take time but can move like lightening between people through activating relationship. While I felt strong but distant before, I was now grounded and present. Others described it back to me as a religious awakening, but to me it felt like a calling to being whole. As time went on, it took the form of permanent becoming – a mission and purpose. This was not a belief system I had downloaded, but a new connection to life itself. I was re-wired and switched on.

A spiritual journey in public

As I described in the introduction, meeting the Nichiren School of Buddhism helped me to frame and activate my spiritual life. Our group – up to 12 million practitioners worldwide – chanted rather than meditated, channelling our spiritual insights and energies into what was described as 'soka', a Japanese word for the 'creation of value'. The lay movement Soka Gakkai was committed to culture, education and peace, and even gave rise to a political party in Japan. Their ethos was that of the bodhisattva: serving the Buddha nature – creative life itself – present in every human being. It was great for us as adolescents, looking for both training and meaning in life.

But not everyone in the broader society was up for it. Spirituality was and still is a tricky word in early 21st-century UK. It is too nebulous for the religious, and simply deluded to the atheists. When I came back from Indonesia, I found myself living a double life of sorts: I was inside and outside of the movement and there was little overlap. In my work with Conflict and Peace Forums, including the Peace Journalism Project, I would never draw on a spiritual perspective – however relevant or helpful it may have been in describing the loss of integrity in the media.

In the late 1990s, I was offered the chance of a two-year bursary by the innovation foundation NESTA to explore – in their words – anything I wanted. But when I proposed an exposition on spirituality, the offer was swiftly withdrawn. It was a blow. Yet in the midst of disappointment, I could see the problem as one of language and disconnect. In my later letter to them I suggested: 'You clearly all live spiritual lives. Wondering, experiencing art, sensing and intuiting, connecting with people and events in unexpected ways. These all seem spiritual activities to me. Ways to see and feel beyond the material reality that is described by science and logic.' I got no reply.

One of my portfolio jobs at the time was as Associate Curator for events at the Institute of Contemporary Arts (ICA). Even though the then Director Philip Dodd was highly sceptical, he gave Director of Talks Rachel Cottam and me permission to pull together a six-part series called 'The S Word: Grappling with 21st-Century Spirituality' (I still have the leaflet[88]). We curated events with the legendary Brian Goodwin on Science and Spirituality, Esalen guru Erik Davis on Spiritual Tech, and Annie Lennox talking to Rupert Sheldrake about sex.

Even in its hey-day the ICA was rarely sold out, but every one of the S-Word events was. Not that we came to any conclusions or that any measurable assessment was made – it's difficult to know what that might have looked like as it was just rooms full of people enjoying conversation. Nonetheless, a second series was deemed too risky for the ICA, which was wary of becoming a home for hippies.

So how has that query into 'the S word' changed in these intervening years? It seems the market for an enhanced understanding of the value of spirituality, in helping us create value in our personal and civic lives, is still unpopular.

The following is from E.O. Wilson in 2000, but it could be today's advice: 'It's got to be done in a way that touches what people like Joe Six-pack are thinking. We've got to get moving on an effort to spiritualise the environmental movement – not in the sense of starting to offer up prayers – but with a sound empirical base.'[89]

This may be why, 15 years later, the Chess Grandmaster and philosopher Jonathan Rowson began a similar – though far more intellectually rigorous – investigation at the RSA, called Spiritualise. That six-part series gave rise to the research institute Perspectiva, where I am now a Senior Associate. Perspectiva's 'urgent 100 year project' seeks to articulate the relationship between our internal spiritual system – which might be captured by the idea of a soul – and the external socio-economic-political system in ways that reframe the climate discourse and help it to have more agency.[90]

Mindfulness, once an esoteric Buddhist practice, is now a billion dollar business.[91] For example, following its launch in 2010, the Headspace app has been downloaded by 36 million members across 190 countries. In the UK Parliament, almost a third of all MPs have been on a mindfulness course and the practice has been introduced into the ministries of education, health and crime.[92]

Extinction Rebellion (XR), the international uprising against ecological and climate breakdown whose surging popularity took everyone by surprise, is explicitly driven by spiritual insight and connectivity. Co-founder Gail Bradbrook attributes the initiative to visions experienced while taking the plant medicine ayahuasca, something she has written about often.[93]

XR's symbolism is heavily influenced by spiritual indigenous rituals. And at the heart of their vision for the future is a regenerative system, capable of reconnecting the people to nature and the planet. How this embeds itself in a new politics is a challenge that Green socio-economic projects like Transition Towns have been exploring for a decade.

But can we also 'spiritualise' the other two dimensions of our current crisis – that is, social division, and individual psycho-social health? From our research on The Daily Alternative, the answer would be: maybe. There's an important conjunction, for example, between the plight of alienated workers – instrumentalised by a relentless growth model and the gig economy (often described as an existential crisis) – and the search for spiritual growth.

On the one hand, 'spiritualising' implies the need for more personal and political agency: a new connection between our inner and outer capacities. This would demand a new socio-political settlement that gives citizens an enhanced role based on their growing response-ability. But on a more personal level, the call for more self-control, self-sovereignty and reclamation of the mind is also increasing.

While some prefer to talk about mindfulness as cognitive, its powerful language of internal and external connectedness creates an easy bridge to a relationship with the non-material. When we bring attention back to ourselves and are able to observe our own thinking, we come into relationship with a very different self than the one which is routinely instrumentalised by the public space. We are less the consumer client, on a treadmill to keep the system going, and more the autonomous agent, free to reconnect with other realms and realities through thinking and feeling.

More challenging might be the common language between technical and spiritual exploration – captured by Erik Davis in his book *Techgnosis*. Davis connects the drive towards what the tech-literate call 'the singularity' – the ultimate coming together of all our tech solutions – with the desire for transcendence. Notions of interconnectedness, interdependency and ultimately inter-being are all shared evidence that the human race can evolve beyond a crude Cartesian duality.[94]

In the meantime, does the virtual nature of the net – game playing, personae adopting – also mean that we are now able, in a very practical sense, to live and experience life in other dimensions at the same time. Is techgnosis the front line of spiritual development? Or is what we are witnessing mostly tech engineers high on substances, projecting their own sensibility onto a shared internet? I'm sure Erik Davis would allow both possibilities. At my ICA event he admitted that the techgnosis exploration is largely pursued by men from the global North. It might be that they are sensing something subtle missing from the historically dominant worldview and are using technology to try and trace it and then mimic it in order to master it.

The existential challenge of Burning Man

Similar questions might be asked of the Burning Man Festival. To all intents and purposes, this is a socio-political innovation space for the creative community, held annually in the Nevada desert since 1986. Predicated strongly on self-reliance within co-creative communities, Burning Man Festivals are 'temporary autonomous zones' that use the creation of extraordinary works of art and the new relationships arising from their impact as a vehicle for spiritual transcendence. It's described by one participant as a space where 'Why not?' overwhelms 'Why?'[95]

Yet how do the skills and new sensibilities learned at Burning Man transfer to the mainstream? Back in 'real life' it's easy for 'Burners' to return to business as usual, taking part in the old system as vigorously as ever. Except maybe in those moments that they meet and find each other again – such as in the annual gatherings known as Alter Ego.[96] Does that make their spiritual odyssey any less valuable?

What is remarkable to me is that the language of personal, social and planetary transformation appears in so many different places at the same time. Not just geographically dispersed, but also in the kinds of communities that gather. The new sense of deeply connected autonomy that is happening at Burning Man sounds oddly similar to what is happening within the various independence movements – from Barcelona to Scotland to Frome, as well as within the civil society sector at the grassroots, and within care and social work in the heart of big cities. This change of culture has also been happening in business for more than 20 years, particularly visible among those that are now identifying as B-corps or 'for benefit companies' who develop with a triple bottom line of profit, people and planet.[97]

All these groups talk about self-knowledge, authenticity and autonomy and about awakening to a more connected system where relationship plays a crucial role. At the same time, there is still a division between the hard power of money and vertical leadership and the softer power of connection and behaviour change. For example, at the charitable trust called Power to Change the language of connectedness and well-being is now at the heart of their literature on collective empowerment.[98] Yet the call to action is focused on the government. Hope, rather than concrete action, is increasingly evoked as the vehicle for multidimensional and connected change.

This moving into a collective, co-created yearning for something that might help us in the face of existential and material crises feels as close to a modern-day spiritual journey as anything. But to get somewhere original, we will need to seize on the new language and build the new systems and structures these fresh ways of seeing imply. But we will also need new ontologies and new ways of capturing being and feeling that help us put new markers down at every stage of the journey.

A virtual self: what happened during Covid

I'm sure I'm not alone in having experienced the Covid lockdown as taking us a few essential steps along that road. The increased quiet on the roads and a more active pursuit of nature where we could breathe, better pushed us towards 'spiritualising' more. But more than anything, the heightened intensity of a new sort of connection with others made an impact on the spiritual shifts taking place.

For example, the sudden popularity of Zoom rooms that, despite being virtual, were strangely intimate.[99] Not only were employees meeting their bosses in their homes, with children and favourite bits of art in full view, but for the first time people started meetings with an earnest 'How are you?' and listened attentively to each other's answers.[100] It was as if people were seeing each other for the first time. In addition, there were immense efforts to bring people together for virtual choirs, exercise classes, cooking lessons. It evoked the possibility of rising to the crisis through people power.

Witnessing even wealthier and more developed governments face the unknown enemy made the pandemic more surreal. It was like we were on the *Starship Enterprise* heading for new territory. It took me back to the earliest days of my spiritual journey when I was standing in front of a void, not knowing how to make sense of what was going on. Yet just as I had then, there was also a feeling of deep connectedness with life itself, and a readiness to be with whatever emerges. To use a Buddhist metaphor, we were in a state of stirring the inner warrior for the fight ahead.

4 The Story of 'We'

4.1 Our failure to come together till now

Sometimes I sit alone in my room, just thinking. It's so intense, I can feel the thoughts tumbling into my head, uninvited. I know this thing – this life that we live – is not how it should be. It should be so much better. We could be so much better. My parents think I'm mad, but I'm sure I'm not the only one who thinks like this. How can I find the others?

He couldn't contain his fury. After all the hours he'd spent carefully creating the conditions for a deep, sensitive discussion among this important group of thinkers, here's this equal rights activist banging on about the lack of diversity in the room. She's ruining everything.

By the time they had got to Session three of the Zoom gathering, something new had appeared between them. Gone was the impatient needing to be heard or the spiky reactions to each other's comments. Instead they seemed to be enjoying each other's jokes and jibes as they gathered, but listening – really listening – to each other's anxieties and hesitant suggestions for a better way forward. Years later they would remember this moment as a rare coming together of strangers to find deep common ground. Although it was difficult afterwards to know what that added up to other than a feeling of love and respect.

As I began to explore in Chapter 2, one of the biggest falsehoods of political culture is that individualists and socialists are separate tribes, implacably opposed, which is why in Chapter 3.2 I described our constantly evolving ability to relate to wider perspectives beyond our egocentred instincts, while still being capable of looking after ourselves.

When we live in conditions that get our emotional needs met, looking after the self does not conflict with working well with others. Why would it? Our interdependence seems obvious as soon as you are part of a family, group of friends. Or among any people standing in solidarity with each other.

Multiple forms of agency

Within the integral model, different expressions of the 'we' reflect different expressions of agency. Inside the first tier, life is perceived as a zero-sum game and competition is unavoidable. With that mindset you can only construct a 'we' when you have a clear opposition. Left v Right, unions v the bosses, 99 per cent v 1 per cent. There has to be someone to beat to generate the motivation to act. As David Merrick famously said: 'It's not enough to win, my enemies must lose.'[101]

At the level of consciousness that Ken Wilber and others describe as 'green', this competitiveness dissolves into relativism. We are all equal, and different: others have a right to disagree. There is no objective right or wrong: the hierarchy disappears. For many this is an ideal way for society to co-exist, in mutual tolerance. At the same time, this new distribution of power does not mean greater coherence or even community. It's more of a right for people to live as they choose, and often they choose to do so in closed, siloed communities.

From this perspective multiculturalism is still distinct from integration as a way for society to cope with diversity. Multiculturalism upholds the right for everyone to hold on to their cultural roots without adapting, which sometimes leads to isolated communities unable to communicate unless the local council provides interpreters. Integration suggests acceptance on the condition of replacing the old with the newly adopted home culture, a common cause for grief and tension – two choices rubbing alongside each other, competing in the party-political discourse. What often occurs over time is a hybrid solution, with the children of second- and third-generation immigrants holding their cultural heritage easily within the nationality of their birth. A more self-organising politics would see all of these options playing out across society, enhancing cohesion through cross pollination – but we're not there yet.

Within the first-tier context, where the majority of society is still competing, 'green' looks like a surrender to chaos. It's an interesting test of the integral theory. Too often we see those who are trying to uphold the rights of the previously excluded – the newly woke – being derided by those who otherwise describe themselves as teal (or 'second tier'). I've experienced this often in otherwise warm, spiritually open – even promiscuous – gatherings: a woman or person of colour describes the overly male or white gathering as limited, then is aggressively rejected by the crowd. As if their needs cannot be held there alongside those of others.

What is at issue here? In the rooms I am now recalling, this was unlikely to be racism or sexism: the emotions being expressed were highly defensive. If anything, it felt like an unwillingness to share the space with different expressions of agency – a competing legitimacy of need. Like the older brother who refuses to take care of the younger siblings, crying out instead, 'what about me?'

Does this inability to hold plurality suggest that those criticising the 'woke' had not yet experienced 'green' fully – what Wilber describes as 'the inner shift past the egoic self'? For those who have done so – be it parent, social worker or teal organiser – the overreaction to those newly discovering their identities seems unnecessary, ungenerous and potentially dangerous.

Herding cats is old school

In the second-tier context, best understood as a more aerial view, it all looks different again. The notion of herding cats – trying to control the diversity and autonomy of others – becomes old school as everyone self-organises. Tolerance of difference, even chaos, becomes an active embrace, a seeking-out of diversity. From this perspective, it's not difficult to find an individual direction and purpose while remaining connected to the whole. Multiculturalism and integration interweave, becoming aspects of each other. The old see the young as their own future. Leadership becomes possible without followership. The 'we' is no longer tribal, nor rejected as illusory, but returns as one's identification with ever bigger systems grows stronger, more complex.

We begin to develop a thinking and a feeling of *belonging with the whole human race.* And then the domains are ever-widening: all humans on the planet, then the planet itself, then the universe of planets and so on. In many ways this completes the Russian doll effect of the integral vision. What might be described as a spiritual quest for ever deeper and wider connection in the adult is often compared to the instinctive, unarticulated experience of the newborn child: curious and in awe.

It's possible that spiritual institutions, such as Church, Synagogue and Mosque, hold the space for the whole of the integral spectrum in our society – keeping a constant relationship with the unknown of the sacred, as we journey through life. But their institutional power also evolves and changes, as our culture does. Today more and more people challenge these institutions' authority and take on that integrating task for themselves, as described in Chapter 3.3. But these islands of self-organisation are not yet working together to offer a broader solution for the whole of society.

The result is that today our Western society is fractured and hard to bring together, much exacerbated by 'first tier' politics and media, which thrive on division. Particularly in the UK, a crude winner-takes-all electoral system (known as 'first past the post', see note 5) denies any possibility of the country being governed as a complex whole. Every politician is required to put party before country, in a daily fight for dominance.

In the midst of that, the people have no collective agency – there is no way for us to work together. That only 2 per cent of the potential electorate are members of the same political parties that prevent this system evolving is barely remarked upon. We give away our power, as millions of citizens, to tiny numbers of people who decide how to run our world.

As we face a climate catastrophe capable of making our species extinct, we have no integrated alternatives to the failed system that caused it. Worse, we do not ourselves have response-ability. For all the reasons I described in Chapter 3.1, we are mostly in *tharn*: the term used in *Watership Down* for 'toxic immobility' – the rabbit frozen in the headlights.[102]

I say mostly, because if you step outside the mainstream headlines, you will find pockets of people around the world responding to the best of their ability, yet with limited success. Social justice warriors are trying to be seen and heard because people are dying of neglect in prisons and slums. Environmentalists are trying to wake people up because the building is burning. But barely anyone moves. Those still seated continue to look around to see if enough of the others are moving, before they break from their own position. We don't have a developed-enough 'we' sensibility, giving us the confidence to act on what is necessary for us together.

Compare that to the stories we hear about animals collectively sensing that a tsunami is about to happen and signalling a retreat from the coastline, larger animals taking smaller ones with them.[103]

New forms of organisation, sometimes combined with technological solutions, try to address what a new collective action might be. But it's early days. After centuries of an economic system that has reduced complex humans to being machine parts for the growth economy, no one thinks that reversing the damage is an easy task. Few think it is even do-able. While each phase of our social development brought extraordinary benefits, they also document the collective trauma of men and women (in different ways) becoming increasingly disconnected and mechanistic, serving what emerged as a global economy.

Agriculture, colonialism, industrialisation, the military complex, free market capitalism – each in their turn robs us of our ability to come together as naturally autonomous adults, and to make decisions for our collective good (never mind the tarnishing of 'social' agency under actually existing Communist and Socialist regimes). If nations were ever intended to offer that container, politics prevents it happening. We are, mostly in ignorance, the major polluters of the earth. It is the shopping, driving, flying and wasting involved in industrial and consumerist modernity that has caused this problem. Yet we cannot correct ourselves.

When we see our situation in these quite simple terms, it also paradoxically becomes easier to see what could change and be effective in the future. If we, as people of every kind, are becoming more self-aware – response-able – we may also be learning to collaborate better with others. Not so much to start from scratch in finding solutions, but by organising ourselves better to connect to the best solutions available.

We could defy an old economic system that gives us poor access to it. In the near future, we may simply rely less on the system that has failed us and more on ourselves, individually and collectively, to find ways forward. Less supplicant, more creative.

New forms of 'we' appear in virtual spaces

Once we start looking at our chances in this more developmental way, the whole landscape changes. We can look at the advent of the internet 20 years ago as the starting gun for power becoming better distributed around the world.

In a very short space of time, ordinary people have moved from having little or no access to the information they needed to make change happen, to almost unlimited access. Today any person with a computer, or even smartphone, can be taught by Harvard University. Or pick up an invention from the other side of the world, increasingly for free.

This is not everyone's experience of the internet but it's my intention here to keep hold of the evolutionary possibility for the broadest swathe of people. We have all seen how the early days of the internet as commons – a shared space where people connected and exchanged freely – has been taken over by the same dynamics as our physical society. We are back in the world of predators capitalising on our energies for private gain and worse, highly intrusive surveillance of our private lives by those who seek to control us.

Many books and countless articles are written about our vulnerability in the face of surveillance capitalism, but not enough about our growing ability to resist and respond. Life has a cyclical aspect to it and we would be right to say there's nothing altogether new about the internet in terms of its ability to change everything. The rise of print literacy was just as revolutionary. Yet despite all these systems of accumulated knowledge, we teeter on the edge of environmental oblivion.

Yet I prefer to think of the circular nature of development as in fact spiral – moving forwards then backwards but always a little higher than before, knowing a bit more about ourselves and able to reflect more. We were reading books alone, with only the most educated having the chance to sit and discuss their deeper meanings and implications, while the internet is a social phenomenon. We read, we discuss, we react, we perform – all in the spotlight.

For that reason, I see the evolving phenomenon of the internet as driven by humans in search of getting their bio-psycho-social-spiritual needs met. It is technology but, as Erik Davis describes, echoing ever more our desire for transcendence. That we should give rise in the midst of that to the very powers that have always sabotaged our progress, is something we have to own and design solutions for. To do that we have to get hold of our own developmental process in relation to the internet and try to develop resilience.

This is not a simple task: social media in particular has accelerated our addictions to consumerism and following strong opinions. But we shouldn't ignore that it has also created the conditions for these new levels of self-awareness. We talk a lot about our own behaviour, our perceptions of how relationships work, how we succeed and fail – none of which could be discussed by previous generations. Alongside that, we are now able to connect to others with shared interests at the drop of a hashtag.

In other words, however imperfectly, multiple new forms of 'we' are appearing. Does this in any way change the status quo? If we continue to look at power as 'hard', meaning the ability to force outcomes, either with money or military might, then maybe not. Business continues to hold sway through politics – a cartel system that keeps them in hock to each other.[104] Our economic system – capitalist, neoliberal – has most of us in its grip, as I've described above.

Yet we increasingly see groups of people with relatively little hard power make massive impact upon our lives. Take Nigel Farage, whose UKIP never had more than one MP in the House of Commons but who managed to sway public opinion with a call upon people's emotions.[105] His Brexit Party in 2019 pulled off the same trick, paradoxically gaining seats in Europe and ceding his UK ones to the Conservative Party, while shoring up the Leave mentality.

While operating in a different universe of meaning, a similar tactic was used by ISIS, who changed the geopolitical landscape with a single gruesome video.[106] It will surprise most people to learn that their greatest recruiting tool was not the promise of dominance over Western values, but poetry: what the young men lacked was meaning and purpose.[107]

More progressively, movements such as Black Lives Matter, Greta Thunberg's School Strikes and Extinction Rebellion have captured the public's imagination and put pressure on government to change. This is the soft power of activism: not force, but attraction – the ability to pull people into relationship through spectacle and a good story.

Once, we might have also called it propaganda and the power of the media, and even earlier, the power of elites to define the dominant narratives of the age through culture. What we might have once thought of uncritically as our common values will likely, over time, be recognised as constructed by those in power. It was only until very recently, for example, that we rarely questioned the BBC's claim that their journalists simply report the facts. Today, through our shared learning, we understand much more about how that truth is constructed and by whom.[108]

The era of the non-state actor points at people power

The examples above, varied as they are, point to what Joe Nye describes as the era of the 'non-state actor'. It used to cost the US military millions of dollars to design, print and drop leaflets over enemy territory.[109] Today any teenager can do the same from their bedroom for nothing. That ability to share story, image and information instantly led to easy mobilising. In a short space of time we witnessed the Jasmine Revolution in Tunisia, the Arab Spring (2010) and then the Occupy movement (2011), which eventually spread through 951 cities across 82 countries.

People power, which tends to describe large numbers in the public realm more than individual actors, has undeniably become a modern phenomenon. Uprisings occur all over the world, albeit with varying effects. While Egyptian protesters were able to topple the government, it was only a temporary victory, with a new version of the old guard resuming power soon after. Occupy may have changed global culture – landing the notion of the 99 per cent in Western society – but it had no concrete plans to restructure democracy.

However, borrowing from the new practices of digital connectivity, experiments in political parties began to happen across Europe – each remarkably different. Like a series of lab tests we saw the Pirate Party in Iceland experimenting with liquid democracy, and Podemos in Spain operating through People's Assemblies and circles.[110, 111]

Two radical Green parties – Alternativet in Denmark and Five Star in Italy – played with crowdsourcing their political programmes through local 'laboratories' and meetups. In Taiwan, the youth-led Sunflower Movement occupied the parliament and achieved an astounding digital transformation of democracy almost overnight.[112]

History will surely record a remarkable rise in people's power in the first part of the 21st century – although with variable results so far. But how does that register in the face of the news, reported by the IPCC in 2018, that we are now in an unprecedentedly perilous state, with environmental collapse threatening our entire existence? Can the humane, developed and reflexive forces that we have seen arising over the past 20 years accelerate rapidly enough to shift power away from the elite-run system that has destroyed our planet?

4.2 Everyone has a story

They looked at each other with a deep frustration bordering on loathing. 'How could he not see that it's just not that easy?' she fumed. 'People can't just pull their socks up and do better.' But how could she not see that everyone is free to do what they want, he thought: 'They just don't want it enough.'

She'd revisited that awful moment a million times – with friends, Mum and now a psychotherapist. What good would it do to keep going back there? If anything, it was making things worse. What happened to the girl they used to look up to and admire, she wondered? She's gone.

We need a new story. How many times have you heard that recently?

In *Out of the Wreckage*, George Monbiot dedicates the whole of the first chapter to illustrating how the story of our inherent competitive nature sabotages our ability to find effective solutions for the problems we face.[113] And then he replaces it, using as much evidence as he can, with a story that says we are, in fact, inherently collaborative.

Yet for all Monbiot's inspiring persuasiveness, it is actually not that easy to replace one story with another. People working in communities, care professions or any large organisation where quick methods of cooperation are relied upon (such as an army) would say: we already know that people can work together when necessary. On the other hand, it is very common to hear, in the history of the cooperative movement, that people are just as likely to be difficult – for reasons of ego, cultural differences or economic barriers – as they are easy to get along with.

You can't just make it up

As described in the previous chapter, what might hit home as a description of our common reality differs according to your experience of agency. Systems thinkers are less affected by the call to 'take back control' than those working in mechanical or routinised jobs. Equally, as described earlier, our different emotional needs make us vulnerable to stories that trigger pain or excitement.

Our need for security, for example – most essential to our being – has become the whole business model for our mainstream news. The more fearful we are, the more dependent we become on the up-to-the-minute details of what our leaders are up to.

Crude, evocative headlines keep us transfixed. They tell a meta-story: that we are mostly helpless in the face of the unreasonable people 'out there'. At the same time, our need for status is constantly exercised by the social media model, offering 'likes' and 'friends' as measures of how well we are regarded in our community. When we have more balanced lives, are able to get our own emotional needs met using our inherent resources, we care less about occupying this persistent echo chamber.

Yet none of us are immune from the power of these tales. The deeper reasons are as much physiological as psychological.

Pattern-matching and emotional authenticity

Over a lifetime as a storyteller, Human Givens psychotherapist Pat Williams (90 in 2020) has always paid attention to the micro-stories we are telling ourselves every minute of the day.[114] She explains that information is captured and transmitted neurologically in our brains.

Not as straight lines delivering data in 0s and 1s from one part of the body to another, but as patterns of emotions that prompt our body to find the right conditions in which those patterns match.

For example, the body's need for privacy, in order to repair and maintain equilibrium, sends out the neurological pattern – the feeling – which is matched when we find privacy. This constant pattern-matching way of moving around our environment is what constitutes well-being. We have a small story to tell about everything we perceive. If you doubt that, just stop in the middle of any conversation you are having, or thought you are entertaining, and check. That moment is made up of a series of small truisms that you jump between, using them to architect your well-being.

Every one of us is telling an overarching individual story, based on our past experiences of what counts as conducive to thriving, and what to avoid. This can be straightforward, for example, some people feel happy in crowded rooms, others constrained. Other stories are more subtle, carried as rich metaphors in our minds; they explain our internal workings back to ourselves as we pattern-match with our environment. Our dreams are a good place to catch ourselves operating in this way. They throw up often obscure stories that, on examination, are telling us how we feel about the events of the day before. They help us see how we could reframe experiences post hoc, to support us in achieving equilibrium.

But often these patterns of feelings are hard to decipher. They are complex packages, made up of multiple layers of emotional responses that cannot instantly be read for their meaning. Phobias and traumas are the extreme manifestation of these packages, leaving us quite unable to pattern-match in our environment. What is often quite an innocuous event – for arachnophobes, the appearance of a small spider – can trigger extreme fear. The story in their heads is: 'spiders are life-threatening'.

The origin of arachnophobia is a common human story that has been traced back to prehistoric times, when spiders were in fact life-threatening. But whether the story is now part of our DNA, or just a hangover from a bad childhood experience, is hard to tell without paying deep attention to the individual.

Tribes are glued together by myth

While much of our story-life is unique to each of us, there are wider patterns of common stories that bind us together in tribes. They appear in our environment as myths – deeply held explanations of what we believe to be true. Some myths are held together by fantasies, for example, the 'myth' of our hidden potential in the story of Superman. Or the myth of American exceptionalism, mediated through the American Dream. But others are less exotic and have a mundane grip on our daily lives.

For example, material inequality is made rational by narratives of power – the system of stories which make it credible that a small number of people could dominate the rest.[115] Some would object fiercely to that notion – on the grounds that it seems to trivialise the complexity of inequality. But the same people might well agree that inequality is culturally constructed, measured by the prevailing language of economic priorities, and confirmed by our belief about where power arises.[116]

Of course, over time, that belief system has been institutionalised. Those 'born to rule' or who 'have more merit' are networking constantly, commanding the seats of power in law, politics and even the military. They defend their cultural assets and send their children to the schools where the stories which underpin their self-belief are reinforced. What began as a story of the divine right of kings has been held strong through the centuries to keep everyone else in their place, within a hierarchy that stretches down to the most underprivileged.

When Occupy reframed this economic reality as the dominance of the 1 per cent over the 99 per cent they undermined the story of meritocracy by revealing its gross unfairness.[117] However, they also revealed its absurdity – like the spectacle of a grown man afraid of an insect. That hugely accelerated a new story about people power: a new rationality wherein the sheer numbers of the oppressed are bound to overcome the elites. Of course, none of these narratives can 'win' conclusively over others: it's not a zero-sum game but a landscape of co-existing, often overlapping, stories.

Soft power wraps hard power

As described in the introduction, the ability of story and narrative to change reality was originally described by Joseph Nye as soft power. While hard power is force – guns and money – soft power is the ability to influence behaviour through narrative. I have already mentioned that Hollywood, in this sense, is the US's greatest asset: mythologising the alpha male as the saviour of all mankind. But these are not tales of equality; on closer inspection, only those of exceptional character or talent are depicted as thriving, the rest are losers. But as with any addiction, the possibility of being lucky has us hooked. As long as people want to be part of that story, the US will continue to dominate the globe.

It's no longer just huge countries that can generate soft power – as described in the previous chapter – since the advent of the internet it's equally (if not more so) the province of what Nye calls non-state actors: those who are easily identified as operating from outside the status quo who bring their own networks into view.

I've already mentioned Greta Thunberg sitting outside the Swedish parliament, creating enough of a spectacle, shared on social media, to cause 7.5 million people to come out in sympathy. But that story did not succeed in a vacuum. It is currently succeeding where previous attempts to mobilise people around climate action failed. This is not because of its singular quality as a story but because of a complex set of conditions that made it more likely to be heard. It's likely those conditions include the publication of the IPPC report and the decades of slowly building climate grief, arising from the insistent provocations of Green activism. Add to that the spectacle of Greta's vulnerability and courage in the face of established authority. And the clarity of her integrity (enabled, she tells us, through her Asperger syndrome) when most of us have been living with compromise. Out of all this, you have world-changing possibility.

However, soft power – a name we could give for these strategies of persuasive storytelling – is a neutral phenomenon, neither good nor bad. Over the past ten years we have seen effective public narration from every corner of the political spectrum – from ISIS, who changed foreign policy agendas across the globe with one horrific video, to the picture of the queue outside a Northern Rock ATM which acted as a major trigger for the global economic meltdown in 2008.

None of these stories are random. Their success depends upon their ability to trigger deeper stories already existing in the public sphere, which in turn depend upon enough of their truth resonating within individuals on the receiving end.

Sci-fi is not doing its job

Knowing that, what kind of story could dig deep enough yet go high enough to change our current trajectory towards the cliff? Many turn to indigenous tribes to offer us alternative language that carries ancient wisdom connecting I, We and World. Yet in the face of the techno-revolution moving towards us at speed – artificial intelligence, automation, bio-enhancement – that may not be enough on its own.

If there are science fiction writers doing a good job of this, they are not being picked up often enough by Hollywood. How often are we subjected to futuristic stories of cities devoid of a blade of grass and characters that show no sign of evolution whatsoever? Even Avatar – after a promising start – descended into too-familiar aggression and an outbreak of war.[118]

I'd single out Spielberg's and Kubrick's *A.I.* for making us confront the coming humanisation of machines, envisioning a future with human values but no surviving human form. In his film *Her*, Spike Jones imagines loneliness in a post-digital era – predicting the wholesale departure of women from the man's world. Or, *Black Panther*, which told the Marvel Comics story of a fictional African country 'in hiding' called Wakanda, where Black people enjoyed the fruits of their own highly advanced cultural and political system.

In contrast to films like *12 Years A Slave* – itself important but in different ways[119] – *Black Panther* told a story of Black confidence and ingenuity that changed the way Black people the world over could expect to be seen. None of the qualities exhibited by the characters were unfamiliar to us – which is why it resonated. But the context in which they were played out was the land of dreams. When Chadwick Boseman, who played the main protagonist, died suddenly in late 2020, he was credited with changing history.[120]

So the next time you hear the call for a new story, and it sounds like an inventive, creative task – be wary. It is more likely to be a challenge to our capacity to listen deeply to people's needs and desires and our sensitivity to prevailing as well as traditional myths. We should also keep in mind the subtlety of our task. It may be our ability to intuit what people are capable of as a transformative response to our current complex problems: their private sense of what is possible (if only), in the face of what is probable.

4.3 Relationship as the rebel act

*Occasionally they disagree, sometimes forcefully. But instead of
standing behind the brick walls of their competing rationales as they
used to, they now take the time to hear each other out. Both listening
intently for the words that speak to them directly, make sense on
their own terms. So far it hasn't failed. One of them always sees
something in the other's explanation that hits home. At which point
he goes, yeah, ok, I get it. It's still a miracle to both of them that only
one year ago they were looking at each other as 'the enemy'.*

*She always dreaded that moment when the homeless person would
get on a train and start to talk. Explaining why they are standing
in front of you, dirty and ragged, needing whatever coins you might
have to get a bed for the night. She hated the way everyone looked
down at their hands. The stories they were telling themselves that she
could hear loud and clear in her head. Professional beggar! Druggie!
I deserve to keep the money I made through my hard work! It always
took every bit of courage she had to reach into her pocket, look the
poor person in the eyes and say, 'there you go, good luck mate. I hope
you find a bed tonight'. And it breaks her heart every time when the
look she gets back is gratitude. As if that tiny bit of attention meant
everything.*

WHEN WE talk about the causes of our multiple crises –
environmental, social and personal – we often hear the blame
laid at the door of neoliberalism or market capitalism. At the
same time, in other quarters we will hear the same answer being offered

to the question: how did we achieve the magnificent progress of the past century?

What both are pointing at is the Darwinian, survival-of-the-fittest logic that promotes the global growth economy. This logic justifies the cities we have built, the freedoms people enjoy, the amount of choice we have around what we can buy. All depend upon an idea that nations and groups of nations should be free to keep generating more and more money to keep us in the manner to which we have become accustomed.

The flip side is that such growth has only been possible as a result of beating nature into submission. We could be working with the natural bounty of the earth, receiving its gifts of food and energy and living in abundance, existing in a regenerative relationship with nature.[121] Instead we have ripped from the earth its resources and burned them once and for all, in an extractive way. We devoured the goose that lays the golden egg.

No one is immune to success

The question I have been posing throughout this book so far is: how and when did we give permission for that to happen? It's not enough for one side of the political divide to blame the other, because whichever side you align with, no one is immune to the effects of the success of the growth economy. (Some more than others, granted). But we have all benefited from the illusion of abundance it brings. And we are now all suffering from the reality of the damage it's done: the climate, the social division, the addiction and depression. When did we say yes to all of that and how can we now say no?

In Chapter 3.1 of this book, we focused on the sharpest point of the workings of the growth economy: its attraction for individuals – how our given emotional needs are harnessed by an ingenious advertising industry to turn us into consumers. When a handbag can give us the vital status we need within the society we depend upon for our survival, we have no qualms about buying it. We are hooked and enslaved.

Later in that chapter, I suggested that we could develop our internal resources to become aware of our collusion with the external forces designed to harness us. In so doing, we can free ourselves and get on the road to better balanced lives where we use our own, inherent resources to get our needs met.

But the vast majority of people live in circumstances which prevent that development: it's very hard to even imagine getting off the conveyor belt. How can we bear to give up what have become the small joys of life – eating and drinking what we want, spending what we've earned – when they are the only rewards we have for our slavish work? Our kids would hate us for pulling them out of the rat race, even as they suffer from the endless competition between friends that this consumerism fosters.

An economy built on disconnection

On deeper inspection, the whole edifice depends upon multiple levels of disconnect: the disconnect within ourselves around our desires and drives and how we can get them met; the disconnect between each other as we constantly compare our relative success at securing the tools we need to thrive socially; the disconnect between our immediate group of friends or family and our community, as our lives – harnessed to this consumer cause – leave us little or no time to spend together and understand each other's conditions.

Follow the trail of disconnect upwards from there: the disconnect between cultures, classes, levels of agency. If you think this is inevitable – after all, birds of a feather flock together – then consider how birds themselves occupy the skies freely. They don't live in ghettoes of alienated species as we do. While birds of prey are able to victimise the smaller birds, there are great illustrations of how swarms of birds – murmurations – come together to foil the predators.[122]

Our fundamental disconnects at individual and community levels are amplified massively by a political system that thrives on opposition, while holding in place the growth economy. This is aided and abetted by a media industry whose business model is to generate emotional reaction – and which then feeds off the disruption it causes. While some political parties are less friendly to large, manipulative corporations than others, they all continue to describe the human being within it as simply homo economicus: driven by material needs.

Politicians do not talk about the bio-psycho-social-spiritual human being that is still, in the 21st century, being instrumentalised by growth, despite all the evidence of the harm it is doing. The day after the tragedy of the Twin Towers on 11 September 2001, George Bush said the most patriotic thing every citizen could now do in defence of their country was to go out and spend money. In the second wave of Covid, UK PM Boris Johnson fined people for gathering as families more than six – but sent people back to work and kept shops open.[123]

Each of us lives in ever-smaller bubbles: physically better off than we were centuries ago, but now operating as alienated individuals in service to the socio-economic machine that is killing us. We walk around our towns and cities, convinced that the people we see around us are either our competition for resources or a threat to our survival.

Even the most educated people will look at those who vote differently from them as dangerous, or evil – unable to see that each one of us has been absorbed into an all-pervasive narrative that divides to conquer.

Relationship hacks the system

Is there any way out of this (now deeply entrenched) systemic disconnect? Can societies that are completely curdled ever get back to being rich, coherent mixes of people working together for their mutual benefit? To find the answer to that we might have to look away from the mainstream news that is over-invested in 'business as usual' and look at examples of social innovation that make a difference, of which there are many operating as experiments at different levels of society. Each of these prioritise making new *relationships* to build trust.

Community organising has long been undergoing a transition – from mobilising methods that lead from the top and front, to forms of spontaneous self-organising that depend more on the facilitation of all the voices in the room. Transition Towns, Flatpack Democracy, Collaboratories, Commoning: all use and promote listening, relating and co-creating tools in their strategies for change.

At the civic level, plenty of examples of participatory methods are arising. Framing them is a changing story about the importance of relationship as constitutive of mental and social health. Hilary Cottam, who, together with her team at Participle, gave rise to the notion of 'relational welfare' is beginning to have influence at government level – though she would say it is a long, slow journey.[124] Ironically, but usefully, the best case for moving from treating the vulnerable in society as isolated units in the care economy to inter-dependent citizens in an ecosystem of health is – financial. Their mutual self-care costs less to social services.

All these slow-burning developments have been accelerated by the sudden and growing awareness of the 'climate window' – 12 years the IPCC gave us in 2018 before the point of no return. Movements such as XR are having remarkable success in cutting through the consumer trance to wake us up to the environmental emergency we are in, with the upheaval of Covid only redoubling the alarm calls.

A rapid loss of trust in our politicians to act in the interests of future generations is throwing people back on their own resources at the community level, where they can prioritise their shared resilience in the face of the coming turbulence. For some, the combination of this climate horizon, and the strange rearrangements of pandemic living, is bringing people together in ways they've never experienced before. As mentioned earlier, Covid mutual-aid networks are springing up in neighbourhoods all over the country, doing a better job than the local council and getting a taste for their own autonomy too.[125, 126]

Key to this will be the growing awareness among all of us, that we can get our own emotional needs met in ways other than through buying and consuming stuff. This was reinforced during the Covid lockdowns, which thrust us into existentially acute situations of isolation, creating new value where there's neither demand nor supply. In these conditions, we discovered (or rediscovered) our built-in resources, such as our ability to empathise, to have rapport, to understand each other and imagine new futures.

For many, this was a new level of waking up, experiencing through the emergence of community itself – even online – the joy of being in connection with others, and discovering that building trust and co-creating is not only the means to our survival but is also built in to our design as psycho-social beings. In that sense, just reaching out to someone outside your bubble, breaking the trance of disconnection, is the most revolutionary act of all.

4.4 Feminising the future

The stress and confusion on his face was palpable. Knowing him as she did, it was obvious he was crumbling inside as he rose to the pressure of the lads around him, already pissed with half an hour to go before kick-off. Please don't give in, she thought, I won't forgive you. Help me, his eyes pleaded: I don't know what to do.

Mum, you're wrong about this. There's no reason at all to think that women are any different from men. Especially when it comes to having babies. I'm all up for blokes getting pregnant if science helps them to do that. Let them do all that home-making stuff. Let them do all the emotional labour of being there for them, putting them first above any career, spending the best years of my life getting them to stand on their own two feet. I've got more important things to do.

Did you see what she did? She was sitting on the top deck of a bus and looking out the window minding her own business. Then she saw what was happening on the street. The guy had already knifed two victims and was waving it around, looking for who to attack next. People screaming and running away. She leaped off the bus and stood right in front of him. She looked him right in the face and said, 'What do you need? What is it you need?' It was enough to stop him in his tracks. He skipped a beat and then someone knocked him to the ground. When others asked her later why she took such a big risk, she said, 'All I saw was someone in pain and I had to help him.'

ONE OF the most difficult challenges I faced in writing this book was how to talk about womanhood. On the one hand, I have a history of working as a woman in the male-dominated spheres of politics and international relations. Noticing and assessing the limitations of our current ways, I have long believed that women can bring much of what is missing from a public space designed and built by men. On the other hand, I have the history of feminism to champion and support: one that focuses more on equality and the right not to be discriminated against and less on the differences between us. Yet that feminism itself is undergoing such a profound development of its own in a post-binary, even post-gender age. That deserves a whole book, not simply another chapter.[127]

To make a start, in July 2020 I wrote 'The Feminisation of Politics: an Alternative Journey' for the German publication *Integral Forum*.[128] I looked at the history of global feminism, my relation to it as a global citizen and the crucial work of 'feminisation' initiated by Ada Colau, Mayor of Barcelona, as well as Laura Roth and Kate Shea-Bird within the municipalist movement. They are calling for full participation from women, not only for equal numbers but to change the political discourse, moving past old ideologies and embracing all that is common in the daily life of communities.[129] It's early days but their effect on both men and women is tangible, not only in the new European but also in the Latin-American political spheres.[130]

Outside of these political circles however, the broader questions still persist. What is it that women bring that will make a difference to our individual and collective agency in times of crisis? Within that, what does the term *feminine* mean to you? One hundred years after women got the vote in the UK, the feminine itself has become much more difficult to define.

According to the historic popular narrative, the feminine was the domain of women and used to reside at home: where the children were, or where privacy and intimacy was possible. It was where the internal life of contemplation and self-knowledge found its space. Womb-like, 'feminine' spoke instantly of nurturance, supportive structures and the freedom to ask questions: the idea of becoming whole. If the public space was where you would put on a performance to earn a living, home is where the outdoors costume came off and a return to the evolving, complex self was possible.

According to this view, feminine language allowed feelings, intuition, caring – capabilities not measured for their efficacy, but valued highly as the thing that Mum brought, different from what Dad brought to the home. Both men and women, boys and girls, saw and needed them, not because these capabilities were an end in themselves but because they were the gateway to children becoming whole individuals – their full selves – whatever form that might take.

However, that popular narrative has since been discredited. Through the power of communication, we know so much more now than we did once. Mum often worked outside the home, already subject to the values and structures created for industry and economic growth. Moreover, women who stayed at home were often abused and badly used for the services they gave – often by the children as well as the men. The idealised relationship between the Mother and the Feminine was always strained, even in the most privileged homes. And it became increasingly challenged by women themselves, as they fought for equality in what was once a Man's world. They wanted the right to be an agentic self, not tied to the home, with access to power and greater resources. Surely this should belong to everyone?

Where can we find the conscious feminine?

In the future, history – or herstory – will show the transformation better than any one of us can describe it now. We are looking from within the eye of the storm. But the phenomenon of women moving out of the home into public life – whether that began with, or was simply accelerated by, the vote, the contraceptive pill or the feminist movement – has left us without anywhere clear to locate the ideal of the feminine, its values or ways of being and doing.[131] As a result, the feminine becomes harder to find and grow, while the need for it is becoming increasingly clear.

Women did not move into the public spaces of work, institutional life and politics and easily bring their particular feminine qualities and capabilities with them. They had to 'fit into' public life as it had been constructed over centuries, even millennia, by men. In this world, what women might have brought specifically and originally was demeaned. As Scilla Elworthy describes in her book *Power and Sex*, softness, the ability to empathise, the attentiveness to emotion, the sense of complex wholeness: all these were seen as weaknesses that got in the way of action.[132] So they were marginalised – often by women too.

This overly masculine mainstream culture also left men disconnected from their inner lives. There was so much demand on their physical and material capabilities. Men, as well as women, had a feminine, more 'feeling' self that also needed attention and care. These selves also yearned for more complex understanding and relationships, within which they could be confirmed and grow, but also cooperate better. If they were lucky and could support mothers to stay at home, some men had somewhere to go and find repair, become whole again in their homes. If not, there was little respite from the endlessly performative demands of public and working life – the narrowing down of the self.

Is the suppression of the feminine why we have the multiple crises of depression, addiction and suicide in our society? When our daily lives do not support the need for self-development, full expression and wholistic vision – through offering enough time, space and reward – we end up getting it where we can.

So, while it was both necessary and much to be desired for women to move into public life, that move has not provided a simple counter-balance to masculine domains of power and industry. Instead it has deprived all of us of somewhere to find that wholeness. We need a commitment to actively re-locate the feminine in the public space, in ways that provide sustenance for all of us: to make it more conscious.

In public life, it is difficult to make a call on modern women in ways that emphasise the feminine without suggesting a return to the old divisions of labour. For example, if women draw attention to the need for more time with children to help develop their emotional lives, there is the immediate assumption that women need to be exempted from work to do so. And once they are, they will resume responsibility for everything domestic as their mothers did.

In societies like ours that are dominated by economic priorities, it is hard to promote the logic that all parents ought to shift into a better work-life balance, with shorter working weeks or even shorter days. It's hard to convince privileged men that it is important to develop their relationships with their children and support the flourishing of their home life as a path to a more stable society. However, it is important, not least because returning to the feminine reconnects us all to the experience of wholeness – the loss of which has damaged our relationship with the environment.

Similarly, it is difficult for women to bring the feminine values of self-care and flourishing without over-emphasising the cosmetic and fashion industry as the vehicles. Both of these industries in themselves are overly defined by the disconnectedness of the extractive economy, as well as playing a key role in amplifying female objectification. We could all benefit from taking our bodies more seriously, not just for health but for the sheer joy of vitality and sensuous interaction. But within this culture it is hard for women to do that without sacrificing the power of the conscious feminine in the process.

Instead, there are many calls for equality, for entrepreneurship, for more fluid sexual identity, each of which are vital for the advance of women, both emotionally and socially. But they rarely properly consider what is consciously feminine and why it matters. Instead it is often diminished, even delegitimised entirely.

Consequently, modern female success has largely been measured on the same terms that men set for themselves. This means through the achievements of status and financial reward; through hard power (the ability to lead and force others to act); through measurable impact (most often meaning economic growth).

Where are the prizes for the most wholistic, most magical, most loving actions in and upon the world? When do we consider the economy of emotional labour? Women have been generally required to downgrade the genius of their own conscious feminine, in order to make advances in the existing order. And the dominance of masculinity in the public space has only increased as women have legitimised those values of success. They have played by those rules, celebrated the wins in that game, and thus intensified the feedback loop.

When masculine culture destroys men

It wasn't always like this. Although there is no unanimous consensus, some scientific studies argue that men and women lived equally during the hunter-gatherer era.[133] Alongside pair-bonding and language arising from the enlarged social brain, equality was one of the key behavioural traits which distinguished humans from animals in those early days. Living closely to the land, settlements followed the cycles of nature, moving on to new pastures when the local resources were depleted and allowing periods of fallow before returning. When women and men had equal decision-making power about who joined their community, they became much more diverse as women looked beyond their own family responsibilities to create society.[134] It's a value that is borne out until today: where women lead, inclusion rises much higher up the list of political priorities.[135]

It wasn't until the agricultural era, when we began to accumulate resources and capitalise on them, that men became dominant – particularly in public life where the transactions were being negotiated.[136] The public sphere became increasingly disconnected from the natural cycles and the wholism that the conscious feminine guaranteed. What are the cumulative effects of a barely mitigated growth of masculine values, by means of a hard power now 'owned' by both men and women in the public space, on our society and planet?

Maybe it's the same as any description of the loss of wholeness and subsequent growth of alienated activity. Could we include in that: the birth and continued logic of militarism; unsustainable business growth at the cost of the planet; mass incarceration of healthy adults needing rehabilitation; epidemics of mental illness; the persistence of a work ethic that leaves 85 per cent of people disengaged with their jobs;[137] and the growth of violent crime on our streets and on the internet.

We are living in a global story of collective self-destruction through disconnection from life's natural and human resources. Male suicide is on an ever-steeper curve upwards.[138] Young women choose early not to have children because it would only add to the unsustainability of a planet burning.[139] Nuclear warheads – the weapons of mass destruction – are given spending priority over solving food and water crises across the planet.[140] And too many of us have disconnected from our own resources for meeting our emotional needs, mesmerised instead by the speed and excitement of the 'daily news agenda'. Scrolling down the screens of our devices, we rarely stop to notice our societal drive towards the cliff.

Yet the conscious feminine is not something that can be eliminated. While it no longer has a clear location – nor even a gender or a sex – to guarantee its attention in the media, it persists and grows in ways we don't readily acknowledge. As if it's waiting for its moment to regroup and become visible again. Like nature's own cycles, the greenery of the conscious feminine may have disappeared for all to see during winter, but it's gathering its forces for spring. And while we may lose the sensibility of all that is verdant and beautiful in the cold months, the eternal rhythms of nature persist and the yearning for it increases.

Networks, emotional literacy, relational structures

Any new politics that has as its goal the flourishing of people and planet will be committed to the re-balancing of feminine with masculine values in the public space. How else can new forms of agency arise? From that perspective, and for at least the past 20 years, what we understand to be feminine forms and behaviours have been making their mark – though largely unrecognised as feminine per se.

Within this framing we see that we have moved from a logic of hierarchies to one of networks – which is the same way that women always worked in their circles and communities. We talk increasingly about soft skills and soft power – the powers of attraction and connection – as the missing factors in our strategies for flourishing.[141]

Our self-awareness has grown massively through the use of social media, even if we don't yet know how to create value for others with that reflective knowledge. In our public services, we are beginning to prioritise relational over transactional practices – slowly understanding that the logic of economising costs lives rather than saves them.[142]

Publishing is always a clue to where the public imagination is drifting. We are reading more and more about how to regain our humanity in the face of our soulless workplaces – and even beginning to restructure them for better work-life balance.[143] When we work online we are giving increasing attention to our emotional needs – for intimacy, self-development, community – and becoming slowly more psychologically literate, as we watch ourselves and others perform.

In a public sphere where most of what counts as new was constructed by men, these developments are too often missed. Sometimes they are actively dismissed as soft and fluffy, or self-indulgent. This still follows the logic that human beings are most useful when efficient in a machine-like, robotic way, rather than when they are efficient in a complex way that involves personal and social development. Nowhere is this more evident that in the economy, where presenteeism – people turning up for jobs even when there is little to do – is paid for and care for the elderly or disadvantaged is often not. The whole realm of what is now described as 'emotional labour' (the important work of understanding why relationships don't work or trust is missing in a society) has never been measured. The loss of this can lead to conflict and loss of cohesion – even full-scale social breakdown – that will ultimately have to be paid for by our services.

As touched on earlier, Hilary Cottam describes this very well *Radical Help*, when she draws attention to social care systems built on time slots: a service economy that depends upon measuring minutes spent on each task rather than outcomes for the person in care.[144] What she demonstrates is how, once someone in need is entered into the system, it's very hard to get out again because there is never enough time or attention given to the problems they face. Instead, everyone ticks the time-boxes to satisfy the management and the workload keeps growing. Those with complex problems can remain in care most of their lives.

Radical Help describes a three-year experiment – in partnership with a number of local councils – by her small but 'ninja' organisation Participle, which adopted the practice of 'relational welfare'. Under this approach, those in care participated in the design of their own services, working closely with a 'family' of care givers. As their relationships developed – with all the hurdles of mutual understanding in focus – those in care became more independent and were eventually able to leave the system altogether.

Feminine leadership saving lives

Once you have trained your eye on the development of conscious feminine practices within our institutions, civic life and education systems, you begin to appreciate them – and actively frame them – as signs of a public space coming back to wholeness, back to life. A great example of this came during the early days of the Covid crisis when all the examples of good national leadership came from women – Jacinda Ardern in New Zealand, Angela Merkel in Germany, Tsai Ing-wen in Taiwan and more.[145] Unusually, their *feminine ways* were directly credited for saving thousands of lives.

So will the conscious feminine slowly assert its logic and burst forth alongside the masculine, bringing us back into balance as if by magic? Sadly, there's no guarantee of that. This is the Anthropocene – nature's tendency towards balance is not *in charge* of the public space. Unless both men and women take affirmative action, it's entirely possible that the sheer force of masculine values – advancing and growing irrespective of connectivity – will prevail. Guaranteed by men dominating leadership positions and women having no economic choice but to leave the feminine to fend for itself, they will lead us onwards in the same direction we have been going since the birth of agriculture – in which we cannot discount the possibility of human self-annihilation, within the history of a planet which continues with or without us.

5 Where is the World?

5.1 What planet are you living on?

Eavesdropping on her son playing Xbox in his bedroom, she couldn't make sense of what she was hearing. He was such a quiet boy, even at the dinner table. Yet now she was listening to a confident, even authoritative voice, speaking to what seemed like quite a crowd of participants in the game. Who were these lads from Cleveland, Nairobi, Tokyo? And how do they know my boy?

I can't ever get a grip, a real grip on what's happening. It used to be simple: we know who our customers are, we run ourselves ragged on the farm, we sell our produce the best we can. But it doesn't work any more. On so many different levels. Not only new rules, different subsidies, disappearing markets. But now I've got animal rights protesters setting free my cows! Who's even a vegan in this farming town? It's just nonsense they've heard on the internet. Then this summer we lost an entire crop of cabbages through endless rain and frost in June. Even the weather is against us. Maybe we should just let this pandemic wipe us all out and start again.

N THIS third part of the exploration of the I–We–World axis for a new politics, I have a question for you. When you think about what lies beyond the towns, cities and nations you know exist, what do you refer to?

Some people think about the *globe* – a spherical object mapping continents and seas. For them it's a geographical, organised space, managed by those with power. Globalisation implies multinational corporations with spider-like capabilities, driving outcomes from a central hub. Prioritising growth and efficiency for the stakeholders, this kind of 'big picture' threatens the autonomy of local enterprise and imposes homogeneity on the diverse cultures settled there. At the same time, it can generate jobs and income on a scale impossible for a small community on its own.

Some people would use the term *planet*, or *earth*, rather than globe, because they are thinking about the living organism that frames human settlements, on whatever scale. Their view of the system we are living within is governed by a nature which has laws of its own. In their view, people with power – governments, corporations, individuals – can hack the natural system but not fundamentally alter it. When humans abuse the system (extracting its resources for finite gain rather than nurturing them for infinite gain), nature suffers, but is unlikely to be destroyed. Instead of corporations, they might imply Gaia as the ultimate decision-maker – who might be equally merciless when it comes to the survival of the human species.

Still others would use the term *world* rather than any of the above. While it's hard to distinguish these terms, world probably implies the people and societies inhabiting the planet or globe. While the term recognises diversity, it also suggests that humans constitute the environment collectively – through their ideas or consciousness. World is the province of soft power rather than hard power – governed by narrative and storytelling rather than measurements.

In the notion of the American Dream, for example, Disneyland offers unity across the cultures in its long-standing theme tune 'It's A Small World After All' (despite our economic power over you). At the same time, Hollywood classic *Wayne's World* offers a 'worldview' to every individual. Everyone has their own way of looking at the world – what's yours?

Globaliser, Earthling or Worldist?

The internet has dramatically shifted the relationship between one person and the world they inhabit. Historical perceptions of the physical limitations between nations and cultures have been both challenged and deepened. We no longer have to travel to Brazil or Lapland to hear Brazilian or Lappish voices, for example. But the more we listen to the wide range of perspectives coming from all over the world, the more we have to let go of assumptions that to be human is to share values. In the era of national and global polarisation, connecting to the world can be both exciting and threatening. Although for anyone with millennials or RegenA around them, those poles are receding: having never really inhabited homogenous worlds, they take extremists and tribes more in their stride.[146]

So when politicians invoke the entity bigger than the nation – globe, earth, world – their use of language betrays their personal experience and often their sense of agency. There's no hard and fast rule here of course, but an integral perspective (see Chapter 3.2) does help us see the diversity. Invoking globalisation, for example, often suggests more machine-like distributions of power in a 'first tier' zero-sum game. More for them – the elites, corporations – means less for us, the people. Local communities are seen as victims of globalisation; elites are masters of that domain.

Talking about the planet earth conjures up a shared space with more equal responsibility for our outcomes. That in turn implies collective values, social justice and rights not just for humans, but for all living things. Within this terminology, the internet can be seen as a mobilising tool, a way to connect feelings as much as ideas. It is a phenomenon that mimics nature with its networks and complex fractals. Ideally, this would lead to the lack of a need for control, as people and their environment would be urged to come together autonomously.

World, on the other hand, implies worldly – carrying the bigger picture around with you while acting in real time, on the ground. Although it's by no means universal, world implies an easier shift between an individualistic focus, a more community focus and a much wider focus that includes countries and continents. There is no hard line between an individual and a world perspective. They are more like different realms or worldviews, to occupy where appropriate. From this stance the 'personal can be political' without diminishing geopolitics as having a logic of its own.

The ambition of cosmolocalism

 It's here that the terms *glocal* or *cosmolocal* offer themselves as the architecture of worldliness. These are ways to connect the big picture to the more time-and-place-specific so that different kinds of intelligence can be drawn upon in any situation. While expensive tech, for example, can only get cheaper through scaling up orders, some of the biggest shifts in economy occur through sharing experience and insight. Rob Hopkins, co-founder of Transition Towns, tells the story of planting an idea for kinds of social enterprise in Liège during a brief visit, and returning there a few years later to find a thriving and sustainable sector.[147] Since then Rob has written a successful book on the power of imagination, *From What Is to What If: Unleashing the Power of Imagination*

to Create the Future We Want, which documents how dreaming together is the first step to radical, concrete change.

Until now, this more comprehensive idea of politics has been hard to experience, largely because the dominant narrative of top-down power has kept local communities thinking that they are irrelevant. Even the most willing of grassroots organisers can be heard to say, 'yes but'. What good is it to repeat the mantra that small is beautiful, if it means nothing without scale?

However, since the information revolution began over 20 years ago with the birth of the internet, the new connectivity has demonstrated that networks have a very different dynamic than simply prototyping and scaling through central distribution. The way even small projects launch in one part of the world and suddenly appear almost identically in another suggests there is a more *fractal* quality to the relationship between the local and global. Fractal means having similar principles and patterns of activity, without necessarily appearing exactly the same.

Take for example how the rash of new political movements and experimental parties I mentioned in Chapter 1 appeared across the globe during the 2010s – without being directly involved in organising each other: the 15-M movement which led to Podemos in Spain; the Five Star movement that led to the Five Star Party in Italy; the Pirate Party in Iceland which came out of networks of tech entrepreneurs. Each in turn had elements of the Occupy movement in common; each had new, flatter forms of self-organised communities rising up against dominant elites.

Since the major 2011 uprising in Tahrir Square, Egypt (an uprising that was itself only one of many less visible revolts in the Middle East and North Africa region), the world has been in constant turmoil. That image of crowds of unarmed people bringing down previously untouchable governments has inspired countless others to emulate them – with varying results. Until now, none of these truly bottom-up people's movements have been able to follow through entirely by bringing in new, fairer and more effective systems – although Tunisia has begun.[148]

But it seems ever more likely that they will. About a year after the uprisings began in Hong Kong, the changes they demanded became more permanently effective by standing thousands of anti-government candidates in local councils and winning. Again, a year later the revolution was brought to an abrupt halt by Chinese intervention, but the move into the local councils has, for the time being, grounded it.[149] Was Hong Kong's strategy inspired by the Flatpack Democracy model in the UK? It is possible, but unlikely to be a direct adaptation. My point is that copying and sharing new models of people's power can accelerate their adoption; the fractal nature of their similarity does not depend on it. More often it reveals a similar stage and patterns of development occurring across different territories.

Organising co-evolves

A good example of such similar stages of development occurring in quite different places would be the coincidence of Nikola Tesla in New York and Guglielmo Marconi in the UK appearing to invent the radio simultaneously – although the latter, with much better communication skills in general, was awarded the patent. Their rivalry was documented but only after both were ready to launch at the same time.[150]

More intriguing still are the many legal cases over the years where two parties have come up with almost indistinguishable original works and one takes the other to court for stealing their intellectual property. For example, George Harrison of Beatles fame, was fined $1,599,987 when found guilty of 'subconsciously plagiarising' Ronnie Mack's identical song 'He's So Fine'.[151] The judge found no intent to steal on Harrison's part, who claimed that at any given time there are songs waiting to be written by whoever gets there first.

However at other times, the phenomenon of same action, same time, different places is less easily explained and might be attributed to serendipity. For example, a colleague from the integral Leadership for Transition (LiFT) group in which I am a participant, Harald Schellander of the Institut für Zukunftskompetenzen in Austria, spotted a remarkable similarity between two drawings he had done to describe his work with the '16 Capabilities for Transformation', with two completely disconnected drawings that innovator Alana Bloom had done in her work for Enrol Yourself's Huddlecraft handbook.[152] Anyone who studies serendipity will not be surprised to hear this: it is a common phenomenon. However, when we link that to our intuition about fractal growth – the sense that similar developments are occurring in similar patterns all over the world without any centralised agency – our reading of what is occurring becomes more familiar, even logical.

In the meantime, global movements of elective citizens from diverse countries, sharing values, have developed a form of soft power (see Chapter 4.2) through mobilising. As in the case of the petition platform Avaaz, these can add up to as many votes as a small nation: these numbers have been shown to have real influence.[153] Every time someone on social media signs a petition to challenge a government policy or an atrocity in their own country or abroad, they are exercising their agency beyond those accorded by their current national politics. Similarly, when they adopt a practice locally that gets picked up and developed in another town or city abroad, they are taking part in a global co-creation experiment.

These new behaviours are changing us in ways we could not have imagined 20 years ago. Unintentionally, we have nevertheless become seamlessly local, social and global operators. But what has that done to our *world* (as distinct from our earth or globe) and our story about ourselves? What has it done to the way we experience life physically and emotionally? And how we treat each other in the streets and on social media? Without a better understanding of the psychological impacts of these hugely expanded realms, we are always in danger of becoming more vulnerable to outside forces.

For example, the images shared on social media of the collapse of the Twin Towers on 9/11, the hideous videos of ISIS, Telling the Truth about climate change – these become existential threats to our daily lives, 'rocking our world'. Newspapers amplify these stories because they know that fear sells copies and drives clicks. Consequently politicians don't hesitate to trigger emotions, knowing that doing so guarantees column inches and wins public attention. In this sense, populism is the deliberate manipulation of emotionality in this newly expanded public realm.

But it's not all about the danger. There is also the good growth implied and invited in an age of rapid transition. Over the past decades our relationship to the globe has changed. Once, the citizens of a nation only responded to the news of our collective actions all over the globe (using military and economic force) in an arm's-length way – applauding or protesting to government, maybe sending aid. Now we increasingly embody our relationships with different parts of the world. Some travel to be there in the struggle, standing alongside in solidarity: this runs the full gamut of involvement, from joining uprisings to building schools in remote places. Others share learning and experience, offer open-source access to software in what many are now referring to as a cosmolocal way.[154, 155]

As explained earlier, cosmolocalism is more than the familiar term global-localism – or glocalism – in that the relationship between the two domains has become more integrated. Rather than having a global mindset while acting locally, which can leave the local actors powerless and small, cosmolocalism concretely brings together the 'light' resources of ideas of all kinds arising in the global commons – including all the free tech and prototypes now available – to meet the 'heavy' production resources unused in your town or city. If once we may have reached for our challenged imaginations to solve a problem, we can now call on the imaginations of millions of people willing to share. This is both inspirational and material. With design comes a whole range of cultural creativity embedded in systems thinking from all across the world. It is cosmopolitanism in your home town, on your terms, to suit your needs.

Still others take part in global initiatives connected by online technology. Again, not in the old, centralised way, with one country defining the rules and structure, but in co-created, emergent ways that allow each country to retain its own cultural characteristics, while still sharing goals. Take, for example, the Neighborocracy project, a system of local-to-global community parliaments, which started in India but is now taking shape in Nigeria, different parts of Latin America, Portugal and the UK.[156]

Hashtag global emotions

But even more prevalent are the global waves of those identifying with others' emotional realities – whether it be joy or pain – that cause social shifts to actually materialise. An example is the #MeToo movement that captured the systemic abuse of women in both industry and society across the globe and has led to new laws and procedures being adopted in 84 countries, including the many countries where women's rights are despairingly unmet.[157, 158] These are not primary emotions (like fear) travelling at the speed of light, actively generated by the mainstream media making victims of us all, but complex patterns of emotions indicating long-standing power systems that successfully engage authority and result in change.

It's possible that everyone sending out #MeToo tweets was imagining their deeper impact. Yet they are generated by a system now capable of reflexivity, as if the globe itself is doing self-development work: each wave of tweeting out taking on deeper and deeper meaning. Another contrasting but strong example of a narrative that takes on a life of its own is the Brexit campaign to #takebackcontrol, which was originally meant to liberate the UK from the European Union. I say 'meant' because the function of such a narrative is simply to trigger emotion and manufacture demand: #takebackcontrol had no direct relationship with what could be delivered in reality, as we have witnessed. However, since then the hashtag continues to generate an appetite for more freedom and autonomy at every level. These self-repeating patterns of emotions, the relationships and networks they give rise to have a fractal quality: able to generate whole new systems of thought and action. These dynamics are neither good nor bad in themselves; they are mechanisms for action and can be used by anyone.

In this way, talking about the future has become as much a question of ontological shifts – how we are being and feeling differently – as epistemological development: the new theories of change. In Section 5.2 I'll look at the new initiatives arising that could lead to institutional change as well as changes of attitude.

The signs of a new architecture that can hold this more complex awareness of the relationship between I, We and World are there. Ada.

5.2 A new global architecture

Tweet on Jan 4th 2020, 12.53, from @bestofbritish
Jan 1 – HNY everyone. All going well so far :-)
Jan 2 – Australia is on fire
Jan 3 – WW3 just broke out [159]

We love our community. Small but kind of perfect. Don't get me
wrong – we have our ups and downs. But we've worked out a way
to talk things through. One of the things we all decided long ago was
to stop reading the news – it was messing too much with our minds.
Between the 1,500 of us, we've got enough news of our own, believe
me! Occasionally my sister comes to visit from Brum. She's full of
this drama and that – violence and destruction, all doom and gloom.
As much as I love her, it's a relief when she's gone. Her world is so
… negative.

I N SECTION 5.1 I discussed the waking up that allows us not only to notice how we experience globalisation but also to think about our own agency, and how thinking about the conceptual distinctions between the terms globe, planet and world activates different thoughts and mechanisms for change.

When there is an environmental crisis – whether it's planetary boundaries, or the spread of a pandemic bearing down on us – what kind of actions can we take that make a tangible difference? Whereas we once felt powerless, today the possibilities for some sort of response are many, even if they continue to be framed and constrained by personal and social capacities as described in Chapter 3.1–2.

Our individual agency depends upon how we look at that agency and feel it to be true. What we believe is possible is tested by our investment in those possibilities. And that belief is sustained by our experience of the outcomes.

On the one hand, that seems banal: in our personal lives we test ourselves continually. If I work hard, what kind of results do I get? How does that compare to how much I pray, or organise or – conversely – stop trying to control my outcomes? Even within formal belief systems, each of us has our personal 'belief system', our core convictions that keep us going through each day. We also have gaps that need to be filled, causing us anxiety and conflict with those close to us.

Yet even those who have a strong personal ethos are routinely challenged by the scale of our global problems – hunger, environmental breakdown, organised crime. In the past 25 years I have taken part in worldwide Buddhist communities, in NGO communities built on care and conflict resolution, in arts movements and political parties. Each has been effective in its own way. Yet we are now at a serious impasse – the rapidly shrinking climate window, and the damage already done – as a result of our collective failure to change our actions and arrest our self-destruction.

Has anything changed in that quarter-century? In terms of our tools and practices, very little that is really visible and accessible. Although acts of care and compassion have never lost their efficacy, we remain locked into poor systems of resource distribution.

What has changed is our ability to communicate better with each other and unlock our collective imagination. The 20th-century public space was controlled by a small group of power elites able to harness the skill and capacities of citizens and workers, in order to build the industrial and post-industrial power bloc that is largely responsible for how we live today. The 21st-century public space is a battleground for control on quite different terms.

As I have argued throughout this book, since the birth of the World Wide Web the framework of industrial modernity has been called into question.

By means of these communications networks, populations have been waking up to the bigger picture of the produce-to-consume lifestyle they've taken for granted.

Developed nations have become inescapably aware of how their habits have had dire consequences for the rest of the world. Across the globe, citizens of different nations have begun to see their own culture as only a part of a multicultural landscape of cultures. Surprising commonalities across these differences have also appeared – enough for hugely diverse, but commonly purposed movements of people to arise. Some have been united by one taste in music, fashion or even games (such as Pokémon Go).

At the same time as these benign meta-gatherings have occurred, more aggressive mobilisations for power have gained international momentum. Among these are neo-fascists of all kinds, suicide cults, terrorists. Consider also exploitative porn, gambling and other addictive means of taking money from vulnerable people.

And faltering before our eyes, we have a last-century political system that is slowly self-destructing in the face of its historic and manifest failures. After almost 70 years of a free-market system of economy and governance that has harnessed our energies and plundered the planet for constant growth, there are uprisings on a near-weekly basis.[160] The peoples of this planet are learning how to protest, not just against economic inequality and social justice, but also against the very destruction of the biosphere that makes any economics possible at all.

Ever stronger attempts to keep us on the path of business-as-usual are manifesting in overtly manipulative campaigns of mind-control by major political parties, in the US, Brazil, Australia, Ukraine, the UK – with the perpetrators sharing their tools between them.[161] And while there is no sign yet of a proper challenge to their power, the search for alternatives is taking shape everywhere. There are new-style political parties in Hong Kong and Taiwan, across Europe and the US, too many to enumerate here (90 in the UK since Brexit alone) but reviewed in Chapters 1, 2 and 3.

Scaffolding for the new system arising

So while not much has changed in the daily lives of most of us, facing a planet that continues to burn, the *scaffolding* of a new way to act globally is beginning to appear: popular virtual platforms that bring people together in novel, attractive ways. In their leisure practices – including festivals, games, movie channels, interest groups – people are interacting, sharing creativity of all kinds.

Even in our political lives, these new platforms enable petition sites, movement hubs, learning spaces – new ways of building personal and collective agency. Social media connects all of these, forging the wisdom of the crowd – though not yet in an integrated way. It's more like many short tributaries of logic and meaning leading to a sea of possibilities.

Scaffolding implies a shrouded building, or a set of global institutions to come. This structure also appears under wraps, yet to emerge and disclose itself. Will it be a reformed United Nations or something more like the intergalactic governance board – the United Federation of Planets – seen in *Star Trek*?[162] No one has made a convincing proposal yet although some (including The Alternative UK) are on the path.

A skeleton of global governance

What is coming into being, however, is something more like the skeleton of a global body of actors. This includes people acting locally, forming town-level groups or city-level governing bodies – often independently of government, or in a flexible partnership with them. At the city level these are fast becoming global networks of municipalities – for example, Fearless Cities – that are aligning on policy and sharing resources.[163]

Organisations like SIMPOL – interested in global-level 'simultaneous policymaking' – are working hard to connect their work to individual MPs, who might shape government policy at national level.[164] At the community level, we could point at Transition Towns or the commoning movement.[165, 166] Feeding into these, and bringing tech solutions and new tools for citizen participation, are groups like Flatpack Democracy, Citizens Action Networks and XR's Future Democracy Hub.[167, 168]

Key to all of these new 'constitutes' is the quality and substance of the relationships between the people involved.[169] If there is little or no interpersonal trust, the ability of the group to grow and proliferate is minimal, held back by internally competing forces. That could mean the overbearing egos of leaders that stifle the creativity of others. Or it could imply tensions between cultures that were never given the chance to understand and appreciate each other.

Even more than that, as described earlier, relationship is the conduit for previously disconnected worlds to reconnect. It's important that these are not simply lines on a map connecting two sources of information in theory, but two whole worlds meeting and interacting. In other words, not Facebook friends who only exist to 'like' each other's thoughts, but real-time friends and associates who work to understand and collaborate with each other.

Fractals spontaneously scaling

For that reason, probably the most important element of this vision of a more successful global, planetary or worldly connectedness are the *fractals* of this complex system. These fractals are new units of action – be they initiatives, organisations or networks – that have a pattern of relationships that can deliver agency to people. As discussed, these fractals are appearing everywhere of their own accord and they also have the virtue of being able to be copied and replicated easily. But can they come together, and how?

In the last section, I made distinctions about the different terms globe, earth/planet and world. The first relates principally to a geographical map, the second to a material natural phenomenon and the third to the subjective experience of our environment. Globalisation tends to think about the scaling of local activity as something that requires concerted, centralised planning. The more wholistic earth/planet orientation would see the whole of the natural world as built on spontaneous fractal emergence.[170] A worldly approach would combine the two by decentralising the process of scaling, using not rigid but liberating structures – loosely held supportive forms – that help groups with similar patterns of relationship to keep innovating, networking, collaborating and learning from each other. These high-energy interactions are very attractive and create fertile conditions for expansion.

Therefore, within a *globalist* paradigm, the best level at which to observe, and encourage, this fractal behaviour is in community groups. These can develop in the fully relational ways required to make a human fractal powerful and influential. The patterns generated at a community level can inspire copying – both in other communities and at larger (regional or national) levels. In turn, these levels can begin to offer new forms of global governance. The macrocosm can mirror the microcosm – containing any healthy turbulence in the system.

When we are talking about the *planet* – a different term for the same essential entity – fractal behaviours are triggering energy, nutrition and health subsystems, interconnecting with each other from the home to the city, or regionally, nationally and internationally. Although we may still be far from it, we should seek to find a pattern of relationships with the *earth*, nature and all sentient life echoing throughout these systems, helping us establish principles we can aspire to. For example, the importance of biodiversity to promote healthy human growth is still not commonly understood.[171] We still rely on chemical interventions, designed to fix discrete problems, not considering how that disrupts the complex natural systems in place.

When we talk about the *world*, we refer more to new patterns of human-to-human connection. These can give rise to networks of social trust capable of solving our problems of psycho-social health, crime and exclusion. This depends much more on the internal lives of humans being much better understood and self-developed, to give rise to more autonomy, capacity for collaboration and therefore agency.

How each one of us takes part

Awareness of the complex, exponential and fractal development occurring at every level is what would help any human being to act more confidently, whenever invited by others to consider events happening physically far away but impacting upon us wherever we live. That personal sense of 'losing control', when faced with circumstances we cannot affect, can be managed with the right tools and practices, set within new patterns of relationship.

None of these 'ideas' of what Buddhism calls the third realm (alongside the personal and community realms) can work independently of the others if we want to properly rise to the multiple crises we face. Each one of us is acting within patterns of relationship and behaviour that are either aligned to the old system, or, when consciously improved, can be part of new systems arising. What creates the change is the understanding that these are not simply technocratic problems to be solved by government, but they are also challenges for the culture and the collective will.

Each one of us can play an active part in triggering and nurturing these waves of change – by doing our own work of waking up, becoming response-able and moving into action.

6 From the Map to the Territory
6.1 The story of Alternativet DK
and The Alternative UK

Part of him loathed her. So easy for her to say, you should have done this, should have done that. But she's just in the audience, not the person having to take these shots. She's never stood in front of any kind of formidable opponent, serving straight aces at you. Or back-handing from god knows where. The speed of it is disorientating. She'll never know what it actually takes to respond.

No one could really talk. No one felt they could put words to the misery they all felt at yet another defeat. They were sure they had the right ideas, the best policies, the most credible leaders. All that time they had spent thrashing out what the people wanted, how it was all going to be different. Yet still they voted for those bastards.

I N THE last few chapters of this book, I'm going to answer the big question – so WHAT? So what if we have a bigger evolutionary picture of the present moment, understand the motivations of human beings, accept the reasons we feel powerless and grasp our planetary existential crisis? What does that mean in real terms?

One of the allergies I began to develop during my time within party politics was to the language of projection and intention. MPs stand in front of microphones claiming, 'What the people want is xxx', followed by a clear exposition of the desires of voters everywhere. This is generally followed by, 'What the people need is xxx', and then a prescription: 'We (whatever party) promise to xxx.' All of this without any direct access to hearing what people want from people themselves.

For those prone to respond that polls, focus groups and questionnaires can provide evidence of people's wishes, I would refer you to Chapter 4.2 and the power of framing questions: it's not enough to ask people to comment on subjects of your choice. If you want to know what they want, you have to let them frame the conversation. This is not only fair – and that would be enough reason – but people's input is *the* information missing about what matters and what motivates them.

As a corollary of not being connected to the true needs of the people, policies are designed without knowledge of what would work in practice. It's one thing, as described in Chapter 3, to fail to plan to meet the complex bio-psycho-social-spiritual needs of people. It's a double fault to fail to create the conditions in which we can all use our inbuilt resources of imagination, reason and creativity to design good lives. Instead, from theories of change often written by men unaware of what it takes to raise children or build community – or how real security is achieved – policy is shaped by ideology. Such policies too often land in communities without instruction manuals – how to get this idea to deliver the impact its inventors imagined.

This disconnect has enabled the construction of entire systems of care, housing and employment, despite the policymakers' inability to deliver on their promises. It has deepened the crisis of disconnection rather than healed it. Hilary Cottam's work on relational welfare mentioned earlier brilliantly exposes the wastefulness of our current care system. By measuring help for the vulnerable in minutes and seconds rather than by effectiveness (such as lives saved or people freed from the system), we have trapped millions in a permanent cycle of dependency on discrete injections of care, which never quite deliver.

The Covid pandemic has given us a particularly strong lens on the fragility of our National Health Service and on the growing factor of poor mental health in our society. In a report by the British Medical Association deep concerns were expressed over the vulnerability of economically disadvantaged communities, whose members can spend long periods of isolation in cramped spaces and are under acute pressure to earn enough to eat.[172] The pandemic has also caused a significant rise in mental health problems for children in lockdown, who suddenly are unable to play with friends and end up spending too much time mindlessly in front of computers. Coming out of lockdown does not fix these problems: the poor will continue to be at the extreme end of care services, with their mental health being impacted while unable to move on from badly designed living spaces. Nor is young people's dependency on their screens diminishing.

Despite being the sixth largest economy in the world, the UK hasn't used its resources well in the face of the crisis. We have amassed fortunes but at the expense of the people's well-being, not in service to it. And that in turn has sabotaged us. For more on this, spend some time with the Wellbeing Alliance (WEAll) – a collaboration of organisations, movements and individuals working towards a well-being economy. You will find that the evidence is overwhelming on how human and ecological flourishing was marginalised, in order to construct the still dominant global economy.[173]

If our care system only reflects this poorly designed society, unable to register the failures of mechanistic responses to complex human problems, where can we look for alternatives?

What is the politics of all this?

If we add up all the factors described so far in this book, how might it look *as a politics*?

How could we somehow capture the complex lives of individuals, working together in fluid community both on- and offline? Can we use the soft powers of play, storytelling and experimental prototyping to build new kinds of social enterprises – what we've been calling constitutes (fluid institutions), or cosmolocal networks of governance? Could these allow everyone to participate in decision-making? And could it bring the full psycho-social health of every citizen into alignment with social and planetary health? Sounds ambitious?

Yet you could argue that this is how public space is actually unfolding, right now. If we think of the rapidly evolving well-being sector now reshaping our health services; the proliferation of social media channels, offering learning and connection to people whatever their conditions; the TV reality shows turning us all into observers of human social behaviour; annual real-time festivals that draw people into play spaces from across the world; the petition sites that mobilise opinion at national and global level …. It could seem we were, even before Covid, already in a planetary revolution. People everywhere – not just in the white Western nations – are developing their capacity for agency. We're either getting ready for something new or we're already lost to chaos. Covid, if anything, has accelerated that.

How does all this land helpfully in 'the real world' of people going about their daily lives – and increasingly stressed by the impact of their own 'waking up'? Maybe they suddenly grasp why they have been so disadvantaged in the race to succeed in life? Maybe they come to own their culpability in creating the economic and environmental crises we all face? What do we do with all this new awareness – this wokeness?

Thirty years on from that moment in Telawa when I saw that remarkable change could happen magically – that is, without being able to see clearly what the cause was for that effect – my question has been: how can we make this magic 'of seeing' happen everywhere? I have explored and articulated until now the conditions in which significant developments are occurring and told a new story of possibility. What is still missing, clearly, is the political action that can integrate this diverse activity, so that its burgeoning, human-centred soft power can meet the hard power available. This intermeshing can deliver much better results for people and planet than ever before, although not as a homogenous entity (the illusion offered by the American Dream). Rather, we can have a fantastically diverse global citizenry moving into relationship for the first time, as each town, city and region delivers its own vision in ways that benefit all.

Politics in this sense are the governance systems that link the deliberate will of the people to institutions with sufficient resources to help deliver on that will. That may or may not point directly at government as we know it – some might describe Facebook, for example, as that kind of governance. However, I'd suggest that absorbing the newly liberated energies of billions of people, and linking them in all their diversity to corporations intent on capitalising on them, is only accelerating the crises we are in.[174]

What is needed at this point in history, with the multiple crises fully in view, is a new kind of democracy architecture: one that connects the flourishing of the people to the flourishing of the planet through the flourishing of communities. To do that, it has to bypass, or hijack, the current political and corporate cartel which is failing to deliver for all of us.

Uffe Elbæk and the politics of human agency

As I described in my introduction, I first met the founding leader of Denmark's Alternativet Uffe Elbæk in 2015 while I was on the management board of British progressive think tank Compass. I was already disillusioned with mainstream politics, having written two papers – 'New Times' and 'Is the Party Over'?[175]– which drilled down into why Westminster was neither representative of UK citizens nor capable of responding adequately to their needs or potential (Introduction and Chapter 4.1).

Uffe had been invited to speak at one of our events because he was leading the 'fastest growing party in Denmark'. When he spoke he didn't sound like a politician – he had a playful, creative energy that engaged each of us personally. He shared his dilemmas, didn't have all the answers and talked as much about why he loves to dance as what 'a radical Green party' might mean. And indeed, Uffe's history and progress did not climb the usual political ladder.

Above all, his career had been shaped by developing human agency – particularly among the young. He started life as a social worker because he needed a job: here he came face to face with exclusion, vulnerability and alienation. Informed and inspired by the wasted potential he saw, Uffe founded a series of youth organisations – the first called The Flying Piss Beans! – and developed a training to build confidence and creative capacity from the streets upwards. This eventually took shape as the Front Runners, which continues to thrive.[176] Working from reclaimed buildings such as the old slaughterhouse in central Aarhus, they developed a unique form of cultural entrepreneurship involving the most diverse parts of the community. The wildest thing they ever did while Uffe was in charge was to help organise a convoy of 3,000 young people, starting at different points in Europe, to put on a concert in the Kremlin – before the Iron Curtain fell.[177] Just, in his words, to impress 'the one girl who wouldn't join in'.

Uffe went on to found Kaospilot in 1991, a master's-level three-year training course that equips young people to live creatively and effectively in the 21st century.[178] It's worth sharing here Kaospilot's own description of what continues to be their 'raison d'être':

> The Kaospilot school was founded … as a response to the emerging need for a new type of education. With roots in activism culture and with inspiration from the Danish folk high school and the Danish co-operative movement, the Bauhaus School in Berlin and the Beatnik movement in San Francisco, the school helps young people navigate the changing reality of today's society.

> The intention was to create an education for action-orientated people who seek out and utilize new knowledge. And for those who understand changing needs and shift systems to fit changing cultural, social and economic realities. It was also about creating a learning environment where students could learn, lead and be enterprising – essential skills that would enable students to work towards an unknown future.

Rather than a static, exam-based course, KP is project- and context-led, moving each cohort of students into different hot-spots around the world. They are taught to learn from and respond to the global cutting-edge of change. That eventually spread to hubs in 20 countries and schools in Norway, Sweden and Holland – and continues to thrive.

Having undergone an inner revolution of his own – coming out as gay to his wife and two children – Uffe became CEO of the World Outgames, at once an international sports, cultural and human rights event.[179] In what was to become his trademark style of symbolic action, Uffe explained, 'We are trying to build a bridge between the LGBT [lesbian, gay, bisexual and transgender] community and the rest of the city …. Our intention is to make this a celebration and a signal to the rest of the world that this is a tolerant city that we are proud of.'

Having served as an Aarhus city councillor from 2001 to 2007, Uffe was poached from Kaospilot and World Outgames by the Social

Liberal Party in 2011 and in a hop, skip and jump became Denmark's Culture Minister. But before the year was out, he was completely disillusioned with what could be achieved in that position and left to create a new party of his own. Pulling together a team of like-minded political entrepreneurs, he launched Alternativet, with Josephine Fock, on 27 November 2013, with only a minimal manifesto and a set of six values:[180]

Courage. Courage to look problems in the eye. But also courage about the future we share.

Generosity. Everything which can be shared will be shared with anyone interested.

Transparency. Everybody should be able to look over our shoulders. Both on good and on bad days.

Humility. To the task. To those on whose shoulders we stand. And to those who will follow us.

Humour. Without humour there can be no creativity. Without creativity there can be no good ideas. Without good ideas there can be no creative power. Without creative power there can be no results.

Empathy. Putting yourself in other people's shoes. Looking at the world from that point of view. And creating win-win solutions for everyone.[181]

Uffe won his seat and then began the process of building Alternativet (The Alternative Party). He opened political laboratories around the country with the invitation, 'Come to a Party!' Directly from this grassroots activity, his small team crowdsourced a political programme. It turned out the people wanted a radical Green party, capable of connecting the health of the people to the health of the planet. In their first general election – under a proportional system – they won nine seats in parliament.

Of course, there were early limitations to how much one new party could fundamentally change politics. Taking part in the establishment meant submitting to its rules and structure. The voting system of proportional representation (PR) obliges every party to compromise and fall under the old banners of Left and Right.

Yet Alternativet decided they didn't have to buy into the political culture. In the aim of establishing a genuinely new politics, they seized on every opportunity to take symbolic action. Crowdsourcing the political programme was a clear first step. But infecting the political culture with everyday actions that indicate change – this could be done in much smaller ways too. The change initiated from such a visible place was more to do with how to *be with* power – about your behaviour, the feelings you generate, the space you offer others.

For example, Alternativet challenged the Danish parliament's seating conventions. Instead of their MPs being arranged in a point with the leader at the front, Alternativet MPs sit in a straight line along the back. Another example would be how Uffe manifests his own power in the public space. In interviews, he rejects the idea that MPs are the experts, the holders of knowledge and wisdom. Instead he suggests a more fluid and reflective kind of leadership – often replying to hard questions with 'I don't know' or 'let's see what the people want'.

The famous Alternativet campaign video presented the candidates as circus performers – able to fly through the air and perform amazing stunts, as they narrated a steady, solid political message.[182] What was on offer was what philosophers might call an ontological shift – a new way of being and feeling in the public space. A new reality of what could be understood as political.

Yet Alternativet also found traction. Representing the people in such a novel and original way gave Uffe and colleagues the momentum – and the attention – to really shift the dial on climate awareness. In 2019 they published 'The Next Denmark' that described radical shifts not just in tackling the crisis, but also in transforming the whole socio-economic system, so it could deliver on the necessary targets – including ideas like universal basic income.[183] On the strength of the popularity of that paper, Alternativet decided to stand as independents in the most recent election – with Uffe standing for PM – in the hope of really raising the bar of political ambition in Denmark.

It did – but not quite in the way expected. Every other party matched Alternativet's climate ambition, almost robbing them of their USP. As a result, they lost rather than gained seats. Even so, with a net gain for Denmark, the party was satisfied. After announcing he was stepping aside as party leader, Uffe was proud to point at a transformational Green budget as his legacy.

Soon after standing down, due to serious differences with his successor, Uffe left Alternativet, and with two of the remaining five MPs he launched another party called the Frei Grønne (Independent Greens), with an ambition to take things even higher.[184, 185] Calling themselves a 'responsible, climate-conscious and anti-racist party', they named five points of focus for their new party:

1. Nature is sacred

2. Diversity breathes life into our society

3. Art and culture are the soul of our society

4. Civil society is democracy's immune system

5. The future is green, feminist and democratic.

Why and how The Alternative UK was born

As I described in the introduction, my first encounter with Alternativet was dramatic, especially as it coincided with the murder of Jo Cox one week before the Brexit Referendum. However, when I returned to the UK, it became clear that we couldn't easily replicate Alternativet's achievement. British political history and baggage makes for a very different landscape. Our winner-takes-all voting system means any new party will suffer a similar fate to the Green Party in the UK.

Therefore, with Alternativet as a model of how challenging it can be for a political party to subtly change politics from the top down, The Alternative UK began its work at the other end of the spectrum. Without the pressure of competing for parliamentary seats, we took space and latitude to consider and develop the infrastructure of a new politics from the bottom up. We explored questions such as what kind of incubators and architectures are needed to bring a new kind of agency to people? And what new intelligence about human capacity and needs should power these systems?

We concluded that we need to operate on three fronts at once. Firstly, at the level of narrative – it was vital to offer alternative media. As I keep reminding you, 2 per cent of the people are members of political parties, which means the political discourse is very narrow. What lies outside the Westminster bubble that might give people a very different idea about power and agency? Hence, from March 2017 we began delivering a Daily Alternative – seven posts and an editorial per week, adding up to a Weekly Newsletter where we join the dots on solutions to our crises that are already available.

The point of structuring the newsletter this way is to bring all the solutions into relationship with each other. We therefore, secondly, committed to 'networking the networks'. By this I mean that we brought together not just the actors in a new political system, but also all those that might comprise what architect Buckminster Fuller once described as the new socio-economic 'system that makes the old one obsolete'. It's this next system that a new politics should serve.

Thirdly, as described in Chapter 9, we sourced and created the conditions to launch CANs (Citizens Action Networks, or Community Agency Networks, and probably more referents to come) in towns and cities around the UK. In a time when the climate crisis, the pandemic and the divisions caused by Brexit are competing for attention – as well as the longer-term crises in poverty and well-being – the urgent challenge was to bring all the solutions into better relationship with each other, as mentioned above. And then how to connect all the people in a city, town or region to that ecology of cosmolocal actions.

It was important that CANs were not a campaign, a protest or even a movement, but rather 'containers' for people power that hold relationship and give traction. Like Alternativet – and maybe even more so Frei Grønne – the required focus was as much an ontological shift (of being and feeling) as it was a structural shift (of doing and acting).[186] In so doing, they enabled a new, collective grip on reality, distinct from the old political one which was so tainted with failure. CANs are, therefore, a major tool for the age of waking up.

6.2 Containers, constitutes, platforms

I've been doing this for ten years now and to be honest we don't seem to have got very far with it. It's not that people don't like what we do, but everyone's doing their own thing, no one's got time to really listen. A lot of people seem to be doing stuff quite like ours, but they don't really want to talk about it when we go for a drink: I reckon we're all up for the same funding. Every time I'm on Facebook for a bit I come back and think I should change jobs altogether: so much going on, but I just can't see how we can break through.

They were slowly getting the hang of it. Talking to each other on Slack was never going to be the same as talking in person, but on the other hand it was quicker and easier and you could look back at what you'd signed up for. It blew their minds that they could change the shape of things and the whole way they were working together just by altering the templates. When he put the energy business on the website on one page and the whole newspaper on another, just two clicks away, he felt so much more in control of things.

WHEN STARTING The Alternative UK political platform, we had an early realisation. It was exciting to set processes running that exploded citizens into imaginative action. But for all this new meaning to find focus and purpose, our collective emotions and new theories of agency needed to find a *container*. By this we meant a specific physical space, capable of holding these new and different energies for development in relationship with each other. We imagined boundaried, wholistic and systemic outcomes for the people and local resources within that space. Without them we would never have traction in the wider world where the old culture is in breakdown.

This would not necessarily be measurable by any of the old criteria, such as numbers of people involved or wealth generated (though those are also relevant). But we would find a way of manifestly answering the broader needs people have for belonging, agency, autonomy. For better lives.

We also knew that there were already communities of practice, like Transition Towns for example, that were holding similar kinds of visions and values I've been describing here – if not all of them. Yet for one reason or another, they were meeting unforeseen limits and not proliferating sufficiently to prevent the multiple crises we are now facing. When Brexit happened in the UK, it became clear that something more was needed to reach those alienated by the strictures of our socio-political culture.

Getting traction

As many have done before us, we imagined community spaces that could hold people from across the political divides – and beyond that, people who never considered politics at all. Like the Alternativet party in Denmark (see Chapters 1 and 7), we opened collaboratories around the country – Eastbourne, Birmingham, Brighton – to get a feel of what the needs were. However, no matter where we landed, we found that we were attracting mostly those who had been in many of these conversations before. There was very little progress other than to come to some basic agreement about what was wrong and needed addressing: but by whom and how, it wasn't clear. After all, the local councils had been diminished by austerity over the past decade: they had nothing new to give.

Our sense was that we needed to pay attention to one or two places for a longer period of time and help build something new in these post-Brexit moments. And that whatever that construction was, it had to answer more of the emotional needs of the people living there. In doing so, at that social level, they would be less vulnerable to manipulation and instrumentalisation – from outside and top-down – than they have been in the past.

We were drawn to the South West, home to many of the socio-political entrepreneurs mentioned in Chapter 5. But it was Pam Barrett, the charismatic Mayor of Buckfastleigh, who advised us to connect with the more diverse, working-class city down the road: Plymouth. This is a place with a massive history; among other things it was the Mayflower's last stop before heading for what we now call the United States of America. But the city had undergone repeated efforts – and failures – to really lift off the ground in the first decade of the new century, despite lots of sporadic government grants.

We started by what we call 'deep hanging out' – just spending time in bars and cafés, chatting with people and finding out which micro communities made up the larger ones. We allowed each conversation to lead us to the next one, moving into new circles we could not have imagined, such as the hospital workers community or the Navy wives. We found out pretty quickly who the 'usual suspects' were. By this we meant, and in an appreciative way, the people who always turned up to share practice, give freely of their time and were already active in community organising. These 'bodhisattvas' are the glue and the engine of social change.

We also found out who was currently excluded from that group – not because they held different values, but because they lacked direct connections to the network or didn't see themselves as activists. We also saw distinct groups of people who would shy away from any public conversation – doubly so if they thought it was 'political' – as they were not interested in politics and/or were distrustful of 'politicians'. Invitations to a conversation that you framed around your own interests rarely tempts such groups. However, they still came because we made an effort to understand their lives, and the listening provided a corridor and a place to meet on equal terms.

Co-labs: experimenting with collaboration

Working with facilitators and artists, some for the local area, we designed a 'collaboratory' (what it sounds like: a place to experiment with collaboration) made up of three stages. These could be repeated in a cycle, which we sketched down as follows:

The Friendly: 100 people in the widest possible mix of the three groups mentioned above. Offer food, drink, arts, games. Practices deployed go from deep listening to shared appreciation and energy building.

The Inquiry: the same people meeting the same facilitation team, both coming together to think about the future of their locality. What are we yearning for, what can we dream up? What could be created that would help everyone look forward?

The Action: bringing ideas to meet cosmolocal resources (of wildly varying kinds, from traditional to relational). Then build a Citizens Action Network (or CAN). Much more on this in the following chapter, but suffice to say, the co-creators of this 'constitute' (see 'A skeleton of global governance' Chapter 5.2) quickly start to include the networks of the originators as well as others who can help to build it.

At first the CAN is simply the container of all the projects that the participants dream up to lead the community from the present to the future – from food or energy initiatives, to talk and deliberation spaces, learning clubs or new transport routes. But over time they produce events, products or even opportunities for investment. For that reason, it needs to have an agreed legal form and constitution – ideally one that can remain flexible while being accountable. For example, Coalville CAN (Communities and Neighbours), whose main focus is to reclaim empty buildings for shared use, set itself up as a Community Benefit Society. This allows anyone paying a pound to become a member, but reserves all the profits made for the benefit of the whole community.

Once this 'constitute' is agreed, it can start to attract people who might never have thought of being part of the original conversation and help them see some concrete benefits from the resources and services it now provides.[187] For example, setting up a CounterCoin currency allows anyone to join who is willing to do a bit of community work in exchange for free food, transport or cinema tickets. Others might simply want to take part in the learning clubs or get cheaper energy. Whatever their entry point, they will meet the culture and structure of a new system and begin to participate. For a pound they can 'belong', participate in the discussion and begin to have a say.

At some point, after a strong ethos and sense of trust has been built among the members, they might want to digitise their operation and become a voting platform. To date there is no ideal technology that keeps the deliberation process close to the decision-making, except where the questions are coming from a centralised body – for example pol.is or all the forms of liquid democracy mentioned before. I've no doubt it's coming down the line. However, we need to watch out for the inertia of old ways. Unless the decision-making arises from the relationships developed in real time, generally but not exclusively in person, then online voting is likely to mimic the old system, easily polarising along old divides.

A fourth-sector platform shaping up

So while The Alternative UK is not a political party – taking part in elections or party-political culture and structure – it is using the platform as a vehicle for broader change. Some might see it as an ark they can climb aboard. Psychotherapists might describe it as a 'transitional object' – the thing you invest with emotion and identity so that it can coherently carry you from one complex reality to another. The platform currently has a news media group telling a new story about power, a network of networks initiative (The Elephant) captured in Zooms and podcasts, and the CANs network. In the future anything could appear on the platform – from an energy or food project to a festival or a political party.

To that extent The Alternative UK is en route to delivering what Uffe Elbæk imagined as a fourth-sector platform (although the economy is not yet fully formed). Alive in this space are cooperatives, commoning platforms, Transition Towns, social enterprises – many different CANs – as well as members and leaders of B-corps, NGOs and Community Interest Companies.

In the pipeline is better structure for linking the CANs to each other, sharing information, methods and practices, possibly governance systems. When enough of them are voting, we will be able to vote together on how to develop a CAN of CANs, giving rise to a shared manifesto and a strategy for change.

6.3 Citizen/community action/ agency networks: CANs

I'm not a joiner, that's my problem. I love the idea of meeting up with people and doing stuff together, but I don't join groups or anything. I'm not a member of anything, except my family – and even they make me feel trapped sometimes. That's why I loved Second Life, I could just play at stuff like getting married or starting a company but just switch off when I'd had enough.

She felt guilty saying it, but she loved the lockdown. All those times she'd tried to get people to come together to do something but they wouldn't, just because they voted for the other side or because they hate politics. And now, here they all were in this Zoom room, working out how to help Joan at No.32 get her groceries. Getting to know each other a bit and even having a laugh. Magic.

WHILE THE CAN started out as a simple idea – connecting the people to each other and to the resources and solutions already available in the town/city/region/globe – its action and purpose keeps deepening with every step forward. And with that, its potential for agency.

Meeting our emotional needs

Arriving after the Friendly and Inquiry stages of the collaboratory, the CAN is conceived as an answer to the desires expressed by the people who took part. Hence it intends to meet the following needs:

1. A local community place where any person can go (physically or virtually) to participate in the solutions to the multiple crises we face, in a way that comes naturally to them, while finding belonging, meaning and agency.

2. Where local civil society organisations can go to collaborate with other local, national and global organisations to find real, creative and effective solutions, while prototyping new forms of governance.

3. Where we can get on with building a healthy environment for flourishing without waiting for Westminster.

Instead of being an extended network – flat, peer-to-peer, local – CANs are emerging as a fractal of the bigger global system of development. Within each CAN are the same elements that would, on a global scale, address the multiple crises we face: understood in the framework of I–We–World, integrating the otherwise competing parts. CANs are a microsystem that both imply and constitute a macrosystem.

The whole world is too big a location to work actively on integrating these parts. It needs smaller containers to resolve the dynamics and to give rise to the best of what is possible in each place. Precisely because it is built on face-to-face relationships between diverse groups of people, the CAN gives rise to a new system in its core processes, one that (to quote Buckminster Fuller again) 'outmodes the old one, making it obsolete'.

Principles, values, affordances

So what are the characteristics of that micro/macro system – locally or globally? The list below is shorthand, but each point is covered in previous chapters as indicated.

- Makes space for the more complex human being's bio-psycho-social-spiritual needs and capacities (Chapters 1–3).

• Offers an open, friendly culture, emphasising the inter- and intra-connectedness of individuals to communities within a more coherent idea of society, itself deeply connected to the planet we all depend upon. New social patterns are revealed; and new 'constitutes' (fluid institutions) are formed, which become the vehicles for regeneration (Chapter 4).

• Holds diverse forms of agency – civil society, social entrepreneurs, activists, wholists (including spiritual and indigenous), carers and more.

• Has a new understanding of power as both soft and hard (Chapter 4.1–4.2). It's not all about guns and money. How we think and talk about ourselves – the stories we live by – are shaping outcomes all the time. Independent, local media becomes a vibrant participant in holding the conversation, linking conflict to transformative possibilities for the future (as Johan Galtung would, see Introduction).

• A new dynamic appears between the feminine and masculine in both public and private space (Chapter 4.4). Women are natural leaders here, but (if conscious of their feminine power) they bring everyone with them. With this balance, we understand better that progress depends as much upon the conditions and capacities of the citizens as the mechanisms for change. More than that, putting relationship at the heart of a dynamic system of change offers something like the possibility of a quantum shift – a new foundation for socio-political transformation (Chapter 2).

• Partly as a result of this and partly because of new creative facilitation by artists, we develop a new 'feel' for gathering and collaborating, both locally and virtually. This signifies an ontological shift (a shift of being) without which an epistemological knowing (what counts as true) cannot land. This emerging 'feel', or sensibility, is deeply relational, excited and experimental – full of possibility, rather than suffused with dogma or convictions. Excited for the future unfolding. More on this below.

These systems also have physical components that are vital for their growth:

- Well-designed places to meet, talk, play – on- and offline; the written word is not enough to carry the message

- Learning clubs of all kinds – from self-development classes, through uses of drama, games and immersion, to tech enablement

- Social enterprises that draw on cosmolocal talents (available people operating at a global and spiritual level), rising to the emergencies we face

- Digital networks, giving rise to tools for participation and sharing of insights, tools and practice; also for effective governance: integrating the importance of participation with the desire to meet urgent targets

- Energy, food, housing projects that do the job that government (and the corporate sector) has failed to do

- Festivals, markets, experimental spaces for large-scale gathering

- New currencies, registering many different forms of value, that can bring people into relationship with the place they live.

All of these are led by the collective intelligence of the people, remembering that includes people capable of many forms of agency (Chapter 3.2), who are gathering explicitly with a view to overcoming old divisions. These groups would be working in partnership with the local council but not led by it, so that people can hold on to their own power and develop their autonomy. In addition, as has been occurring increasingly in the UK – and more recently in Hong Kong – they might be putting up their own representatives to take over the party-led councils as independents, thereby ushering new ways of working into the old political culture.

As such, CANs are new units in a changing political system, a 21st-century politics that embraces the people waking up and – in friendly, connected and planet-positive ways – enables them to take back control of their own futures.

Feminisation of culture and form

What if, I hear you say, the people involved in these processes turn out not to be friendly and planet positive? Then, I would say, they are not truly connected to the needs of the people where they live. Where there is division, then friendship and trust need to be built. Wherever there is concern for each other's well-being, there will be a reckoning with environmental urgency. If that is missing, there will always be conflict: the world is on everyone's doorstep and has to be reckoned with.

While The Alternative UK helps to create conditions for CANs to take shape through holding Co-labs off- and online and offering tools for building the narrative, we don't see it as a central body controlling the process. At most we ignite sparks, through the sharing of the achievements, tools and practices of others. The strength of a CAN lies in its ability to hold and facilitate the native energy of a town, city or region. Participants need to own it themselves, precisely to experience their autonomy. If it is initiated and then held from the outside it never quite does the job of releasing the *diversity of energy* from within.

An example of the latter might be the wonderful work that Participatory Cities are doing in the borough of Barking and Dagenham and, in fact, all over the world.[188] With a grant from the American media group Bloomberg, they have created the much-needed infrastructure for citizen participation in cities that have suffered from the challenges of austerity and social cohesion. It's a beautiful vision of flourishing and inclusion, slowly taking shape.

Quoting Elinor Ostrom on their website, they say, 'We can't keep blaming each other for materialism, cynicism or laziness when the practical tools simply don't exist to enable us to step forward'. This echoes the aims of The Alternative UK and many of the values I have been expressing in this book.

However, if you look at the metrics published in their annual report, they are not yet succeeding in bringing the people to their project.[189] The Every One Every Day response to the pandemic, which added the National Lottery Fund, Esmée Fairbairn and more funders to the network, had 2,000 people signing up, less than 1 per cent of the local population. Compare that to the completely unfunded Covid Mutual Aid network in Hackney that had 7,000 people sign up overnight.[190] The difference is unlikely to be due to any lack of planning or creativity on behalf of Participatory Cities, but rather a lack of soft power – attraction – arising from the lack of a pattern-match with the energies of the people living there.

Indigenous design and development

To become a people's initiative, a CAN of the kind I am describing here must arise from the available energies, including cultures, of the people living there; it can't be some ideal form, designed and imported from outside. In most cases, that will mean a bringing together of the different groupings already gathering, each with their own pulling power.

One of our favourite CAN developers in the UK is a group of self-styled 'community transformers' who first met each other at Extinction Rebellion. When the task of growing the movement outside of London began, they quickly saw that they had to work together with people in the smaller towns, rather than simply enrol them. They also saw that there were a number of different starting points available to answer the question of how to bring people together in service to a common cause. For that reason they work more at engaging with multiple communities than harnessing them or bringing them into a pre-designed home. This set of activities now *brings into relationship* social entrepreneurs, activists and movement builders, permaculturalists, educators, well-being initiatives (from sport to therapy), care professionals and lots of people without a group, who feel attracted to the sense that something is going on. They call their movement Trust the People.[191]

In that sense, the idea of a CAN is a generic term rather than a formula for system-holding and cosmolocal containers of people power. Yes, we are working on successful prototypes in situ. But like any fractal anywhere, each one will look and develop differently, according to the people's character and make-up. Through an integral lens this would describe being able to hold diverse forms of agency alongside each other, allowing each to self-organise within a relational culture. From a narrative perspective, it means allowing more than one story of change to describe a common goal.

At the same time, when we look around us we can see CANs already established and evolving according to their circumstances: when you observe with a more wholistic perspective, they are akin to a natural phenomenon. Those we consider at the forefront of actively developing CANs worldwide would include: Cooperation Jackson in Mississippi;[192] Civic Square in Birmingham;[193] Frome in Somerset;[194] Regenerate Devon UK;[195] the Neighborocracy system in India;[196] and Transition Town in Tooting, London.[197] Prototypes we are co-creating are taking shape in Plymouth[198] and Stoke-on-Trent.[199] As a new picture begins to take shape, these very positive responses to the narrative of powerlessness that party politics generates make them core to any possibility of a genuine alternative.

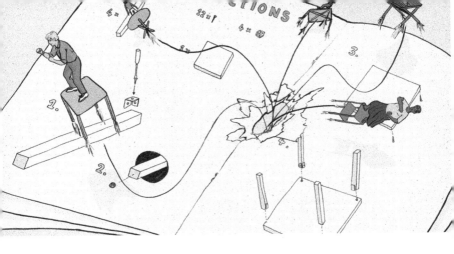

7 The New Socio-Politics

7.1 Freedom and Independents

Most of the time I don't know what you're talking about. When you say you're on the Left I feel like you just pushed me into the Right – which is where the racists are. I'm not racist! But I don't agree with your way of doing things either – makes me feel oppressed.

Trying to stay true to myself is like spinning plates and juggling at the same time. Every day I read something new that rings a bell, resonates deeply in the depths of my being. But it also invites me into a new group or media stream to explore that further. Trying to keep up with these new kinds of belonging and all the possibilities is exhausting and confusing. I try to bring them back to the inside of myself, so I can just be with that new me emerging. But, you know, FOMO.

He had her in his grasp. The politician was floundering, clearly unable to answer the question. He repeated it again, still nothing but obfuscation. As he saw her squirm, he knew this was great TV: time for a pay rise!

IN THE party-political battleground between the Left and Right, both sides have had to cede important language and ideas to their opposition. I won't start with any overarching definition of their positions here, but will only draw attention to the heavy costs both have paid to stay in this binary division. The Left, for example, cannot use the word 'freedom' because it implies that the state should reduce its role in running, sustaining and defending public goods. The Right on the other hand cannot talk easily about 'care' or 'welfare', without reducing their traditional emphasis on individual and family self-reliance.

At the heart of everyday society, these distinctions often find their equilibrium, but in politics and the media they are polarised. Because the Left sees caring for the most vulnerable as its primary duty, its regulations – designed to offer the best protection – are caricatured (by the Right) as the nanny state. Because the Right sees the family as the front line of care, with the state withdrawing from the private life of adults, the Left charges them with avoiding their responsibilities. Of course, any of these accusations can also be true – and often are. But on the whole, they are false divides. Neither set of voters or politicians would willingly give up any of the values mentioned by either side.

Rather than try and find a compromise – a centrist position that trades one policy off against another – can we not transcend and include those positions? Can we find a new starting point to think about what we need to develop, individually and collectively, that would make us capable of meeting the current crises? That doesn't mean starting from scratch or reinventing the wheel. It means, rather, bringing all our capacities into relationship and collaborating for ingenious leaps forward.

Flatpackers make democracy look easy

Easier said than done, naturally. Yet in some parts of the UK that is exactly what is happening, in the phenomenon known as Flatpack Democracy. Seventeen residents of the town of Frome, each coming from a different ward in the parish (a small political unit that maps to many English towns) stood together as independents for Frome. Among them were previous rivals – two ex-Labour councillors, two from the Lib Dems. The rest had never stood for public office before; some were Conservative voters.

What brought them together was a long-standing impatience with the local council. Despite being led by different parties at different times, the council had never shown an interest in the views of the local inhabitants. Local money was poorly spent, with no consultation. Any attempt by citizens to offer proposals was routinely stifled by protocol.

Independents for Frome had a simple campaign message: vote for us and we'll tear up the local council rule book and involve you in decision-making. The first time they stood, they won ten of the 17 seats – enough to take over the council. They did exactly as promised and radically changed the culture by introducing participatory budgeting. In addition, any good idea any local citizen had to improve Frome for all its inhabitants, which could not be funded within the budget, would be connected to possibilities of outside funding.

The second time IFF stood in local elections, they won all 17 seats. The first Indy Mayor, Peter Macfadyen, wrote a short manual on how to take over your local council, which he called Flatpack Democracy. Today there are 21 Flatpack Councils and in May 2021 – with hundreds of these manuals now in circulation – they are running a campaign for more.[200]

But of course, like Ikea flatpack furniture, Flatpack Democracy is not always as easy as it sounds to put together, or to maintain once it's up. Standing against established parties in your home town can look like a betrayal of good principles and 'the greater cause' to long-standing supporters on the Left, Right or Middle. In addition, while the prospect of winning the council is attractive, the job of running it is demanding. Even when you have a new, exciting relationship with your own constituents, you are obliged to have an old, entrenched one with all the layers above you. Fighting for independence often leads to a loss of freedom at another level.

A friendly kind of anarchism

Like the concept of freedom, independence is always relative. Even so, it remains a siren call – and for good reason. As explained in Chapter 3.1, the need for autonomy – the ability to have control over our own circumstances – is one of the nine essential emotional needs specified by the Human Givens framework. From birth onwards we struggle to become capable of standing on our own two feet, as a means to survival and then fulfilment. To bring a child up is more than a challenge of feeding and housing; it is the task of moving them through the stages of total dependence to independence. If they mature well, they will propel themselves to interdependence, understanding that their well-being depends upon the general well-being of others.

Losing our freedom, as we would if we were imprisoned for example, is seen as the ultimate punishment for a living human being. That is why the idea of anarchism – citizens simply responsible for their own self-governance – keeps making a return, most recently in Brett Hennig's book on sortition, *The End of Politicians*.[201] Consider also Carne Ross on why and how he left the British Foreign Office and landed in the (self-described) democratic confederation of Rojava, according to his book *The Accidental Anarchist*. But anarchism is a term that conjures as much fear as yearning: within the zero-sum game, one person's freedom can so easily be another person's prison.

In the meantime, the essential emotional need for autonomy can be temporarily met by illusions of control, for example, by giving people infinite choices in a supermarket – such as hundreds of biscuit brands without ever giving them the healthy choices they desire. Or the illusion of a clear choice between Leave or Remain in Europe – when, either way, we need to have solid, ongoing, material and cultural relationships with our continental neighbours.

When you have lived a life with only superficial control over your circumstances, genuine independence can seem very daunting. We might be constantly calling for free choice, but there are risks if the conditions under which it can be achieved do not yet exist. Within a large community of people – a city, region or small nation – there is always a broad range of capacities sitting on the continuum between dependent and independent, according to the circumstances people have been living in. These are not simply material conditions, they are also emotional and psychological.

In a single town, you might have the privileged safe, the privileged unsafe (freelance/entrepreneurial, physically challenged or simply unhappy), the workers and working poor, protesters, counter-culturalists, civil society actors, activists, social entrepreneurs – all seemingly calling for change, but with vastly different capacities for responsibility. A broader social independence cannot be achieved unless there is at least enough of a core of responsible actors capable of supporting the rest on their journey. Wanting transformation is not enough: it needs organisation.

Yet, as Brexit proved, 'taking back control' can always be played upon as an essential need within our individual and collective psyche. What might be more surprising is that the instinct for independence is synchronistically emerging all over the world, if for different reasons.

A rising tide of Independents

Scottish and Catalonian Independence are both popular movements that have grown in significance, as the larger states that contain them show their inability to cope with the multiple crises of democracy and development. In psychology, what's known as self-determination theory shows how feelings of meaning, mastery and autonomy are sustainable resources for personal well-being. As for individual people, the call to national self-determination can breed a deep sense of confidence and purpose among aspiring regions and stateless nations.

Independent activists and candidates are sure they can do better for their citizens. Isn't this evidence that our growing development, both as individuals and groups, makes us more responsible for overall outcomes in our society? The key question today is less about whether or not that instinct for independence is positive – and more about the optimum size for self-organising units of governance.

Cities are increasingly acknowledged as the new frontier for healthy citizen engagement. But can municipalism really thrive without a strong localism, which builds trust between the metro-lands and those living side by side in smaller towns and villages?[202] Equally, how can we avoid excessive competition between cities for resources that, at some levels, should be shared nationally? Each level of independence from the upper tiers has to be carefully worked out.

Movements and uprisings bring a mixture of offers. Within each seems to be some elements of pure anger or frustration that demand a response from higher authorities as the answer to the problem. But these movements also tend to carry new methods and practices that would deliver solutions somewhat more evolved than the authorities can bring. The movements often demand that those with power be more sophisticated than they currently are (or can be, within the structures and cultures they inhabit and maintain).

Routinely, these new elements are carried forward by the increased diversity of the new compared to the old. More young people, more women or people of colour that the establishment has not included. They also include less privileged people who bring with them insights from the wider population. It is their intelligence that is usually missing from the established system. This was originally designed to deliver on their needs (like the welfare state) but tended, instead, to maintain the established order in which everything is measured in numbers only and where people are seen as recipients of services rather than as their designers or envisioners.

Until now, the successful movements – those that have successfully pierced the public imagination – have been top-heavy on protest. As a result, when they are in the eye of the media, it is difficult to land the innovations they are bringing. While Occupy, for example, introduced new ideas about democratisation, they couldn't influence the general public with the new culture.[203] This was largely because they didn't have a strategy within that vision which could be offered as a route to power for those watching.

As I began to describe in Chapter 6, some elements of Extinction Rebellion however (who have many Occupy veterans within them) have been steadily organising for the future beyond protest. First with the establishment of the Future Democracy Hub at the tail end of the first Rebellion and later with the clearly evolved 'community transformers programme' called Trust the People – a form of citizens action network, or CAN.[204] They have evolved the People's Assemblies into Community Assemblies to attract a broader range of civil society organisations to take part. In so doing, they are entertaining broader action, such as reclaiming empty buildings on 'meanwhile contracts' rather than simply squatting.

Some think of this kind of radical change taken in stages as r-evolution! The neologism seems appropriate for the way that Trust the People stitches together different pieces of the broader demand for better democracy, helping them to add up to more than the sum of their parts. They are currently putting their weight behind Flatpack Democracy to help reclaim local councils for citizen participation. This is not with the intention of transferring all the energy built up within a community into the hands of the state (or the party currently leading), but rather to have a genuine partner in the existing system that acknowledges the two different ways of working and their need to collaborate. Two but not two ... or what I increasingly think of as parallel power.

Forging parallel power

The notion of a second, autonomous socio-political system running alongside the state party-political system is not at all original. For example, if you look up the term 'dual power', you will quickly run into the violent history of Leninist workers' councils (Soviets) partnering with the Bolsheviks to smash the Russian Provisional government of social democrats. Or Mao Tse Tung's Chinese Revolution in 1949. In both cases, the duality describes the growing people power alongside the state, followed by the sudden shift made possible by the people partnering with a smaller party and overthrowing government to become the state.[205]

With a nod back to Chapter 3.2, where I describe the *strategy mindset* (first-tier and orange in Spiral Dynamics terms), this is how dual power manifests in a zero-sum game: a pincer movement using people power to overcome the incumbents. How would that look with a green or second-tier mindset? Writer Václav Havel, the last President of Czechoslovakia from 1989 and the first President of the Czech Republic until 2003 – 14 years in total – had a similar but more benign sense of what the people's will required.

In the mid-1980s, during the oppressive years of Socialist 'normalisation' in Czechoslovakia, Havel and his philosopher friend Václav Benda imagined what they called a parallel polis – 'a space for informed, non-bureaucratic, dynamic, and open communities' (to some extent prefigured by his secret life with dissident friends) to develop independently of the state. Explicitly opposing the 'demoralisation of the consumer value system' of capitalism, as much as the fake solidarity of communism, Havel wanted to deeply address human powerlessness, the 'machine-like' nature of politics, and sought a return to love as a political language.[206]

Havel's parallel polis never imagined building a parallel power system, not least because it would challenge the very establishment that Havel was elected to lead. Instead, the possibility dissolved in the crass materialism and market exuberance of liberated post-communist societies. Yet the concept, as we face our own sclerotic, gridlocked and creaking political establishments, may very well be worth the revival. Can we imagine how the relationship between the state and a parallel polis might look with a 'teal' approach? One that looks at power as constantly redistributing itself across the whole polity as people become ever more self-organised in the task of meeting the multiple crises of these times.

My sense is that as we enter the fractal age – where people take it upon themselves to build new socio-economic-governance prototypes to help them face the crises – we will need national- and international-level CANs and constitutes to maintain the integrity of the new socio-political system that they are building. Otherwise it will simply be sucked back into the old – the fate of almost all the 'new politics' parties arising over the past ten years. Podemos, Five Star, Alternativet and so on, are all now part of the frozen system we need to transform. Another test case is Komeito in Japan – a Buddhist anti-corruption 'peace party' that has now been in coalition with its previous enemy the Liberal Democrat Party since 2012, losing many loyal supporters in the process.[207]

The closest initiative I've seen that points at this parallel power is the call for a permanent Citizens' Assembly at the national level.[208] However, while there is no doubt that Citizens' Assemblies are an important development in people power, they are not enough. Citizens' Assemblies only involve a small number of citizens directly (albeit others indirectly). And until now in the UK they have only had advisory power, with no opportunity for the citizens' decisions to be put to a referendum whose results would be binding. And anyone reading who thinks it would be mad to allow the process to be binding should read about the successful process in Ireland which led to the legalisation of abortion, or the many times Poland took that risk successfully.[209, 210]

Even that, however, misses the main opportunity and advance of what CANs offer, which is the collective ingenuity of people living in community to design and enact new self-governing, cosmolocal, socio-economic-political systems – ones that they take part in directly as much as they wish. Once these are up and running at the town or city level, where can their power be felt at the national level? If they hand it over to the old party politics they will simply become political footballs, like the NHS.

As mentioned briefly above, one of the most promising developments over the past five years is municipalism, which has platformed significant socio-economic-democratic developments in cities like Barcelona and Madrid. Much has been written about Kate Raworth's *Doughnut Economics* and the plan to unfold action-labs in 40 cities around the world.[211] However, for every kind of person to have access to the fruits of that, and even to play a role in co-creating how it might land in your community, we need CANs to be held independently from even the best of city states.

If you doubt that, see how coastal cities currently intent on innovating economies will be hijacked by the race for jobs and tax-free investment that the UK government's Freeports policy will offer.[212] As many jobs could be generated by a Green New Deal or possibly more in the long run by a transformed notion of livelihood altogether, over time. But the dualism of party politics will find it easy to polarise the Freeport narrative between those who are 'for' or 'against' immediate jobs.

So why not create a permanent space for CANs by replacing the House of Lords with a People's Parliament? Not a group of people elected to represent us in the old way, but a constantly evolving body that is part of a variety of new forms of decision-making, linking CANs on the ground to CANs at the national level (see India's Neighborocracy for inspiration). That might include elements of sociocracy (structured deliberation), liquid democracy and even pol.is (collective sensemaking technology) to have a more plural – yet still direct – means of hearing the will of the people.[213]

This 'house' would be seen not as secondary to the House of Commons, but in a constantly evolving partnership – between the wholistic people's movement already taking decisions at city level, and the more vertical structures of government that deliver on services paid for by our taxes. In a radical redesign of our political system, this would bring socio-politics, the connection between I–We–World, into line with party politics.

While government within this transformation would have more hard power for the time being, that would guarantee a gradual transition to the next economies. At the same time, the People's Parliament is likely to have more soft power, as everyone will have a chance to be directly involved, whatever their historic privilege. It will be the story of stories, an ambitious new narrative of all of us. And as we know, soft power trumps hard power in the way that paper wraps stone.

But what about Me?

How does all this impact upon any one of us, as individual human beings, obliged to enter into the voting booth on our own to make decisions about the future? Watching my own next generation of youth grapple with a very different balance of personal and public power than I grew up with, it looks complicated. While there is a new culture of self-expression and individual creativity championed by the internet, there are also much more intensely applied efforts to capture our attention and control it.

Our new-found freedoms are potentially a sham when we find ourselves playing ever more deeply into a digital public space still owned by those who have always been in power, only now in league with new corporates like Facebook and Google. They're the same as the old corporates, and see people only as data waiting to be mined for their financial gain.

On the other hand, our personal and collective self-awareness is also growing rapidly. We understand more about fake news than our parents did (see Chapter 4.2). We are in better touch with our health – including our mental and, to some extent, social health. We are more involved in debates about identity, whether gender, sexual, cultural, class, age or national. And we are more capable, through all the forms of media we consume, of observing the behaviour of others.

To be able to withstand the accelerating external pressures from outside, it's clear that we need to rapidly build our internal strength for self-mastery. In that sense, any politics for this new age must understand and serve our urgent need for more personal autonomy. But at the same time, it must do that in ways that create the best conditions for our greater collaboration, locally and globally, as people facing multiple common crises.

7.2 Cosmolocalism and the next economies

Ugh. That annoying thing when someone from the city comes to 'listen to us', really believing he has to fit our local thinking into his big picture. As if we could do any of our work without having a big picture of our own! I'm already working directly with farmers on all five continents, sharing data and best practice – makes me laugh. Our councillors are no better – all that talk of the top-down meeting the bottom-up. Don't they have Wi-Fi?

She loved their get-togethers. At first they only talked practical stuff like organising food and meds. But recently they've spent much more time checking in and hearing how each other is doing. A lot of them have family far away: Amina's family had to leave the city and go back to their village where there's no running water. It's painful sometimes, but it helps make everything more real. We can't run away from the problems we created.

I N THE wake of Brexit and the US Trump presidency, the fake divide I described in Chapter 7.1 nevertheless showed a clear line along which division could be exploited. In the UK we might describe that as the north–south divide – post-industrial towns and cities not yet finding their way after the decrease in manufacturing, versus cosmopolitan cities that have thrived in the better-connected world of an information economy. In the US, the split is between rural and urban areas, most starkly in the contrast between the outward-looking coastlines and the inward looking, vast open spaces at the centre of America.

In a world in which people are measured only by their success in the growth economy, these differences are hard to overcome. However, in an alternative political culture, difference does not lead to division: difference is understood better as plurality – of ages, cultures, genders and so on, and also of kinds of agency. Where conflict or disadvantage occurs, it is a shared problem – and a shared opportunity.

As a more nuanced reading of the election results in either location show, every city or rural area is itself diverse. Cities have inner suburbs that vote Democrat/Remain and outer suburbs that vote Republican/Leave, a pattern that is repeated from coast to coast in a map that turns purple, rather than Red v Blue.[214] Yet if you talk to either 'side' about the other, there is more caricature and prejudice – more othering – than would ever be tolerated if the targets were excluded minorities. Yet those people often share the same streets and shops and local identity. Talk to any of them about the wealth of their town or city and they will want the whole place to thrive.

What is a living?

This is why it's crucial for people to meet where they live – not focusing on the political divide but on a common future they want to build. In the midst of that, to be able to include everyone in the discussion, the question of how a better culture gives rise to thriving is crucial. It has to be real for everyone. The demand for a solid income is uppermost in the minds of most people, but urgent for the less privileged. If the traditional form of employment has gone, and the government is unable to generate alternatives for your town or city based on the old economy, people need access to new thinking, models and support from elsewhere.

Note that I didn't say jobs or specifically work: while that will always be core, it is already the mainstream conversation, filling our news streams every day. There are more ways to 'earn a living' than taking part in the old economy, much of which is built on excessive consumerism and mechanistic, alienated labour in the service of major corporations. A recent event curated by Jay Tompt of the REconomy Centre on Alt/ work for the young and unemployed, encouraged a focus on meaning and purpose while staying local where social entrepreneurship can more easily be incubated.[215] As a report from Dell Technologies claimed, 85 per cent of future jobs have not yet been invented: now is the time to be creative using this moment of uncertainty and with less to lose.[216] The new currencies mentioned earlier – CounterCoin,[217] Mutual Credit,[218] Cryptocurrencies[219] – also help to create some fluidity, as people experiment.

Every week The Daily Alternative publishes seven blogs – each containing a plethora of examples of entrepreneurial initiatives of all kinds – with concrete tools and methods available from all over the world. The growth in the personal and social development sectors (local and global) sits alongside expansion of the green economy or other whole-planet strategies, evidencing the I–We–World connection I'm pointing at throughout this book.

Much of the innovation that will help us transform our system is coming from parts of the world badly covered by the mainstream papers. To give some examples, there's Somaliland's use of iris recognition in presidential elections, prototyping the world's most sophisticated voting register.[220] And Rwanda's use of drone delivery for the health service, saving huge resources of time and energy while saving lives.[221] And Taiwan's use of digital participation in a much expanded idea of citizen-led democracy. And Costa Rica's new ecologically transformed tourist industry directly linked to new biodiversity practices in towns and villages.[222]

This is not to underplay or trivialise the gross disparities still unacceptably persistent around the globe, but to bring them into relationship with ours, recognising the many levels of agency. Alongside the continued reporting of poverty, inequality and injustice, The Alternative UK hopes to play a part in introducing new evidence of agency and creativity arising from those portrayed as powerless or hopeless. For example, in ways comparable to the work in Stoke's CounterCommunity, successful social entrepreneurs Goonj in India 'are building an equitable relationship of strength, sustenance and dignity between the cities and villages using the under-utilized urban material as a tool to trigger development'.[223]

Again, this is not the same as glocalism – where globalisation is taken into consideration when local decisions are made (which could lead, for example to lower wages in the global competition for work). It's called cosmolocalism because it downloads fractals – initiatives shared through story and relationship patterns – directly from one community into another. These are concrete resources, freely offered. *Ada*.

The Three Horizons

Yet how can these small connections and pattern matches add up to significant change in the short time we have? If the dominant global economy stays extractive and growth orientated within the context of continuing division and competition, then how can these small efforts to change the narrative and culture thrive? This dilemma is well captured in the Three Horizons theory, primarily attributed to Bill Sharpe, Senior Associate at the International Futures Forum.[224] The theory describes our current socio-political-economic system as H1, the fledgling new system fractals and the early adapters as occupying H2, and a possible transformed system that can lift us away from the cliff's edge as H3. The diagrams of the growth curves of each of these Horizons show a chasm looming if H2 cannot get off the ground, and the people doing their best burn out.

When facing the challenge of H2, many describe a possible future in which 'top-down devolution of power meets the bottom-up grassroots innovation'. Yet, as I have been describing throughout this book, our current socio-political-economic system cannot achieve that. In fact, our current party politics could be the very obstacle to that possibility. Too often, when local initiatives build up their energy for change there is no way to develop their agency other than through the local council or a political party. These local establishments carry too much of the old divisive structure and culture to be able to run with the potential on offer.

As I describe in Chapters 1 and 7.1, while many local operators cultivate valuable personal relationships with councillors – which in turn create useful knowledge flows between them – there are no mechanisms to allow that knowledge to flow upwards to the policymakers. Instead, Westminster bubbles continue to send their decisions downwards, drowning the new potential. I remember when I had been working on a paper for Barrow Cadbury on community cohesion, researching the many initiatives local communities were taking to bring people together: food events, choirs, experiments with participatory budgeting.[225] Many were swept aside when the New Labour government sent down its paper on communitiarianism, loaded with abstract concepts and new allocation of budgets. It happened again with David Cameron's Big Society initiative, which eulogised the role of community initiative.[226] With its significant resources the Big Society could have given a lifeline to projects that were already working but severely stretched – mostly run by women, often without pay. Instead, completely new start-ups were given huge budgets to lead and incentivise communities, largely led by young men described as social innovators. In that period many long-standing volunteer services had their budgets cut and had to close.

Too many genuinely indigenous community initiatives founder for lack of an external support structure that is not vulnerable to party politics. Ideally this would not be simply peers working at the same level, like so many fledglings flapping their wings on the ground. Cosmolocalism offers the commons not only as a toolbox but also as a repository of stories and the opportunity for relationship at every level of agency.

Even so, we need a better sense of what 3H could be, not overly defined, but just enough to attract more energy that way and to create something of an 'updraft' to accelerate the struggling activities of the 2H activities towards long-term viability.

The blind men and the elephant

In the last gasp of the 2010s, after two and a half years of observing what is emerging in the socio-economic-political field, The Alternative UK called a gathering. Our sense was that there were many of us who could feel a new system beginning to take shape, but each of us only from our own limited perspective. Moreover, while some knew what they were touching on was partial, some thought what they were holding in their hands was the system itself. But when challenged on how it could answer the major global-level crises, they could rarely answer without slipping into dream mode.

This plurality of views reminded us of the Indian fable – versions of which are found in Buddhist, Hindu and Jain texts – of the blind men and the elephant. It tells the story of a group of blind men who have heard of the arrival of a new animal in the town, called an elephant – but none of them know what it looks like. They decide to visit together and learn by touch. But as they stand around the beast, each of them grasps a different piece – one the trunk, one the leg, another the tusk. At first they squabble fiercely, contradicting each other's descriptions. But later, any conflict is resolved as they learn to listen to each other's perspectives and become able to generate a picture of the whole animal in their collective imagination.

In longer versions of the fable, we hear more about the relative virtues of each part of the animal. The tail of the elephant is useful for swatting flies but cannot exercise the intelligence of the trunk, which picks up heavy logs right at their mid-point in order to carry them a distance. Each part depends upon the other, but none can offer the full impact of the elephant walking through the village. When thinking about the bigger systems that we are part of, how can each of us get a sense of the whole – the full elephant – so we can build better on our collective agency?

From the almost one thousand blogs we'd posted in The Daily Alternative up to that point, we invited 30 systems actors with a diverse range of perspectives on the new system arising.[227] Some had been working for more than a decade building alternative structures and cultures. Others were new arrivals, often very young. Together they brought digital and spiritual technology, experimental economies, new democratic tools, theatre practice, existential futurism, journalists and psychologists ... it was a heady mix of inputs.

Over three days we worked with relational systems coach Stephan Kolinsky to see whether we could 'make the elephant appear' – at least in our collective mind's eye.[228] Whether we did or not is a question to ponder. If we thought we would emerge with a blueprint for the future, we failed to do so – but we generally knew that was the wrong objective. However, if we aimed to now sense, feel and relate to the new system – including the disruption that will ensue as it emerges – we certainly achieved that. We could feel the nature of the beast.

In a constellation workshop on Day 3 we were split into small groups to write a short press release on our different versions of this new system arising.[229] However, as we delivered our speeches to an imagined public, it was clear that the language adequate for describing the 'elephant' was not yet available. As we were reaching for it, the words that came sounded overly familiar and idealistic. We wanted to be pure and original. Instead each of us were – and are – part of the culture we are attempting to transform. At first that was painful: I myself felt momentarily hopeless and despairing. Yet ignoring the likelihood of that happening is core to the problem of agency.

If we conceive of the future as made up of the solutions to our current problems, we miss what is truly possible. An example would be that when you have no money, money seems as though it would solve everything. Yet when you get more money, your problems take on a different shape and you realise that money itself is not the solution. Of course this mindset could become a recipe for inaction. Instead, what was precious about the gathering of the 'elephant' was accepting and learning to live with what we sensed was possible without being disillusioned when nothing concrete appears, other than the deepening of our relationships.

Later, I saw more clearly that as a pattern of relationships we were not yet a fractal that could ignite the whole system change we were yearning for. While many of our group were global actors, we were not yet working from the perspective of the globe: for that we needed wider collaboration.

Fittingly, a week before the Elephant I was in Bellagio at a Rockefeller Foundation conference on the fourth sector – a term that describes the social enterprise sector which has developed beyond second-sector (private) market-based practice and third-sector (charities, NGOs) goals for social and environmental benefit.[230] Uffe Elbæk had described Alternativet as a fourth-sector platform and I was attending this event as his proxy. For some time I had been watching the developing fourth sector in Plymouth, with imaginative and human-centred social enterprise groups like the Real Ideas Organisation sitting alongside cooperatives, commoning and volunteer initiatives like Pop Plymouth.[231, 232] My thought was that work could be done to bring that cluster of new economy initiatives into relationship with the global-level 'for benefit' companies – also known as B-corp – to create a wider and stronger alternative to the current economic system.[233]

Among other brilliant participants, I met Steve Waddell, co-founder and lead staff at the SDG Transformations Forum – a rich network of global community transformers working in all fields connected to the UN sustainable development goals.[234] He in turn invited me to Althorp, UK, in January 2020 where The Alternative UK became a founding member of Catalyst 2030, a newly formed network of global social change innovators committed to meeting the United Nations' original target of 2030.[235] Major funders on board included Ashoka, Skoll Foundation and Schwab Foundation – although they were there to connect and support, rather than fund. While it is early days for meeting their targets, you can keep in touch with our high-energy innovations on The Daily Alternative.

Covid opens eyes everywhere

As described in Chapter 1, the global pandemic of the novel coronavirus Covid was an unprecedented shock to the global system, first and foremost in terms of illness and death, cruelly impacting the old and vulnerable the most. How quickly it showed up our value system as those in low-paid jobs and, for reasons of long-term deprivation, the Black and minority ethnic communities suffered the worst – even as they continued to do the badly paid jobs upon which we all depend to keep our society moving.

The most privileged could only observe the crumbling public space, while being themselves discombobulated by having to work from home. For the first time for many, they had to pay unusual attention to their children, who were now themselves vulnerable to loss of education, and to social and mental health problems. In between were the vast majority, furloughed from their regular job, with no guarantee that their position would be there at the end of the year.[236] We witnessed many small to medium businesses collapsing, a leisure industry entirely at rest and atrophying. The global economy was shrinking day by day.

In the midst of this, many reported intense *awakening* experiences. The Alternative UK developed a phone app which invited people to note down how differently they saw themselves and those around them, or what new story of the world they were telling themselves.[237] The entries (which can be read on the app) reveal a strange mix of freedom, reconnection and deep sorrow about the truths coming through the haze of confusion.

Soon after the lockdown began to spread around the globe, I started to meet regularly online with Waddell and members of the Transformations Forum to discuss their long-term project to give rise to a new global economic paradigm capable of shifting us away from self-destruction and towards flourishing. About two months in, we all began to hear a growing commitment from governments to 'bounce back' to normal. But this was quickly followed by a popular call – through polls and social media – for a 'new normal' and to #buildbackbetter than before. Initiated by political progressives who linked post-Covid to a 'green recovery', this positive idea was quickly picked up by governments and civil society organisations everywhere.[238] Yet in the Transformations Forum we knew that would not be enough. Rather than 'bounce back', we had to 'bounce beyond' to a whole new economic paradigm that would make the old one obsolete.

Our chance to Bounce Beyond

As we saw it, for at least ten years, solutions to the multiple crises have been in design outside of the current system. Not just one, but a number of 'next economies' have been taking shape around the world, each responding to a different aspect of the complex problems we face. They are noticeable for the strong role that women have played in defining them, and they include:

- Circular economy, which aims to eliminate waste through fixing rather than discarding broken products (see Ellen MacArthur)[239]

- Well-being economy, which measures economic success by the impact it has on the flourishing of humans, society and planet (in the UK, see Katherine Trebeck)[240]

- Regenerative economy, which seeks to emulate the patterns that nature offers to keep our economies able to renew themselves (see John Fullerton)[241]

- Doughnut economy, which offers a visual and practical framework for how our social goals have to be kept within the boundaries of our planet's ability to renew itself (see Kate Raworth)[242]

- Thrivability economy, which describes a step beyond sustainability within a material world to constant innovation in a spiritual world (see Jean Russell)[243]

- Buen Vivir economy, which sees communities as becoming self-sufficient and fully potentialised through their relationship with the land (largely indigenous wisdom).[244]

Like the blind men and the elephant, they have enough in common to suggest they are pointing at the same post-extractive economy they all see is possible – one that can connect the health of the human being to the planet, largely through community agency. Yet each has a different perspective and hence offers a different entry point for all of us watching.

As each develops their methods within a specific context, they have yet to cross-fertilise, expand and amplify their impact. As the Three Horizons theory describes, there is a real danger that in this crisis moment, their work would be swept away by old economic initiatives intent on resuming economic growth at any cost, while ignoring the true cost to people and planet.

Bounce Beyond then became a 24-month project of system transformation which proposed to bring the 'next economies' into dynamic relationship, thereby strengthening them, but also helping to bring the elephant into view. What might be more than the sum of their parts? Bounce Beyond would achieve this through working directly with a mix of places and sectors now emerging around the world that apply one or a combination of these 'next economies' practices. This would reveal core pieces of infrastructure – such as currencies, governance models, cultures, markets, products – that can be made more widely available to help move any territory out of the old ways of working and into the new.

Wholistic new system projects, such as Regenerate Costa Rica led by Eduard Muller, are already able to demonstrate how working with local communities to renew the biodiversity of the soil has an impact on the wider economy all the way up to the national level where a new eco-tourism is taking shape.[245] Yet Eduard also describes the same unfinished system as the 'elephant gathering':

It's basically a concept of a territory that is managed by the people who live in it and who decide on how to allocate the uses of the land, from protected areas to more intensive uses. It has three functions, which is conservation, development, and education. So we identify the main constraints for a territory and how it can reverse degradation and do regenerative development. And then we bring the different knowledge areas such as sustainable use, regeneration, connectivity conservation, regenerative agriculture, wholistic cattle production, nature-based solutions, ecosystem approach and more, together with local knowledge to solve complex problems in a transdisciplinary fashion.

Over the years, we have tried this on several biosphere reserves throughout Latin America working with different stakeholders, such as government, business, local and indigenous communities, but so far not in a systemic way because we didn't have the resources for it. But I truly believe that's the way to go. I think there's a global tendency in recent times that is strengthening local governance over central government. It's artificial, having one central government.

Through Bounce Beyond, one of our 'elephant participants', Isabel Carlisle, founder of the Bioregional Learning Centre in South Devon, will be able to work directly with and learn from the Costa Rica project, sharing both tools and stories of change. While they have principles and methods in common, the communities they develop will look and feel quite different, each in keeping with their local culture. This is how the fractal is enriched and how the elephant becomes more visible as a complex, working system.

Eduard Muller continually refers to the core importance of women to *lead* the future, an aspect absent from UK governmental initiatives like 'communitarianism' and the Big Society I described above. He acknowledges that our current system has given him more opportunities to take action and be heard, but in my view he uses that to give the women he works with more agency. Not simply in terms of numbers of women employed, but as the holders of the indigenous and feminine wisdom needed to restore whole systems. For example, when invited to curate a week of media events on the Humanity Rising platform to showcase Bounce Beyond to a Regenerative World, he invited Carolina Fernández-Jansink, Melina Angel, Ryah Chandler and Karen Downes to speak on each day and then invited them, as a team, to design the schedule for the week.[246]

From this perspective, the catalyst needed to lift 2H to 3H may not be so elusive after all, but simply be the ever stronger presence of the feminine in the public space. When women are actively supported by men, not to compete on their terms but to bring what's missing, a new dynamic appears. This is not simply balancing numbers of men and women, but, as I described in Chapter 4.4, women bringing the sensibility of wholeness. In the era of waking up to profound internal and external fragmentation, that wholeness creates a powerful magnet for the desires and energies of everyone.

7.3 The feel of it all

Steeling herself, she walked through the door and took a seat four rows from the front, at the end. That way she could be seen if she put her hand up but also get away unseen if it got unbearable. She had her sandwich and coffee, all set up for what she knew would be a long haul. The table on the stage had four chairs and she knew three of the speakers, all blokes. I bet the host is a woman hovering around a podium, she thought, quickly batting away all the resentment that came with it. It is what it is, she told herself, you do what you have to do.

Right here, right now, this is powerful. Just being together under the full moon, waiting for the New Year to begin. I don't know any of you – it's a really diverse crowd – but I know we're here for the same thing. We all want the next 12 months to be the best we've ever had. But it's more than that: waiting for the fireworks to begin, we're all thinking about the world out there, the countries starting before us and then after us. Like this big wave of exploding light across the world. Someone cracks a joke and we all laugh. The music begins: I feel it in my body.

ONE OF the core tests of an alternative politics is how it looks and feels. This is not a cosmetic or marketing issue, meaning how we make it look and feel after everything important has been decided by the executive, but rather the visceral evidence that the power we are now sharing is arising from the people in all their diverse complexity. In other words, is it alive? Is it warm and compelling? Does it hold complexity, multiple forms of agency and tension, as well as the possibility of liberation? Is it intimate – no matter how large the room? Do you want to join in?

Goodbye airless rooms, manels and a fixation on the past

All the years I spent in the old party-political environment were informed by real-life people in real-life dilemmas and opportunities. But the spaces in which the politics of our everyday lives was discussed were largely dead. Airless rooms, row upon row of hard-backed chairs, facing a platform upon which mostly men talked about policy and strategy, often framed by a past that was no longer relevant. The experience of the non-executive participant was, at best, physically uncomfortable. At worst, it was mind-numbing.

Yet it was – and still is – nigh impossible to change. Even when everyone agrees it needs to liven up a bit, the most that can happen is to add a bit of music or comedy into the mix. That does cheer us all up – but it has little impact on the way we interact or where our decisions come from.

Some would say it would be wrong anyway to try and integrate the business of politics with the job of the arts. We need boundaries: leave the arts alone! Good theatre is always political and will have a direct effect on shaping our sensibilities, and I would agree that these two industries as they are currently constituted cannot blend easily. At best one can lend its capital to the other – as happened with Red Wedge or The World Transformed where artists and creatives add their names to a cause or become influencers.[247, 248] Good theatre is always political and will have a direct effect on shaping our sensibilities.

But the kind of new creativity and aliveness I'm describing here doesn't start exclusively in either of those two well-established – and often elite – establishments of arts or politics. It more often starts in very ordinary, diverse gatherings of people who simply want to live life well. They are likely to gather in circumstances that allow them to do that – an independent Festival,[249] a marketplace,[250] around a campfire,[251] a football match.[252] If, while they are there, they strike up conversations with others, share thoughts and opinions, maybe dream together – hopes, wishes, ideas – you have the raw materials for a CAN.

Festivals prefiguring, theatre incubating, music liberating, dance embodying

As mentioned in Chapter 3.3, 'transformational festivals' like Burning Man and its offshoots are successful spiritual-political incubators driven by an artistic impulse – the desire to curate and create future civilisations.[253] Core to their appeal is the building of what Richard Bartlett has described as 'microsolidarities' – groups of peers who share values and practices and are willing to spend time with each other in the nurturing of their imaginations.[254] This in turn (as Bartlett has explored within Enspiral Networks[255]) gives rise to new relational earning opportunities, wherein your community becomes the container for a local economy. That might take the shape of participants offering each other jobs rather than outsourcing. Or even building up shared resources to help community members in need through difficult times.

Among similar creative gatherings, the Noisily Festival, initiated by Lachie Gordon and partners, was the first to articulate a community-driven, socio-political-economic system by founding the Noisily Action Network (based on our CANs concept).[256] Although still in early stages, it invites the many social enterprises that Noisily team members have initiated to form a community of practice, generating a new cultural economy.

Lachie's other focus – holding the same principles – is the Green Heart of Kenya, which involves turning 1,500 acres of monoculture farmland into an eco-village.[257] Its initiators were brought together by the Kilifi New Year festival, which draws young creative Kenyans to the area. Over a couple of years Lachie's work with the local youth will create employment and boast carbon neutral all-income housing; it will establish food sovereignty from agroforestry and sustainable business and employment. It will be the first ecosystem-regenerating social project of its kind in the region.

But these creative zones are not always around music and dance or even spirituality. When we think about how the creative impulse leads directly to social change, we should include initiatives like Fun Palaces – an ever growing annual group of events that brings the arts to science on the very outer edges of our communities.[258] These highly diverse, self-organised events create artful opportunities for the most alienated members of a community to meet and engage with ideas, helping them to hear their own voices in the public space, often for the first time. After opening 364 Fun Palace hubs in 11 nations, founder Stella Duffy describes the events as an 'ongoing campaign for cultural democracy'.

Another great example is Sarah Corbett's mix of craft and activism, called Craftivism, which she calls 'a gentle way of shaking the world' that offers intimate spaces for talking while sewing radical messages on bits of fabric. These might include anti-capitalist, feminist and environmentalist thoughts, beautifully embroidered on muslin or recycled material. She once sent handkerchiefs to every member of the M&S board with carefully stitched, hopeful pleas to pay 50,000 of their staff fairly. Ten months later they changed their pay policy and the Chair of the Board told Sarah her campaign was a direct cause. Her manifesto includes such suggestions as: Solidarity not sympathy. Preserve the dignity of others in your craft. Understand their struggles and you'll understand their solutions. Activism is not about charity.

The long-standing experimental Chickenshed Theatre produces some of the most challenging artistic performances I've experienced – not *about* inclusion, but *through inclusion*.[259] Partly available on the web, the triptych *GlobalEyes*, *Mother of a Brown Boy* and *Crime of the Century* addressed the failings of our socio-political system, casting radically diverse performers – multi-cultures but also multi-abilities. The unfamiliar mix is viscerally shocking, rewiring the audience for a different, more vibrant future.

Each of these examples offers a hint of a new political system in action – a fractal of the new politics emerging.

Living the larger life

Of course, this new political energy I'm describing does not arise exclusively from artistic-creative intervention – that's only one set of tools to reconnect us to the vital energy of life itself. When we launched The Alternative we borrowed philosopher and politician Roberto Unger's famous challenge: 'how can we live in such a way that we die only once?'[260] While each person reads this differently, the unavoidable charge is that we are dying daily, even hourly. As I've described throughout this book, we have trapped ourselves in and enslaved ourselves to a system that only cares for us as cogs in a machine: it rarely acknowledges the transformative potential of our desires that can, if given proper attention, lead us to take on our current limitations.

Unger's exhortation is not mere rhetoric. As Brazil's Minister of Culture he worked all his life to reconnect the people to his liberation agenda. Relying heavily on tech, he welcomed the age of automation, proclaiming that 'no one should do work that can be done by a machine'. Challenging the idea that we can't experience the good life until we have overcome scarcity, Unger believes we are all capable of living a life greater than the context we find ourselves in – what he calls 'the larger life'. In Chapter 8 I look at how it's possible to take that brief and run with it.

8. Now What? The Future Arising

Looking at her, grieving for our natural world, was extremely uncomfortable. On the one hand he knew she was right and they should accept the inevitability of a grim future: the science has it. On the other hand, his body told him he was young! Full of vigour, imagination, arrogance. Surely that counted for something?

How long have I listened to you saying, 'we need a more diverse community? More women, more people of colour or from the other side of town'? You're IN a highly diverse community but you're stuck in your small bubble of what matters to you. What's stopping you getting up out of your chair and just getting to know them – the others? Going to where they meet, listening to their voices and getting involved in their lives? Hey presto, you'll be part of a more diverse community.

WHERE DOES the future arise from? Not a small question and one that touches on every aspect of power and agency that I have been exploring in this book. Can we predict, organise or control the future – or is it determined by a greater force, such as God or fate? Can we know for certain either way?

What is the *relationship between* the present and the future? Simple logic would say that the future arises directly from the now: you can't step into it from any other place or moment. At the same time, the way we run our societies would suggest that we believe otherwise. That somehow, we can give rise to a future by *intending* to change: not 'being the change' right now.

Being and intending

Whether Gandhi ever spoke the famous words 'be the change you wish to see' or not, the call to transformation has resonated through the decades since. It's compelling to believe that simply aligning yourself to your goals will change history: for example, moving towards a greener food and energy plan to save the planet. Yet the specifics of Gandhi's adopted lifestyle – extreme and self-directed – and his enlightened skills in identifying the key symbolic actions that captured the imagination of millions: these are less often talked about and rarely emulated.

We may think it's common sense, but the relationship between intention and action is not straightforward. We all know the difference between intending to get fit, for example, and actually putting those trainers on every day and establishing a routine that would lead to physical health. The difference between embracing an idea and enacting that idea can be brutal: without a clear plan to link the first to the second, there is zero result.

If we believe character is key to agency – as many schools of thought hold – how do we describe the qualities of that character? Gandhi's 'being' was very active, strategic and ambitious. His intellect was fierce. He was different from the gentler, appreciative and forgiving 'being' espoused by some 'change' groups as essential qualities in a leader. At the same time, these two dispositions emphasise a different relationship to the future. Gandhi was an activist with clear goals; other activists might adopt a different approach and address the future as something less goal-oriented that we can't control. Even so, many who have similar strong characteristics to Gandhi will never make the impact that he did.

Others with far gentler dispositions, such as Rosa Parks – who, though courageous, was kind and compassionate in her relationship with those around her – also change the world. And who defies expectations more than Greta Thunberg, who grew up with Asperger's syndrome and came to join up the dots on climate change in ways few others have? It seems there is no formula for being a change-maker.

Integrity and truth-force

What their stories do have in common, however, is the will and capacity to find clear integrity between their thoughts, analyses, desires and actions. Each leader mentioned was able to find the right actions that summed up their deeper intention and brought it into the present moment. In so doing they were already living in a different world. Such was the symbolic power of these actions that, by inviting you in to join them, you were instantly occupying the future.

All are forms of non-violent, non-compliance with the current system: what Gandhi calls satyagraha, or truth-force. An example is Gandhi's 24-day 'salt march' during which he and his followers made salt by evaporation rather than buy into the British state monopoly of essential goods that was keeping the Indian people in servitude. Rosa Parks took a seat on the mainstream bus in Montgomery, Alabama, refusing to be segregated. Greta Thunberg went on strike from school to sit in front of the Swedish parliament to denounce the climate crisis. She halted her own education to 'educate' – eventually – every world leader at high-level places such as the United Nations and the World Economic Forum meeting in Davos.

Yet it's not as easy as it looks to make that commitment. The vast majority of us are left behind by our own goals, be they personal or political – and not for lack of intention, but for lack of capacity. In mundane terms that might mean a lack of resources: time, space and energy. Modern life has designed our days to be enslaved to the growth economy. Most of us are obliged to make money to maintain the consumerist lifestyles we've become addicted to. We have to be in service to toxic businesses seven to ten hours a day, just to put food on the table or to keep a roof over our heads.

At the same time, even those with enough material resources will have limitations on their emotional capacity, hindering them from stepping directly into action. Each of us has a story about our own agency which depends on our personal history of acceptance and rejection, success and failure. It takes confidence and mental and physical space, to make the kinds of changes we know would create a better future for all of us. As it stands, it is mainly people with the means – economic, yet also psychological – who can take risks and change the world as they envisage it.

Creating the conditions for response-ability

For this reason, any alternative politics would bring into its remit the core importance of *creating the conditions* for each person to develop their capacity for self and social development together – what we've been calling response-ability. This isn't simply an education based on absorbing information (although that matters), but rather a lifelong, living, developmental incubation of physical and emotional capacities that makes one resilient and creative. As support for this, think about the grounding provided by a Universal Basic Income, plus the kind of personal and social learning clubs (the German-inspired Bildung folk schools) that the Scandinavians enjoyed in the 19th century.[261, 262] Add to that every citizen who is enabled to take part in a process like EnrolYourself, which uses the power of adult peer learning to take participants on steep learning curves of capacity development.[263] Imagine that the vast majority of citizens saw their own role in shaping their collective future, rather than seeing themselves as powerless, dependent upon those in authority to make all the changes.

At the same time, what shapes those goals we might set ourselves? We may only have access to the thoughts in our head as we go about our pressured lives. So much of what we are hoping for will be defined by what we already know, or what we can imagine from our narrow base of experience. Some of us may demand more and better jobs, while others will only dream of less work and more free time to develop things.

The broader access that people have to the reality of those outside their social and media bubble, the better we can begin to plan for what is needed to create the conditions for general flourishing – the health of a common environment (or 'commons') we all depend upon. Politicians will say that is what they spend their whole time doing: all we have to do is choose between their party prescriptions. Yet, as I have reminded you throughout this book, only 2 per cent of the potential electorate sign up and join political parties. Maybe it's time for the 98 per cent to step into more response-ability for identifying and reaching their shared goals.

On top of the diverse kinds of learning mentioned above, we also need the impetus to think beyond what the mainstream culture believes is possible or desired. In that sense, social media, and the digital imaginarium in general, can be crucial tools, in the way they inform and also stimulate our speculative powers.[264] Anyone with elementary technology (85 per cent of people in Europe, 67 per cent globally, now use mobile phones) can express their own ideas for innovation. Although we are still largely constrained by global corporate control of the internet, there is plenty of evidence that experimental thinking and acting is going on all the time. It's our conscious editorial policy on The Daily Alternative.

As described throughout this book, being open and exposed to new concepts, tools and practices from all over the world is crucial to individual and local development. The point is not for every community to be representative of the whole global system, but for each one to be open to the originality of new sources of creativity. Whether this exposure prompts us to include ancient practices from indigenous tribes, or to leap forward in technological empowerment, will be different in each place. It is how we join up the dots between the cosmolocal and the future-possible that will make the most of our human and social potential, wherever we are.

In that sense, it is crucial that young people are always feeding their imaginations into whatever collective futures the wider society is planning. Their capacity for and therefore access to new tools and practices – often free of what might be seen by their elders as historical constraints – can radically affect the way we think together. At the same time, young people need a good, yet critical, relationship to what's been developed before, saving them from constantly reinventing the wheel or spending too long in rabbit holes.

How to get from here to there

The Covid pandemic was a new low for governments worldwide as it became ever clearer that, despite warnings from scientists for over a decade, they had failed to prepare for a future that experts had long told them was coming. In many ways this wilful ignorance only echoes the bigger picture: our collective lack of political will and capacity to face the ongoing triple crises – personal, social, global – which I have been pointing at throughout these pages.

Yet because this was a virus, potentially threatening any human being and their family regardless of privilege (though social inequalities are shaping its impact), it made these endemic problems more visible. Everyone felt the crisis directly: even if none of your close family or friends were vulnerable, someone you saw regularly was. This was not happening to a far-off country; it was in your community, on your doorstep, maybe in your home.

That countries with inadequate or run-down health services were struggling to cope with the sudden increase of demand should have been no surprise. But the evidence that some countries were clearly doing better than others with similar levels of wealth made the pandemic a very political moment.

Some of the conditions for success or failure were easy to reveal. For example, early in 2020 a medical expert at the White House shared a programme of action that could be quickly implemented in a pandemic, which had been on standby throughout President Obama's term in office.[265] Crucially, that programme was scrapped by President Trump when he took over and then had to be created from scratch in the emergency. In the UK the high rate of death could in part be directly attributable to the number of care beds available which, at the start of the campaign, were the lowest in the whole of Europe (228 per 100,000 of population compared to 621 in Germany and Lithuania).

Styles of leadership came under the microscope: it was interesting to see which qualities inspired quick and collective responses from the people. Attempts at Churchillian (meaning character-led) calls to follow instructions – not grounded in recognised expert advice – failed in the UK. Major institutions decided to isolate well before the government recommended and the PM's serial U-turns caused much confusion and therefore lives.

And, as mentioned more than once in this book, female leaders stood out as successful in keeping down the infection rates and deaths. In these countries, scientists were relied upon for safety instructions, allowing politicians to concentrate on building trust between government and people, with many opportunities for warm and supportive communication. To help parents struggling in lockdown,

New Zealand's Jacinda Ardern held a press conference just for children to help explain and to enrol the children in the national effort.

Taiwan's Tsai Ing-wen relied heavily on community relationships, themselves already well served by state-of-the-art technology. Local leaders delivered food and were in ready communication with citizens. Neighbourhood support networks were in operation and digital tech available to report daily on symptoms. As long as you remained infected you received a daily allowance to stay home – an incentive that the UK later adopted but delivered badly.[266]

Across the world, the whole of society has been asked to play its direct part in protecting everyone else. Individuals and domestic groups were required to self-isolate at home, not simply to stay safe themselves, but to keep the most vulnerable in our society safe from our inadvertent actions. For some, that was a wake-up call, collapsing the distance between personal responsibility and a good outcome for the whole community.

As described in Chapter 6.3, in the absence of an effective, centralised organisation of care across the UK (still poorly organised, at the moment of writing), spontaneous mutual-aid networks sprang up in neighbourhoods everywhere. It's become commonplace to hear people in vox pops say how shocked they were at how much better they were at responding to need than their council.

Where might this new experience of agency at the grassroots level lead to? In The Alternative UK's networks there is plenty of talk of citizens reclaiming more of their power to make decisions and plan action in the future. Some politicians will be happy about that: it has long been their goal to share the costly burden of community care with willing volunteers. Others will be nervous: more community responsibility could end up colluding with the existing system. While volunteers take on the responsibility of caring for those impacted by a dysfunctional welfare state, Westminster might simply continue to spend public money on subsidising the very industries that threaten the health of the planet.

But in the midst of these old political battles, according to a major Sky News report in April 2020, only 9 per cent of people wanted to return to business as usual after the effects of the pandemic are over.[267] Many wanted to keep their temporary arrangement of working from home, organising their own balance between professional and family attention. Others preferred the experience of less pressure from busy streets, constantly compelling them to choose and buy stuff they didn't really need. Still others were shocked by how quickly the environment had improved through the drop in the use of transport and wanted to keep going in that direction. Despite the struggles, if you were looking throughout that period, you could find a hopeful story about awareness of, and increasing sovereignty over, our personal and community realms.[268]

The quantum social change now possible

The insights and new energies that were released during the pandemic moment and are still incubating, are bringing about the convergence of a number of factors: firstly, our collective waking-up to a new possibility for the future arising out of the shifts in attitude during the lockdown; secondly, our own health, all-too-directly related to the health of the planet; and thirdly, a growing sense of our own agency for delivering outcomes. It could be that through the challenges of this pandemic, we suddenly forged the capacity for individual responsibility and a new trust in our sovereign powers.

While the mainstream news continues to ignore the growth of community-led people power that The Daily Alternative, among other independent news sources, focuses on, it's hard to assess the state of play in any given city, country or region until what Malcolm Gladwell once described as a social tipping point occurs.[269] This is when we notice a new normal has been established through the accumulation of many disconnected actions with a similar agenda, but without any explicit agreement from anyone – a phenomenon that, Gladwell suggests, can only be documented in hindsight.

That need not discourage us of course: the more experience any of us have of acting blindly on our instincts – or maybe more precisely, acting without precedent on our inner wisdom – the more we learn to trust ourselves.

Or maybe we should be thinking in even more accelerated terms, such as the alignment of possibilities that Professor Karen O'Brien describes in *You Matter More Than You Think*? As I pursued in Chapters 4.3 and 5.2, new patterns of relationship, occurring all over the world, are triggering quantum social change consciously.

This is working with a fractal sensibility, not a linear one. Not looking at new kinds of behaviour as something that needs to be encouraged or controlled by the behaviourism of nudge teams, but seeing the new formations that arise out of these new ways of acting and being together, changing the landscape significantly, just as how molecules moving more slowly turn into ice. As long as you want ice, it helps to know it is coming when the water gets colder. In a similar way, seeing how these new responses to adversity have led to some communities becoming Citizens Action Networks, bringing whole new micro-systems in their wake, makes it easier to invest in the early signs. Surely, if more of us do that resolutely – working together, to paraphrase Alasdair Gray, 'as if we were in the early days of a new civilisation'[270] – are we not bringing the future into the present?

To be awake today can mean more than understanding how and why we are, each of us, in the mess we are in. Every day and ever more so, it can mean seeing the deeper potential of human ingenuity and what has been forming over the past 20 years. And making that the ground of our action.

9 Backwards and Forwards

No, she said, still trembling; it's more than that. You're not listening. And if you are, you're not hearing, because everything I say sounds like a threat to your steady commitment, your equilibrium. Nothing matters more to you, she ventured, than being able to fulfil your promise to your father to be a great man. I have to listen to you night and day. Even as you push for inclusion, you prevent it, you don't let anyone else decide. Because only you can be the saviour. I feel for you because you never understood that giving me a chance would mean losing some of your own power: that I might stop listening to you.

They sat, amazed. Until that moment they had been prepared to let everything go, just surrender themselves to the unknown and likely death. After the solutions turned out to be just more of the same hype, solutionism itself failed and they didn't dare to believe that anything else could be done. But now for the first time they saw something new but strangely recognisable: a different pattern of activity that made sense of the breakdown and gave them something to work towards. Just faintly, they could hear the first bars of a song in their hearts.

A YOUNG PSYCHOTHERAPY client of mine was experiencing extreme frustration with his school life. At one point he had been challenged by his teacher to explain something and found he couldn't. His shame was palpable – 'why couldn't I do it?' – and worse, it plunged him into a very dark view of his own future, convinced he was never going to be good enough at anything.

I assured him that everyone has moments like this, it's natural. After all, what is school for if not to teach you what you don't know? His emotions subsided but I could tell he was still judging himself harshly. It was not until a close friend suffered the same humiliation that he had his a-ha moment. 'Mate,' he later reported saying, 'you've just got to accept that you can't know everything at once. You've just got to be up for learning.' He seemed to turn a corner there: his demeanour changed and he became confident at school, especially after he became known to his friends as the guy to ask.

Life change can be as simple as that. A penny drops, we re-arrange ourselves, inside and outside, and for a while we feel refreshed and able to take on the inherent unfairness of life energetically again. That is, until we reach the limits of that way of thinking and being and start the cycle again. When we are young, each one of these moments is a Herculean battle for selfhood. As we get older, if we are lucky, we get better at recognising the patterns and even begin to enjoy the ups and downs: feeling confronted, becoming response-able, sharing with others, back to power. Some begin to think of this kind of challenge as the source of joy.

The Mother of all challenges

Even so, the challenges we face are large, and now – the story goes – they are the Mother of all challenges: the battle for the planet that even Superman would be hard pressed to fix. What I hope I have been able to convey in this book is that, firstly, we do have the internal wiring to radically change the way we act and to become response-able for the future. It's there: *Ada*. Secondly, the ideas, resources and prototypes already exist to shift us into a new socio-economic system capable of saving the planet. *Ada*. Thirdly, we do have the technology to bring us all back into connection with each other in varying degrees of depth. *Ada*.

However, what we don't have yet is an effective governance system that would help us to move from the present to the future. Through the internet we have a world of fragmented passions that are represented back to us as competing for attention. We have no clear way to come together as a human race in a form that would impact everything. It's coming into view but, like my young client, too many people are still experiencing the humiliation and grievances of the past few decades to enter into a space of possibility. They may even be getting their emotional relief and solidarity from investing ever more deeply in the pain.

Others still are numb, apathetic. They are either unwilling to look at the suffering of others for fear of getting pulled in. Or unwilling to face their own powerlessness in the face of a system that barely registers their humanity. When someone comes to offer them a way forward, they turn away, refusing to be disappointed again. In my experience, these are the majority, even among the privileged who cover their apathy with escapism and cynicism. Idealists irritate them: they don't dare to believe.

For that reason, the only place to start is where people can meet themselves, and then others, to find their own path out of the mess. For the majority, this has to be on the ground, in communities where they live, building containers for complex community agency, which link every kind of person to each other – in a myriad of loose or engaged ways. This way, everyone has access to the solutions already available anywhere in the world.

We can't give this job to the politicians who are keeping the dysfunctions of our system alive, yet we can't abandon them either: they have their hands on our resources and their finger on the button.[271] We need a new socio-politics that is able to transcend the antagonistic battle between party politics and populism: a system that recognises the real and diverse powers of the people, brings them into relationship with each other and into an equitable partnership with power.

As you are reading, you may well be conjuring the image in your head of CANs in towns, cities, regions, nations, offering the crucibles for selfhood and agency I have described in this book. You may be seeing, quite naturally, how the right technology could connect them and give rise to a very different experience of democracy than we have ever had, until now. In many ways, it's not so different from the billions of Facebook pages we already have, except linked directly to deliberative discussion on the ground, and less vulnerable to polarisation by external vested interests. In another way, it's not so different from a place of worship, where people come together to tend to their spirit. Except that the belief system is more open-source and the agenda goes well beyond voluntary activity.

Back to Telawa

Revisiting Telawa in my mind, I can now see that there were many conditions for the magic to happen that would not have been visible to me as an adolescent, impressionable journalist. Well before the carefully planned visit took place, a young Buddhist scout called Bhaktiar had spent months developing a relationship with the Chief, listening to his thoughts and hearing his concerns about the village he felt responsibility for.[272] Without the trust built up in that relationship, the visit could not have occurred. *Ada*.

Within that situation, there was a prior relationship between the village Chief and the villagers, held within a strong, indigenous belief system. The Chief's gentle leadership, the strong role of the women and the container for trust meant that when he took up the Buddhist teachings, others easily followed. There was a collective openness to the youngsters and their newly inspired self-reliance and a willingness from all of them to be in service to each other when they got down to work. The conditions for agency were there. *Ada.*

What Senosoenoto and his team of young Buddhist anarchists brought was a direct enhancement of that belief system. He was not offering a competing deity or a cult movement to harness their emotions, but a next-level development of their belief in their relationship to each other and to the land. Telling them a new story about their resourcefulness, he was re-activating their connections and inviting them to take that further, through chanting and learning together and then sharing their experiences. In that way, whatever happened after we left was theirs: they owned it.

Poverty and a decade of military rule had reduced their self-belief and autonomy to the point of acceptance of their fate: a bare gratitude for the minimal food parcels and individual withdrawal from collective action of any kind. So the visit from the Buddhists was a rude awakening. Just like the boiling frogs, they had all but succumbed to the reductive paralysis. Senosoenoto was not offering leadership from the front. Instead, with his team of young spiritual activists, he was reigniting what he knew was there but suppressed. At the same time he shared with them the story of how this awakening was happening in similar villages all over Indonesia.

With small exceptions, none of this tends to happen when people are being mobilised by others for a specific party-political agenda they weren't already involved in. Waking up does not occur. Instead, they remain dependent on instructions, have to work within the rules, show up when required. Often the only goal is a demand on the government and there is no tangible experience of agency beyond making a noise for the present moment. At the same time, the complete opposite can also generate frustration; meetings of barely connected people just talking through ad hoc agendas can leave people with too great a gap between their needs and a plan. There has to be some organising principles that can help people to experience agency quickly.

In my experience, there are many factors in a collaboratory that incubate the human potential in the room and help it to emerge. It has much in common with any feminised, deeply and fully connected space: a happy family, a thoughtfully curated social enterprise, a good care home, a sangha. Yet a CAN is unique because of the framing and narrative: the story we tell ourselves about the moment we are in and our growing capacity as citizens to meet the challenge. The emphasis is not on electing compromised representatives to fight our battles, but becoming the people with agency ourselves.

Forward from Telawa

When the Indonesian villagers met in Telawa, it was in the mid-1980s and under military rule. It took 30 years before the first crowdsourcing, tweeting president was elected in the shape of Joko Widodo – known as Jokowi. He had a head start on his counterparts in the US such as President Obama – with a history of grassroots self-organising happening at a variety of levels across the 17,000 islands, of which 6,000 are inhabited – by the indigenous, Islamic, Buddhist and civic community actors.[273]

Today, the conditions for change include both the urgent need for people to come together and the radical possibility for connectivity. When the Plymouth, Birmingham or Stoke CANs meet, it is in the bigger context of post-Brexit, cosmolocally connected Britain – yet until now it is a context that is still largely deactivated, one still in the grip of the old system that has primed us to keep sleepwalking towards the cliff, despite our inner terror. Not yet awake. When Vermont's Front Porch Forums or Cleveland's Community Wealth Building groups meet in New York and Atlanta, it is in post-Trump, cosmolocally connected America, still largely deactivated. When Neighborocracy parliaments meet in Chennai, Tamil Nadu or Lagos, they are in post-pandemic, cosmolocally connected India and Africa, still largely deactivated.

Even so, in all these places there seems to be a new hunger for making sense of the world at a community level – place based and virtual – with the people you live among and a desire for both personal and collective agency. To meet this yearning, we have an immense number of tools, methods and alternative narratives available and a new chance of becoming digitally connected to each other that can change the socio-economic-political paradigm. *Ada*.

As of now

If this book has described the moment we are in and the new conditions for change that are visible below the surface, this final section brings them into the light to activate them: a necessary appearance of the yin (latent) in the yang (performing). Before writing, I subjected several factors to three tests that Buddhists call the three proofs: is it logical, is it theoretically grounded, can you point to evidence it exists? All test positive on all counts.

Ten transformative factors already present but may need amplifying: *Ada*

- Every human being has complex emotional needs and also has the internal tools to get those needs met.

- Every person can 'be' and 'act' in the three realms of personal, social and global: I–We–World. Our mind, body and spiritual capacities are available to us and the technology is ready to connect our thoughts and action.

- Every person needs relationship to activate their agency and those relationships are available in the place you live as well as online.

- The biodiversity we need to guarantee the flourishing of the planet is much diminished, but can, with commitment, still be regenerated.

- The understanding of diversity of agency, wherein each one of us is unique and can contribute something new for the whole to flourish, is present if not dominant in global culture.

- Diversity – wherein every culture has a different history and journey but each is vital for the maximum potential of our globe – is increasingly taught in schools and celebrated widely.

- A new understanding of the soft power of story and influence, outperforming the hard power of guns and money, is changing the way we understand and participate in social media.

- Political authority is failing all around the world as people wake up to the precarity of our future and the dysfunctionality of our past that led us here.

- Community organising and municipalism is resurging following the global pandemic with a new story about people power and the need for self-reliance.

- Following a decade of growing distrust of technology, a new capacity for virtual relationships and digital organising arose during the Covid pandemic.

Ten tools to reactivate our personal, social and global agency: *Ada*

- Embodiment practice assiduously pursued (e.g. chanting, mindfulness, healthy diet, music, dance, loving, caring, dreaming, playing, making).

- Relational tools to facilitate deep connection between those who share values and beyond to those that may not share values but share humanity.

- The learning that encourages 'upgrading ourselves' for the 21st century. From the 'bildung' which offers self- and social development to 'moocs' (massive open online courses) on anything from 3D printer training to classic Harvard degrees. These are largely available for self-study online but are also increasingly taught within communities.

- Citizens Action Networks, aka Community Agency Networks for transforming weak relationships into repositories of deep trust and growing agency within neighbourhoods and communities. There are opportunities for tried-and-tested ones as well as for brand-new prototypes to emerge.

- Fractal organising where people generate micro-systems for the macro system they want to emerge. These can be applied to different sectors such as the economy, social justice or health.

- New media that tells the story generated by the activity of personal, social or global flourishing, thus catalysing even further flourishing.

- Cosmolocal commons where people all around the world share the fruits of their imagination, collaboration and innovation in ways that understand the interconnectivity of human existence as well as the connected ecosystems of humans and the nonhuman natural world.

- Festivals, markets, clubs, choirs, sports and similar spaces for conviviality, which encourage joyful physical interaction and unencumbered but deep conversation.

- Movements that offer entry points for people to embark on personal learning journeys that lead to effective collective agency towards social change.

- Multiple experiments with citizen participation
from the local to the global that actively prototype,
strengthen and expand new forms of democracy.

Ten steps to global change that are already happening at different
stages, in different places, simultaneously. Consciously moving into
integral – complex and enabled – relationship: *Ada*.

- Individuals waking up to the impact of the past,
finding the others and making themselves heard.

- Individuals stepping away from the old power systems that
instrumentalised, triggered and manipulated them, finding others
with whom to explore the social trauma of the past, and with
whom they can form microsolidarities and build resilience.

- Civil society groups present to the possibility of the
future, self-organising and moving out of their bubbles,
fostering relationship where there was none.

- Community organising stepping up from rural neighbourhoods
to municipalities developing community wealth, alternative
currencies, independent banks, open platforms, learning
clubs and designing new democratic practices.

- Cosmolocal CANs forming in towns, cities and bio-
regions all over the world offering a new experience of
participation and generating a fourth-sector economy.

- Women more visible in the public space bringing
wholistic community practice, feminine economic systems,
feminine ontologies and national-level socio-politics.

- A new, big-picture socio-political-economic system
coming into view, arising from all the different forms
of fractal agency moving into relationship.

- The global CAN of CANs facilitated by secure and deliberative technology, simultaneously driving and learning from the 'next economies', capable of regenerating the planet and offering a new form of participatory global governance.

- A new parallel political system forming: fully participatory, interconnected CANs running local, national and international Citizens' Assemblies working *in partnership everywhere* with a fully proportional party-political system delivering services.

- A new story of Us emerging, reintegrating people, planet, cosmos.

Some of you reading this will recognise themselves in these lists; others may not. Still others will look at the list and say, 'what about China, Saudi Arabia, Russia?' (or whatever nation they have decided is the obstacle to our global flourishing). As a global citizen, with Catholic and Muslim heritage, a Buddhist training and a British context, I can see all of them already taking part in this emergence in small or medium ways.

If you are thinking, yes, but what about the Trump supporters, the hopeless liberals, the demanding woke activists, the alpha males – won't they sabotage us? As a psychotherapist with clinical experience of how our emotional needs are exploited by the old system but could also be well met by the new one emerging, I'm hopeful. If the social trends I have been describing keep accelerating, propelled by our increasing need for community and relationship in critical times, then we will experience a growing understanding of each other and a greater willingness to reach for a better future together.

While populism has triggered hurts of all kinds, the speed of social change has also increased noticeably. Today, football teams all over the world 'take the knee' – to symbolise anti-racism – every week, only four years after American footballer Colin Kaepernick lost his career for sitting down during the national anthem. Increasingly, the rewards for victimising target groups are diminishing and new kinds of belonging are appearing.

If you are looking at the lists, thinking this transformation will take forever, then share them with friends and invite the conversation. Maybe the penny has not dropped that this is already happening. Since the Intergovernmental Panel on Climate Change raised the flag in 2018, we have been in a global story of rapid change that has revealed decades of preparation for this moment. Black Lives Matter took it deeper and Covid took it wider. Unless you step right in and immerse yourself in the transformation, it will remain only a distant hope for you.

Hold your nerve

But if you're reading those lists and recognising that most of what is there is live and kicking, then hold your nerve. These next few years will require radical openness and generosity and the courage of your intuition. You will have to forgive yourself for being inadequate and welcome the others who keep you buoyant.

On a circular and regenerative principle, elders must give way to the younger ones, who in turn must keep the elders in view, wasting as little of their wisdom as possible. Those who love the spotlight (yangsters!) must give way to those who avoid it (yinsters!) to create the context and conditions that allow change to happen. They in turn must invite the performers back, so they can prompt action and gain traction. We must get used to noticing that whoever it is we find ourselves othering is the key to our transformation.

Finally, we must dare others to believe the future they dream of is already here by putting it to the test every day. To be alive to our own power and to the power of all to create a new reality that everyone can experience and benefit from. To invest our attention in that new reality minute by minute, day by day, knowing that as our understanding grows deeper and wider, so the movement becomes stronger and louder.

The global revolution is the human revolution you do in your communities of action. To be truly awake is to see the future arising from your every thought and act, knowing your story is shaping the I, the We and the World of our shared reality. Your response-ability and that of those around you changes everything. Together we are enough. *Ada.*

Afterworlds

CLOSE WITH an invitation for you to propel your mind into the future you are yearning for and to look back at the present day. What do you imagine these early days of the 21st century will look like from there?

Seeding the nostalgia of RegenA: some new stories of Us.

Remember when people just did whatever they wanted without noticing anyone else or what it was doing to our planet? Wow – getting on planes just to go to a conference or to meet a friend for the weekend. Spending all their hard-earned pennies on clothes they only wore once and then dumped in the rubbish. Keeping the lights on in all the shops all night, just to look glamorous for the tourists. I know we've got the benefit of hindsight with our solar planes and quantum computing, but how could they have wasted so much time just running the planet into the ground?

Remember when parents used to get up and go to work from seven in the morning till seven at night? They'd come home exhausted and stressed with barely any time to spend with their kids – let alone each other – before it was time for bed again. All this for a pathetic wage that barely kept them going – just enough after food and rent to save up for the latest bit of tat that other kids were getting. Breaks my heart to think about their wasted lives.

Remember when our young men were chuffed to get into the army? It was money and a chance to make something of yourself. But that thrill – that pride – never lasted. All you heard about was the long hours of boredom and keeping your mind small. Watching white kids straight out of college becoming officers, expecting you to take orders. Then out of nowhere you're off to the war zone, expected to be excited about getting some action. Getting killed more like, so Sir can go home and get a medal. But what choice was there? Just as many young Black boys were getting killed on the streets or banged up for years without anyone ever asking why it was all Black guys in prison. So glad we got past that and our boys can be seen for who they are, able to shine.

Remember when everything came in twos? Left and Right, rich and poor, black and white, masculine, feminine, old and young? Hilarious. I can't even imagine how they managed to squeeze all the different kinds of sexes into just two? Or the billions of different opinions or ideas into two – what? – opposing sides? Like goodies and baddies? Sounds mad. But then in those days they didn't have the time to spend together and just hear and see each other properly. Or the tech to really meet people from different places. Everyone was kind of isolated, just trying to get on with their own lives. Sad – so little trust between them.

Remember when no one ever had to make any decisions about what happened in the world? We just left it all to politicians? Who were those guys anyway? I could never work out why I should listen to them or vote for them – even once every five years. They were never especially smart or inspiring. Although they were dedicated – I'll give them that. But for people like me they were just a convenient enemy to blame for everything going wrong. I don't know what I'd do now without my CAN. Just plugging in every day to hear what's going on for everyone nearby, sharing a few of my thoughts. Hearing through the CANs what's going on for people in Juba or Boulder – or wherever I'm connecting this month. Hitting the button once I've made up my mind on things. It's satisfying. And it saved us I reckon – how could we ever have got to the right plan of action without everyone taking part? Without our collective intelligence?

Remember when big corporations – and institutions actually – were allowed to brainwash us, willy-nilly? Like just use their tech to addict us, to turn us into slaves at their command? Wow, the things they got us to do totally against our own interest! I guess it was a godsend that people fell off their Wi-Fi as things got worse. And they had to turn to each other to find out what was going on and what to do next. Thank fuck for the women who had all their neighbourhood networks and clever ways of getting people to talk to each other. Beats me why we didn't listen to them before: they're like the ultimate software! All that time, women were the technology we were looking for.

Endnotes

1   For more on Adat: https://en.wikipedia.org/wiki/Adat

2   Nichiren Shoshu Indonesia was recognised by the Indonesian government in 1983 with an annual Buddhist holiday. This reflected part of an Indonesian constitutional principle Bhinneka Tunggal Ika – Unity in Diversity. The honour was particularly important as it gave Chinese and Japanese Indonesians a way to be part of Indonesian society in a time when Chinese commerce was causing social unrest.

3   Compass was my first UK political home: founded and directed by Neal Lawson and Deputy Director Frances Foley: www.compassonline.org.uk

4   This was the figure at the time of writing Is The Party Over and remains constant, taking the electorate as 47,074,800: https://commonslibrary.parliament.uk/research-briefings/sn05125/

5   First past the post means that in every constituency whoever gets the most votes wins the seat, irrespective of vote share. It's common for an MP, and indeed a government, to be elected with only 33 per cent of the vote but then have all the power. A proportional system on the other hand allocates the number of seats to each party in direct proportion to the overall share of the votes they achieved.

6   Much has been written about the Soka Gakkai since it was founded in Japan on 18 November 1930 (including Levi McLaughlin (2018) *Soka Gakkai's Human Revolution: The Rise of a Mimetic Nation In Modern Japan*, doi:10.1515/9780824877897). For an introduction

to the Nichiren Buddhist practice I recommend Richard Causton's book *The Buddha in Daily Life* (1995). 2nd edn. London: Rider.

7 The Ikeda Dialogues explore how Buddhist principles are reflected in everyday cultural life, including science, arts, governance and institutions: www.daisakuikeda.org/sub/resources/records/dialog.html

8 Johan Galtung founded the Peace Research Institute, *The Journal of Peace Research* and then peace 'chairs' in universities around the world, including Oslo, Hawaii and Kuala Lumpur in Malaysia. His methods of 'peace by peaceful means' generated the Transcend global network of peace practitioners who influenced foreign affairs over a generation.

9 Associate Professor Jake Lynch: Director of the Centre for Peace and Conflict Studies, University of Sydney; Dr Annabel McGoldrick later became Lecturer and Researcher in Peace Journalism at Sydney University as well as an EMDR psychotherapist.

10 The Serbian/Albanian conflict took place in Kosovo between 1998 and 1999. The UK participated in the NATO bombing in 1999, occasioning a lot of protest against the government.

11 'We Will Win', written by Iain Whitmore, Ian Pearce, Indra Whitmore, 1983.

12 Ken Wilber, American philosopher and founder of Integral theory. A prolific author, his first book was called *A Theory of Everything* (Shamabala Publications, 2000).

13 My former husband Iain Whitmore: songwriter and lead vocalist in Starry Eyed and Laughing, also solo artist and musical arranger with Chickenshed Theatre. Very best of fathers.

14 The Downing Street Project was sister to The White House Project (1998–2013), whose successful campaign VoteRunLead resulted in more participation at every level. DSP had a shorter life: after a successful start it became synonymous with women in business and lost its broader appeal. Lee Chalmers has since stood for the Scottish Parliament and co-initiated The Parliament Project.

15 The Feminisation of Politics is a term coined by those around Mayor Ada Colau and the municipalist movement in Barcelona. It refers largely to the change in socio-political culture that occurs when more women are involved in politics. I write about it here: www.integralesforum.org/medien/integral-global/5270-the-feminisation-of-politics-an-alter-native-journey-by-indra-adnan

16 My *Guardian* column is at: www.theguardian.com/profile/indraadnan

17 *Soft Power Agenda* is my ebook containing all my *Guardian* and *Huffington Post* articles, my two speeches to NATO in Brussels and my submission to the UK Select Committee on Soft Power: https://issuu.com/sugarfreedesign/docs/soft_power____indra_adnan_2014

18 Pat Kane and I undertook a two-year project in 2002–2004 for the Scottish Executive called Re-Imagining Social Work, a highly ambitious series of workshops that aimed to reclaim the meaning and purpose of social work from the overwhelmingly negative media headlines of the time: https://newintegrity.blogs.com/reimaginingsocialwork

19 For more information on the growth of ethical marketing: www.theguardian.com/media-network/2015/dec/10/unethical-advertising-outdated-trend-feelgood-marketing

20 Adnan, I. & Lawson, N. 'New Times: How a Politics of Networks and Relationships Can Deliver A Good Society.' *Compass*, 2014: www.compassonline.org.uk/publications/new-times/

21 Saul Alinsky's book *Rules for Radicals* earned him the title of 'father' of community organising: theecologist.org/2018/jul/10/rethinking-alinsky-community-organising

22 Solutions-based journalism is a generic term, but this website is a good introduction: www.solutionsjournalism.org; I explore cosmolocalism in depth in this book, but for an introduction see: www.cosmolocalism.eu/

23 Perspectiva – Systems, Souls, Society, founded by Jonathan Rowson and Tomas Bjorkman, is a research and events platform that seeks to build the intellectual foundations for a more conscious society: www.systems-souls-society.com

24 Alter Ego network, founded by Ronan Harrington, is a highly creative annual gathering of social-spiritual-political transformers, committed to both inner and outer, personal and collective change. Deeply informed by the meta-modern writings of 'Hanzi Freinacht' (the writing partnership of Emile Ejner and Daniel Gorz), author of *The Listening Society* and *Nordic Ideology*, and a stream of latter-day sense makers such as Charles Eisenstein, Daniel Schmachtenberger and Boyo Akomafale, they are calling for a new understanding of how the personal becomes the political. They have been mostly men talking to men, particularly in the early days – fertile ground in the quest for a new masculinity – but not yet wholistic.

25 Transition Towns (2007–today) are the global network of people committed to taking their home town into a community-driven, greener future through a circular economy.

26 The Good Country Index was founded by serial global entrepreneur Simon Anholt. His book *The Good Country Equation: How We Can Repair the World in One Generation* (Berrett-Koehler) describes his fascinating career advising national governments on how to be a good country.

27 Dark Matter Labs founded by Indy Johar addresses civic responses to the climate crisis, proposing smart commons infrastructure for the imminent future: https://darkmatterlabs. org/. London Futurists, founded by David Wood, brings post-human capacities to new political concepts: https://londonfuturists.com. Both are a constant inspiration and valuable contributors to The Alternative UK.

28 Socio-economic-political is a term I explore extensively in this book, but for an introduction see: www.thealternative.org.uk/dailyalternative/2019/2/17/ micro-to-macro-a-kind-of-fractal-growth?rq=fractal

29 I gave this phrase capitals because 'Labour of Love' was also the title of Hue and Cry's first top ten hit: a rare political pop song attacking the UK's Thatcher government in the 1980s.

30 Sonder was originally coined by John Koenig in his Dictionary of Obscure Sorrows: '*n*. the realization that each random passer-by is living a life as vivid and complex as your own – populated with their own ambitions, friends, routines, worries and inherited craziness – an epic story that continues invisibly around you like an anthill sprawling deep underground, with elaborate passageways to thousands of other lives that you'll never know existed, in which you might appear only once, as an extra sipping coffee in the background, as a blur of traffic passing on the highway, as a lighted window at dusk.'

31 Statistics from: https://data.worldbank.org/indicator/IS.AIR.PSGR

32 The UN Intergovernmental Panel on Climate Change (IPCC) 2018 report gave us 12 years to successfully limit global warming or prepare for the extinction of the human race: www.ipcc.ch/sr15/download/

33 Greta Thunberg began her school strike for the climate in front of the Swedish parliament in August 2018. She is widely acclaimed for changing the global narrative on climate change through her speeches at the UN Climate Change Conference in 2018 and the UN Climate Action Summit in 2019. She received many accolades including *Time Magazine*'s Person of the Year (https://time.com/person-of-the-year-2019-greta-thunberg/) and being twice nominated for the Nobel Peace Prize. More on Fridays for the Future at: https://fridaysforfuture.org/

34 Extinction Rebellion began in 2019, taking over the streets of 60 cities worldwide with three demands: 1) tell the truth about climate change; 2) declare a climate emergency; 3)

hold a citizens' assembly to decide our climate future: https://rebellion.global

35 Coronavirus: Covid, later known as the novel COVID-19 pandemic that spread across the globe in early 2020, infecting millions of people. The total death toll is not yet known.

36 Throughout the first official lockdown, households across the UK came out onto the streets every Thursday to applaud health workers: www.bbc.co.uk/news/av/uk-52054745

37 We cover this period extensively in The Alternative UK editorials through what we retrospectively began to describe as The Shift, with week 1 when the UK went into the first lockdown: www.thealternative.org.uk/dailyalternative/2020/7/20/alternative-editorial-scenario-planning. For lessons learned see our Daily Alternative blogs on the pandemic: www.thealternative.org.uk/search?q=pandemic

38 Alexander, Michelle (2019). *The New Jim Crow*. Penguin. Jim Crow laws were state and local laws that enforced racial segregation in the US in the late 19th and early 20th centuries. Alexander's book shows how current forms of drug laws do the same job, facilitating the mass incarceration of Black people in America.

39 Colonisation: the act of settling among and establishing control of an indigenous population, typically replacing their legal system, culture and governance, and stealing their resources.

40 Pollution drop in London from April to August 2020. Study by King's College, London https://airqualitynews.com/2020/05/07/study-no2-falls-significantly-since-lockdown-in-london-but-pm-rises/

41 'We can serve humanity better if we take our anguish for what it is: a sign that in these interconnected days, our responsibility as agents is increasing.' From 'Existence precedes likes: how online behaviour defines us', *Aeon*, 30 April 2019, https://aeon.co/ideas/existence-precedes-likes-how-online-behaviour-defines-us

42 Despite having several million members, Facebook did not make significant profits until it changed its business model in 2012: www.theatlantic.com/technology/archive/2012/12/2012-year-facebook-finally-tried-make-some-money/320493/

43 The comparisons between 2008 and 2020 are still fluid, but see *Forbes* at the point of the first global lockdown: www.forbes.com/sites/sergeiklebnikov/2020/04/03/imf-warns-coronavirus-will-hurt-global-economy-way-worse-than-2008-financial-crisis/?sh=38e92148707e

44 You can peruse the large number of new political parties as they are registered in the UK: http://search.electoralcommission.org.uk/Search/ Registrations?currentPage=1&rows=30&sort= ApprovedDate&order=desc&open=filter&et= pp&et=ppm&register=gb&regStatus=registered&optCols=EntityStatusName

45 Permaculture is an agriculture ecosystem designed to be sustainable and self-sufficient (here's a great piece: www.nytimes.com/2011/07/28/garden/permaculture-emerges-from-the-underground.html?mtrref=www.sustainable.org &gwh=A0E9BCEA99EC86 499B372945946AAE18&gwt=pay&assetType= REGIWALL); Peer-to-peer networks are simply practitioners sharing methods and tools without a centralised body of control and a commons transition describes how a new system capable of transformation relies upon the availability of access to innovation free of copyright (see: http://commonstransition.org/peer-to-peer-a-commons-manifesto/); Open Coops are co-operatives run on open P2P platforms: https://open.coop

46 The Preston Model set the pace for community wealth-building in the UK: www.preston.gov.uk/communitywealthbuilding

47 The Cleveland Model – Evergreen Coops set the global benchmark for community wealth-building: https://community-wealth.org/content/cleveland-model-how-evergreen-cooperatives-are-building-community-wealth

48   Cooperation Jackson, building a 'solidarity economy', is now making its own waves globally: https://cooperationjackson.org/

49   Participatory Cities initiated in Barking and Dagenham, UK, as a transdisciplinary experiment to measure the well-being created through community participation.

50   *Flatpack Democracy* is the name of a manual written by Peter Macfadyen, the former Mayor of Frome, to describe how easy it was for a group of 17 citizens to take over their local council with a view to inviting local residents to take part in decision-making. More in Chapter 7.1.

51   The triple bottom line is widely attributed to John Elkington, who explains it at: ww.23dd. fr/images/stories/Documents/DD/Elkington-Enter-the-triple-bottom-line.pdf

52   Nobel Prize winner Elinor Ostrom's Health Care Commons: https://papers.ssrn.com/sol3/papers.cfm?abstract_id=2221413; Permaculture's earth care, people care, fair shares at: www.permaculture.org.uk/knowledge-base/basics. Transition Towns on how 'everything connects': www.everythingconnects.org/transition-towns.html

53   Fractal emergence describes the way nature, and society, forms out of patterns of relationships repeating themselves again and again – more on this as the book unfolds. See Dr Jonathan Wolfe's Fractal Foundation: https://fractalfoundation.org/

54   Karen O'Brien, Professor of Human Geography, University of Oslo, Nobel Peace laureate with the Intergovernmental Panel on Climate Change in 2007, is an internationally recognised expert on climate change and society. She focuses on themes such as climate change impacts, vulnerability and adaptation, including how climate change interacts with globalisation processes and the implications for human security. *You Matter More Than You Think* (to be published) is paradigm-shifting in terms of how the metaphors and meanings of quantum physics can cause radical social change: www.youmattermorethanyouthink.com; www.sv.uio.no/iss/english/people/aca/karenob/index.html

55   Covid Mutual Aid Networks: https://covidmutualaid.org/local-groups/

56   Much more on liquid democracy: https://wiki.p2pfoundation.net/Liquid_Democracy

57   Blockchain: a digital ledger in which transactions made in cryptocurrency – such as bitcoin – are recorded chronologically and publicly, making everything transparent and easily accountable.

58   Pol.is is a sense-making tool that allows respondents to register their agreement with a statement along a continuum rather than in a simple Yes/No. It also invites participants to offer their own questions to enrich the enquiry: https://pol.is/home

59   One of many great interviews with Audrey Tang, Digital Minister for Taiwan: www.thealternative.org.uk/dailyalternative/2019/2/9/voting-is-just-entry-level-democracy-audrey-tang?rq=audrey per cent20tang

60   Dual power: associated with Leninist revolution, but worth reimagining in a new age of women participating: www.pmpress.org/blog/2019/09/02/alternative-institutions-or-dual-power/

61   In the US the biggest religious category is 'none', with over 25 per cent saying they have simply stopped believing in God: https://religionnews.com/2016/09/22/why-most-people-leave-religion-they-just-stop-believing/

62   Particularly regrettable when it comes to local news: see https://thehill.com/opinion/technology/506947-news-industrys-bleeding-leads-good-for-business-bad-for-the-country; also www.thealternative.org.uk/dailyalternative/2019/3/31/a-better-media-bleeds-leads

63   Socially Engaged Buddhism is the contemporary movement of Buddhists, East and West, who actively engage with the problems of the world – social, political, economic and

environmental – on the basis of Buddhist ideas, values and spirituality.

64 See note 54.

65 See *The Play Ethic*, Pat Kane (Macmillan, 2004: www.theplayethic.com).

66 The frontal cortex, in close association with other regions of the brain, makes up cerebral systems specifically designed for individual mental tasks. It participates with other brain regions in aspects of learning and memory, attention and motivation, in part through its central role in working memory.

67 Pat Kane, 'The "I'm Happy I'm Green" Consensus Won't Placate Our Lust For Novelty', *The Guardian*, 26 April 2011: www.theguardian.com/commentisfree/2011/apr/26/green-consensus-versus-consumerism

68 See Jason Hickel's concept of the 'radical abundance' that lies beyond growth economics: www.jasonhickel.org/blog/2018/10/27/degrowth-a-call-for-radical-abundance

69 Joe Griffin and Ivan Tyrell, *Dreaming Reality* (HG Publishing, 2004) explain the work of the dreaming brain in constructing each of our unique experiences of reality.

70 Anil Seth, 'The Neuroscience of Reality: Reality is constructed by the brain, and no two brains are exactly alike', *Scientific American*, September 2019: www.scientificamerican.com/article/the-neuroscience-of-reality/

71 The Daily Alternative, edited by Pat Kane, began in March 2017 to offer a new socio-political narrative to the 98 per cent who are not members of political parties: www.thealternative.org.uk/dailyalternative

72 'How affluent people can end their mindless overconsumption', *Vox*, 20 November 2020: www.vox.com/21450911/climate-change-coronavirus-greta-thunberg-flying-degrowth

73 Interview with Mike Davis, 'Why Humanity Will Probably Botch the Next Pandemic, Too', *New York Magazine*, 30 April 2020: https://nymag.com/intelligencer/2020/04/coronavirus-next-pandemic-mike-davis-avian-flu-covid.html

74 This list is published on the Human Givens Institute website: www.hgi.org.uk/human-givens/introduction/what-are-human-givens

75 On Cummings' sampling of non-voters, see Paul Goldsmith, 'Why "take back control" trumped "project fear"', UK In A Changing Europe, 23 November 2017: https://ukandeu.ac.uk/why-take-back-control-trumped-project-fear. Also see the Channel Four drama-documentary *Brexit: The Uncivil War*.

76 For a fascinating history of the relationship between politics and advertising read Sam Delaney (2015) *Mad Men and Bad Men: What Happened when British Politics Met Advertising Publisher.* Faber & Faber.

77 A good attempt at addressing freedom from the left comes from Roberto Unger, 'Deep Freedom: Why the left should abandon equality', IPPR Progressive Review, 24 October 2013: www.ippr.org/juncture/deep-freedom-why-the-left-should-abandon-equality

78 See note 74.

79 Douglas Rushkoff, 'We've spent the decade letting our tech define us. It's out of control', *The Guardian*, 29 December 2019: www.theguardian.com/commentisfree/2019/dec/29/decade-technology-privacy-tech-backlash

80 Before anyone was talking much about sugar and addiction, Coca-Cola was linking its product with our yearning for world peace and harmony, 'It's the Real Thing. What the world wants today: Coca-Cola': www.youtube.com/watch?v=KW9cuta7mdE

81 Tim Jackson, 'Paradise Lost? The iron cage of consumerism', 22 September 2018: https://timjackson.org.uk/consumerism-theodicy/

82 In 2004 Pat Kane and I were invited by the Scottish Executive to Reimagine Social Work with six Scottish regions over two years. Our final report is on: https://newintegrity.

blogs.com/reimaginingsocialwork. See my *Guardian* column: www.theguardian.com/society/2004/oct/20/comment.guardiansocietysupplement1

83 How Finland solved its homeless problem: www.theguardian.com/housing-network/2017/mar/22/finland-solved-homelessness-eu-crisis-housing-first

84 There are plenty of books, websites and organisations associated with Spiral Dynamics, one is: http://spiraldynamicsintegral.nl/wp-content/uploads/2013/09/McDonald-Ian-Introduction-to-Spiral-Dynamics-1007.pdf

85 While non-dualism is embraced, it is also debated within the integral world; there is an interesting exploration by Oliver Griebel at: www.integralworld.net/griebel4.html

86 Ken Wilber has been very prolific and somewhat influential in UK and US politics. Both UK PM Blair and US President Clinton were reputed to be aficionados. Here is an interesting assessment of Blair's term in office by *Integral Review* in which he does well overall but finally fails the integral test: www.integralworld.net/vergara.html

87 For more on map-territory relations see: https://en.wikipedia.org/wiki/Map per centE2 per cent80 per cent93territory_relation

88 The S-Word: www.thealternative.org.uk/the-s-word

89 Interview with E.O. Wilson, 'Living in shimmering disequilibrium', Salon.com, 22 April 2000: www.salon.com/2000/04/22/eowilson/

90 Perspectiva is at: https://systems-souls-society.com

91 Mindfulness is worth US$1.2billion and growing: https://blog.marketresearch.com/1.2-billion-u.s.-meditation-market-growing-strongly-as-it-becomes-more-mainstream

92 The Mindfulness Initiative was founded by Madeleine Bunting and Chris Cullen in November 2013 to support British politicians in forming the All-Party Parliamentary Group on Mindfulness. Jamie Bristow took over as Director in May 2015. To date, 250 UK MPs, 14 national parliaments and 40 global politicians have experienced mindfulness training. Bristow and his partner Rosie Bell are also active co-creators of The Alternative UK: www.themindfulnessinitiative.org

93 'How Psychedelics helped to shape Extinction Rebellion', Gail Bradbrook: www.whatisemerging.com/opinions/psychedelics-and-social-change

94 See: www.techgnosis.com. Also, Davis's 2015 afterword to the latest edition of *Techgnosis* is an excellent overview of his thinking and interests, then and now: www.lareviewofbooks.org/article/myth-magic-mysticism-age-information/

95 Erik Davis has also written profoundly on the Burning Man phenomenon. See 'Beyond Belief: The Cults of Burning Man', techgnosis.com, 13 June 2006: https://techgnosis.com/beyond-belief-cults-of-burning-man/

96 For Alter Ego, see note 24.

97 Rapid Transition Alliance blog, 'The decline of the single bottom line and the growth of B-Corps', 16 August 2019: www.rapidtransition.org/stories/new-economics-the-rise-of-the-b-corp/

98 Power to Change is an independent charitable trust that supports community business: www.powertochange.org.uk/blog/from-crisis-to-community-empowerment/

99 Zoom is a video conferencing platform whose revenue quadrupled in the first six months of Covid: www.independent.co.uk/news/business/news/zoom-results-sales-rise-coronavirus-pandemic-video-conferencing-a9698086.html

100 Many reports have been written on the unexpected effects of working from home during Covid, with the result that, in the UK, 91 per cent don't want to go back to the way things were: www.bbc.co.uk/news/uk-53580656

101 This well-known aphorism is attributed to theatre producer David Merrick, remembered

for his love of outrageous publicity stunts! https://en.wikipedia.org/wiki/David_Merrick

102 Richard Adams, author of *Watership Down*, created a whole 'lapine' language for the book, tharn among many terms: https://en.wikipedia.org/wiki/Lapine_language

103 After the Sri Lankan tsunami, the *National Geographic* collected evidence that animals retreated from the coastline before the humans, largely avoiding the catastrophe human settlements faced: www.nationalgeographic.com/animals/article/news-animals-tsunami-sense-coming. More at: www.sciencedirect.com/science/article/pii/S0960982218309382

104 The cartel political theory posits government in league with business to keep the economy growing, but in hock therefore to their special interests: https://en.wikipedia.org/wiki/Cartel_party_theory

105 How Farage hijacked British emotions has become a hot topic for political commentators either calling it out as bad practice or hoping to find the formula: www.theguardian.com/technology/2017/may/07/the-great-british-brexit-robbery-hijacked-democracy

106 Chatham House explanation of how ISIS came to shape foreign policy: www.chathamhouse.org/sites/default/files/field/field_document/INTA91_4_03_Friis.pdf

107 How poetry played a major part in ISIS recruitment: www.newyorker.com/magazine/2015/06/08/battle-lines-jihad-creswell-and-haykel

108 See my work on the Peace Journalism initiative, mentioned in the Introduction, which became Reporting the World.

109 Joseph Nye on The Information Revolution and Soft Power, Harvard Library: https://dash.harvard.edu/bitstream/handle/1/11738398/Nye-InformationRevolution.pdf

110 The Icelandic Pirate Party was led by 'poetician' Birgitta Jonsdottir who, together with Smári McCarthy, Icelandic/Irish, introduced the Shadow Parliament Project for 'crowdsourcing democracy' through liquid democracy. Here is a good introduction from 2016: https://theconversation.com/icelands-pirate-party-what-is-it-and-how-did-it-become-so-popular-67879

111 15-M is a Spanish grassroots movement arising from the protest group indignados. 15-M is prototyping modern democracy through citizens' participation in deliberative circles and People's Assemblies. Podemos is a party that set itself up to represent 15-M. These are historic developments worth a book of their own, for an overview see: https://wiki.p2pfoundation.net/15M_Movement_-_Spain

112 For more on these examples, see the 'Democratic Innovation' category on The Alternative UK site: www.thealternative.org.uk/dailyalternative/category/DEMOCRATIC+INNOVATION

113 Monbiot, G. (2018) *Out of the Wreckage*. London: Verso Books.

114 Pat Williams' work on storytelling is ground-breaking: www.hgi.org.uk/resources/delve-our-extensive-library/society-and-culture/sound-sense

115 For example, Mia Birdsong on the 'story' of poverty: www.ted.com/talks/mia_birdsong_the_story_we_tell_about_poverty_isn_t_true/discussion

116 See Alexander, J.C. (2007) 'The Meaningful Construction of Inequality and the Struggles Against It: A "Strong Program" Approach to How Social Boundaries Change'. *Cultural Sociology* 1(1): https://journals.sagepub.com/doi/10.1177/1749975507073915. Alexander describes how our cultural discourse becomes the table we are standing on that cannot be easily lifted: 'The imposition of inequality, and struggles over justice, inclusion, and distribution, are mediated by cultural structures. Inequalities are nested inside the discourse of civil society, and so are demands for equality.'

117 When the Occupy movement named the 99 per cent of people outside the wealthiest

elite, it changed the public discourse: https://en.wikipedia.org/wiki/We_are_the_99 per cent25

118 *Avatar*, beautiful film, shame about the armies: www.imdb.com/title/tt0499549/

119 *12 Years A Slave* was important for telling the often-hidden history of slavery in the United States: www.nytimes.com/2013/10/18/movies/12-years-a-slave-holds-nothing-back-in-show-of-suffering.html

120 How the *Black Panther* film changed history: https://news.sky.com/story/chadwick-boseman-why-did-black-panther-have-such-a-huge-impact-12059119

121 To see what this alternative economics might look like, go to Chapter 7.2 'Our chance to Bounce Beyond'.

122 'Synchronized defense: How animals move as one to avoid predators', PBS, 9 February 2017: https://whyy.org/segments/synchronized-defense-how-animals-move-as-one-to-avoid-predators/

123 Johnson's Chancellor even echoed Bush's 9/11 injunction. See *London Economic*, 20 December 2020: www.thelondoneconomic.com/politics/use-your-household-savings-to-bail-out-the-economy-rishi-sunak-says/20/12/

124 Relational Welfare introduced at: https://relationalwelfare.wordpress.com/about. More in the following chapter on Hilary Cottam and *Radical Help* (Virago, 2018).

125 Covid Mutual Aid Networks sprang up around the country: https://COVIDmutualaid.org

126 The Alternative UK's report for the Local Trust 'A New Story of Us' showed a reluctance by neighbourhood networks to 'hand power back' to local authorities after discovering their mutual aid networks were more effective than the local council: www.thealternative.org.uk/dailyalternative/2020/8/13/a-new-story-of-us-auk-localtrust-plymouth?rq=local per cent20trust

127 Feminism is disaggregating. On the split between social and individual feminism see: www.theguardian.com/news/2018/may/11/how-metoo-revealed-the-central-rift-within-feminism-social-individualist. On the sex wars and gender panics see Hines, S. (2020). Sex wars and (trans) gender panics: Identity and body politics in contemporary UK feminism. *The Sociological Review*, 68(4), 699–717. https://doi.org/10.1177/0038026120934684

128 The essay, edited by Elke Fein of the Institute for Integral Studies, is at: www.integralesforum.org/medien/integral-global/5270-the-feminisation-of-politics-an-alternative-journey-from-indra-adnan

129 See Alternative UK's blog on Collaboration, dialogue, horizontality: What links the 'feminisation' & 'municipalisation' of politics?: www.thealternative.org.uk/dailyalternative/2018/10/27/roar-feminisation-municipalisation?rq=feminisation

130 The feminisation of politics in Argentina: https://minim-municipalism.org/magazine/lets-feminize-politics-and-politicize-care

131 The contraceptive pill was a revolution for men and women: https://theconversation.com/the-contraceptive-pill-was-a-revolution-for-women-and-men-37193

132 Scilla Elworthy, founder of the Oxford Research Group, Peace Direct and many other conflict resolution organisations, pioneered the way for a more feminine kind of power in the public space throughout her professional life. *Power and Sex* (Vega Books, 2002) is one of her many books on the feminine. She is also co-founder of Rising Women, Rising World and Femme Q.

133 M. Dyble, G. D. Salali, N. Chaudhary, A. Page, D. Smith, J. Thompson, L. Vinicius, R. Mace, A. B. Migliano (2015) 'Sex equality can explain the unique social structure of hunter-gatherer bands' *Science* 348:6236, pp.796–798 DOI: 10.1126/science.aaa5139

134 A *Guardian* review of the Dyble paper: www.theguardian.com/science/2015/may/14/

early-men-women-equal-scientists

135 An important report from the Overseas Development Institute on the impact of Women's Voice and Leadership in Decision Making: https://assets.publishing.service.gov.uk/media/57a08977e5274a31e00000c4/Womens_Voice.pdf

136 According to James Suzman in *Affluence Without Abundance*, hunter-gatherers had a strong relationship with the land, believing it to be naturally abundant and sustainable as they moved around in response to the seasons and depleted soil. The move to agriculture was to take control of nature and force the land to produce surpluses to overcome the possible failure of crops. This in turn led to forced labour and increasing inequality: *Affluence Without Abundance* (Bloomsbury USA, 2017).

137 A Gallup Poll finding from June 2017: https://news.gallup.com/opinion/chairman/212045/world-broken-workplace.aspx?g_source=position1&g_medium=related&g_campaign=tiles

138 According to the Office for National Statistics 2019 report, 75 per cent of suicides are male and only ever steadily increasing in numbers: www.ons.gov.uk/peoplepopulation-andcommunity/birthsdeathsandmarriages/deaths/bulletins/suicidesintheunitedking-dom/2019registrations

139 Wynes, S. and Nicholas, K.A. (2017) 'The climate mitigation gap: education and government recommendations miss the most effective individual actions', Environmental Research Letters, 12:7, https://iopscience.iop.org/article/10.1088/1748-9326/aa7541

140 According to the Stockholm International Peace Research Institute, global military spending could solve global poverty if redirected: www.sipri.org/media/press-release/2018/global-military-spending-remains-high-17-trillion

141 See: https://indraadnan.global/2014/11/04/new-book-the-soft-power-agenda/

142 Transactional leadership is enacted through reward and punishment, well described at: https://en.wikipedia.org/wiki/Transactional_leadership

143 In his 2014 book *Reinventing Organisations*, Frederic Laloux talks often about soulful workplaces: www.youtube.com/watch?v=GxGGkrtKZaA.

144 Cottam, H. (2018) *Radical Help*. London: Virago: www.hilarycottam.com/radical-help/

145 Numerous articles on feminine leadership during Covid are summed up at: www.thealternative.org.uk/dailyalternative/2020/4/11/womens-leadership-coronavirus?rq=-women

146 RegenA refers to all those prepared to move on from Gen X, Y and Z and build a new system together: www.thealternative.org.uk/dailyalternative/2019/1/27/alternative-edi-torial-step-up-regeneration-a?rq=Regen per cent20a

147 Rob Hopkins talks about how Liège decided to resist becoming a smart city in favour of becoming a Transition City at: www.thealternative.org.uk/dailyalternative/2018/5/1/liege-not-smart-city-transition-city

148 Foroudi, L. 'What happened to the Arab Spring?', *Prospect*, 8 December 2020: www.prospectmagazine.co.uk/magazine/what-happened-to-the-arab-spring

149 For more on these interesting local council elections with an unprecedented 71 per cent turnout, see https://en.wikipedia.org/wiki/2019_Hong_Kong_local_elections

150 How Marconi won the credit for inventing radio ahead of Tesla: www.pbs.org/tesla/ll/ll_whoradio.html

151 Much more on this fascinating case at: www.abbeyrd.net/mysweet.htm

152 The two sets of drawings on the German website: www.haraldjschellander.net/inspirationen/

153 Some of the effects that Avaaz claim for their assiduous work: https://secure.avaaz.org/

page/en/highlights/

154 Cosmolocalism derives from the term cosmopolitan localism, describing social innovation through bringing the local and global closer together. Distinct from glocalism, which maintains the different realms of globalisation and localisation, cosmolocalism is acting with a global mindset and within a global culture on the ground in your community. Michel Bauwens uses this term for P2P commoning practices that encourage open-source sharing of global design and knowledge: https://wiki.p2pfoundation.net/Cosmo-Localism

155 See many examples of this cosmolocal effect in The Daily Alternative.

156 More on Neighborocracy: www.thealternative.org.uk/dailyalternative/2020/4/26/neighborocracy

157 While all hashtags are informal movements, here is one website dedicated to its visibility https://metoomvmt.org/

158 For more on the global impact of #metoo, see this piece from *Foreign Policy* magazine: https://foreignpolicy.com/2019/03/07/metooglobalimpactinternationalwomens-day/

159 This was in reference to Donald Trump approving a drone-strike in Iraq that killed top General Qasem Soleimani. Several newspapers reported this as a declaration of World War 3: www.express.co.uk/news/world/1223901/World-War-3-is-world-war-three-happening-WW3-declared-Donald-Trump-Iran

160 See Global Uprising – an independent news site and video series dedicated to showing responses to the economic crisis and authoritarianism: www.globaluprisings.org

161 US President Trump, UK Prime Minister Johnson and Australian Premier Morrison all relied on similar social media tactics (with Ben Guerin consulting both the UK and Australia) to win their elections against the reported odds: www.thealternative.org.uk/dailyalternative/2019/12/14/the-day-after-lets-be-practical?rq=general per cent20election

162 The United Federation of Planets governance board: https://memory-alpha.fandom.com/wiki/United_Federation_of_Planets

163 Fearless Cities: the global municipalist movement standing up to defend human rights, democracy and the common good. Their first summit in 2017 was convened by Barcelona En Comu with mayors, neighbourhood leaders and activists from all over the world.

164 SIMPOL stands for Simultaneous Policy and works as a pledge signed by political candidates to commit to implementing interconnected environmental actions at the same time as other nations to avoid the economic risks of being the first to move.

165 Transition Towns are self-appointed by groups of citizens as those committed to moving their social economies into line with the needs of the planet: https://transitionnetwork.org

166 The commoning movement is committed to reclaiming socio-economic resources, especially land, tools and practice, into the ownership of conscious and active communities. See: https://primer.commonstransition.org; www.freefairandalive.org; our commons tag at The Alternative UK: www.thealternative.org.uk/search?q=commons

167 Flatpack Democracy is the simple way for people to reclaim local councils to be run by people instead of parties: http://flatpackdemocracy.co.uk

168 Citizen Action Networks are cosmolocal containers for community agency: www.thealternative.org.uk/search?q=citizen+action+network

169 Constitutes are fluid, often temporary governance structures which can evolve as new information about what serves the purposes of the group well and what doesn't: www.thealternative.org.uk/dailyalternative/2020/6/20/what-is-a-constitute-re-festival-civic-square?rq=constitute

170 For earlier notes on this, see 'Patterns and fractals', page 41.

171 Biodiversity is the diversity and variability of life on earth, without which we would not have the variety of species that we do presently. Loss of biodiversity is loss of species. Replacing biodiverse soil with chemicals is killing the planet's sustainability. *National Geographic* on why biodiversity matters: www.nationalgeographic.org/encyclopedia/biodiversity/

172 British Medical Association, The Impact of COVID On Mental Health in England: www.bma.org.uk/media/2750/bma-the-impact-of-COVID-on-mental-health-in-england.pdf

173 The Wellbeing Economy Alliance ties many elements of the I–We–World argument together, i.e. how the well-being of complex individuals is interdependent with the well-being of the planet and can be best achieved through the well-being of communities: https://wellbeingeconomy.org. WEAll offers proposals for socio-economic change programmes to governments around the world.

174 Even recently, after many opportunities to reform and redesign, Facebook's relationship to democratic voices and energies is worrying. See 'Facebook is tilting the political playing field more than ever, and it's no accident', The Conversation UK, 27 October 2020: https://theconversation.com/facebook-is-tilting-the-political-playing-field-more-than-ever-and-its-no-accident-148314

175 New Times: www.compassonline.org.uk/publications/new-times/. Is the Party Over? www.compassonline.org.uk/publications/21st-century-politics-is-the-party-over-or-is-it-just-kicking-off/

176 Front Runners: www.frontloberne.dk/about

177 The Frontrunners went up through Sweden and Finland and entered the Soviet Union through Leningrad – now St Petersburg – where they did all kinds of cultural events before moving to Moscow. Another group moved from Copenhagen through Germany and Poland up to Moscow. Uffe writes about this in glorious detail in *Leadership On The Edge* (Copenhagen, Gylendal, 2013).

178 For more on Kaospilot: www.kaospilot.dk

179 The World Outgames were first held in Montreal in 2006, inviting participation from anyone, irrespective of their sexual orientation. The events attract athletes and artists from all over the world, including some where homosexuality is still illegal: https://en.wikipedia.org/wiki/World_Outgames

180 Alternativet's manifesto: https://alternativet.dk/en/politics/manifesto; Alternativet's history:https://alternativet.dk/om-os/alternativets-historie (in Danish) – worth doing a simple online translation for the description of the salons through which the political programme was crowdsourced.

181 For more on the values: https://alternativet.dk/en/politics/our-values

182 Alternativet's first election campaign video emphasised their playful energy and new thinking: www.youtube.com/watch?v=cm68P6Jaj7I&feature=youtu.be

183 'The Next Denmark', Alternativet: https://alternativet.dk/en/politics/next-denmark

184 Despite – or maybe because of its radical nature – Alternativet was never free of excessive media attention which led to many internal tensions. This turned more subtle differences in the party's vision for the future into personality clashes that eventually had to be side-stepped, or risk destroying all the progress made.

185 Frei Grønne (Independent Greens) included in its initial line-up Sikander Siddique as party leader, Uffe Elbæk (now self-styled Elder), Susanne Zimmer and Niko Grunfeld (Copenhagen Mayor's office). Co-founder of Alternativet Rasmus Nordqvist also left to join the Socialist People's Party.

186 David Bollier and Silke Helfrich talk about the importance of an 'ontoshift' (an

ontological shift) in their *Free, Fair and Alive* book (British Colombia: New Society Publishers, 2019), pp. 29–50.

187 What is a constitute? See 'A skeleton of global governance' in Chapter 5.2.

188 Participatory City: Co-creating The First Large Scale, Fully Inclusive, Practical, Participatory Ecosystem www.participatorycity.org/

189 Made to Measure: Year 1 report for the Every One Every Day Initiative: www.participatorycity.org/made-to-measure?rq=Made%20to%20Measure%201

190 Hackney Covid-19 Mutual Aid Group had 9,000 members at the time of writing: www.facebook.com/groups/280285692955390/

191 Trust the People (www.trustthepeople.earth) is a decentralised network that nevertheless offers training and regular gatherings to help develop ways of being and working together. They shifted from being a local to a cosmolocal network during the Covid lockdown. Interviews with co-founders Mags Mulowska, Greg Frey and Hester Campbell among others: www.thealternative.org.uk/search?q=Trust+the+People

192 Cooperation Jackson describes its vision thus: 'To develop a cooperative network based in Jackson, Mississippi that will consist of four interconnected and interdependent institutions: a federation of local worker cooperatives, a cooperative incubator, a cooperative education and training centre (the Kuwasi Balagoon Centre for Economic Democracy and Development), and a cooperative bank or financial institution': https://cooperationjackson.org/intro

193 Civic Square self-describes as a 'public square, neighbourhood economics lab and creative and participatory ecosystem'. Not quite up and running yet, Civic Square recently enacted 'The Department of Dreams'.

194 Frome is unusual in that it is developing a dual power system all at once: a Transition Town generating ever broader and deeper citizen action networks that have already taken over the town council. Now the people can fully participate in council decision-making and budgeting, even before they have constituted themselves. However, it will remain to be seen if the people will be able to hold the council accountable unless/until they create some form of democratic decision-making tool of their own.

195 Regenerate Devon is a network of networks that together hold all the characteristics of a CAN except any form of democratic decision-making across them: https://regenerate-devon.heysummit.com/#

196 Neighborocracy is a sociocratic system of 400,000 neighbourhood parliaments in India, each with a children's, youth and adult parliament designed to tackle the UN Sustainable Development Goals: www.thealternative.org.uk/dailyalternative/2020/7/4/indian-livelihood-self-reliance?rq=neighborocracy

197 I'm singling Transition Tooting out for its strong work on urban living and diversity.

198 See our 'Plymouth' category on The Daily Alternative: www.thealternative.org.uk/dailyalternative/category/PLYMOUTH+LAB

199 In concert with CounterCoin's Mike Riddell: www.thealternative.org.uk/search?q=countercoin

200 Flatpack 2021 Campaign has teamed up with the Trust the People movement for community transformation to encourage people to stand as independent councillors to save the planet: https://flatpack2021.co.uk/home/

201 Sortition describes the method of random selection of participants for a Citizens' Assembly. Using the official electoral roll, those chosen are minimally edited to ensure balance and diversity of culture, age, gender and economic privilege.

202 Municipalism proposes the municipality (often the city) as the vehicle of social change.

Partly because it is a manageable container, partly to suspend the necessity of changing political ideology or legal structure before further change can happen. For more on different forms of municipalism start with: Thompson, Matthew (2020) What's so new about New Municipalism? *Progress in Human Geography*: https://journals.sagepub.com/doi/full/10.1177/0309132520909480

203 An interesting podcast with Daniel Thorson, producer of the Emerge podcasts, on why the Occupy Wall Street movement had limited results: www.whatisemerging.com/updates/a-conversation-with-daniel-thorson

204 The Future Democracy Hub was started by Paul Thistlethwaite (Thinking Box), Sam Weller (acupuncturist and web designer) and myself, after XR co-founder Gail Bradbrook asked us to think through how to help People's Assemblies to get traction. Our idea was that they needed to be better rooted in community life, drawing on the work that local citizens were already doing and co-creating the space for more active citizen engagement. See: www.xrdemocracy.uk

205 Dual power was brought into latter-day politics by US Marxist thinker Fredric Jameson, whose essay on the topic is at the core of *An American Utopia: Dual Power and the Universal Army*, Slavoj Žižek (Ed.). It warns us on the back cover: 'Many will be appalled at what they will encounter in these pages – there will be blood!'

206 Pankaj Mishra, 'Václav Havel's Lessons on How to Create a "Parallel Polis"', *New Yorker*, 8 February 2017: www.newyorker.com/books/page-turner/vaclav-havels-lessons-on-how-to-create-a-parallel-poli. See also: https://en.wikipedia.org/wiki/Parallel_Polis

207 Komeito: https://en.wikipedia.org/wiki/Komeito; I wrote my MSc dissertation on Komeito in 1996 under the supervision of Leftist academic (and guru) Ben Pimlott, just as the Blair government swept into power. It was a time of great expectations, now dashed.

208 Variations on this theme include the Scottish government's ongoing Citizens' Assembly to decide on the future for Scotland. Also Extinction Rebellion's third demand to hold a meaningful Citizens' Assembly that takes 2025 as the year to target for carbon neutrality, not the government goal of 2050.

209 For more on the Irish Citizens' Assembly: www.electoral-reform.org.uk/the-irish-abortion-referendum-how-a-citizens-assembly-helped-to-break-years-of-political-deadlock/

210 Since their inception in 2016 following the failure of the municipality to deal well with the flooding, three major assemblies have taken place in Gdansk, each of whose recommendations have led to over 80 per cent approval by the broader electorate and therefore have been accepted. For more on Polish binding Citizens' Assemblies: www.resilience.org/stories/2017-11-22/solutions-how-the-poles-are-making-democracy-work-again-in-gdansk/

211 Doughnut economics and C40: www.kateraworth.com/2020/07/16/so-you-want-to-create-a-city-doughnut/

212 Boris Johnson had long planned to establish a system of Freeports across the UK: secure customs zones located at ports where business can be carried out inside a country's land border, but where different customs rules apply. They can reduce administrative burdens and tariff controls, provide relief from duties and import taxes, and ease tax and planning regulations: https://assets.publishing.service.gov.uk/government/uploads/system/uploads/attachment_data/file/878352/-Freeports_Consultation_Extension.pdf

213 Sociocracy, also called dynamic governance, is a system which seeks to create harmonious social environments and productive organisations. It is distinguished by the use of consent, rather than majority voting, in decision-making, and of discussion by people who know each other.

214 More on the purple maps: https://purplestatesofamerica.org/; www.thealternative.org.

uk/dailyalternative/2020/11/9/editorial-american-localism

215 Alt/work: www.altwork.live; www.thealternative.org.uk/dailyalternative/2020/10/10/valiakis-on-alt-work?rq=Mary per cent20Valiaki

216 Dell report: www.delltechnologies.com/content/dam/delltechnologies/assets/perspectives/2030/pdf/SR1940_IFTFfor-DellTechnologies_Human-Machine_070517_readerhigh-res.pdf

217 CounterCoin is the ingenious invention of Mike Riddell and his team in Stoke – nicknamed Brexit capital of the UK – who found a way to link excess food, unused seats in theatres and buses with voluntary labour. Since then CounterCommunity has become an online network that enables voluntary organisations, charities, social enterprises, local businesses and individuals, to work together for social change and to boost the local economy, shaped by the community which arises. The Alternative UK works with CounterCoin in developing CAN prototypes.

218 To see how mutual credit can work through open-platforms (as opposed to analogue co-ops), check Open Credit Network: https://opencredit.network

219 Blockchain is a dencentralised digital ledger that records the origin of a digital asset. In this way every bit of information or action taking place can be traced back to its initiator, guaranteeing transparency. Blockchain is commonly used to 'bank' cryptocurrencies such as bitcoins, a form of currency independent of sterling.

220 Iris recognition in Somaliland: www.planetbiometrics.com/article-details/i/6521/desc/somaliland-to-hold-iris-recognition-elections/#.WgWPaiugv0Y.twitter

221 How drones are in active use by Rwanda's health service: www.healthcareglobal.com/technology-and-ai-3/health-stealth-how-drones-are-saving-lives

222 Learn how to regenerate your soil with Costa Rica's ecotourism: www.visitcostarica.com/en/costa-rica/things-to-do/ecotourism?utm_actcampaign=62976&gclid=CjwK-CAiAn7L-BRBbEiwAl9UtkPkkcb6uegCEfbRJbbMlq_xDKlhREdOFVj-UCvr5ggXm-04b5GpoBmxoCqNcQAvD_BwE

223 Social entrepreneurs working in the villages and slums of India to restore dignity and release creativity: https://goonj.org

224 The Three Horizons framework has been taken up in numerous ways. McKinsey & Co global management consulting firm adapt it to help companies create vision for the future. Here I am talking more about how to harness the creativity of cosmolocal communities to step away from the old socio-economic-political system: www.thealternative.org.uk/dailyalternative/2020/10/12/alternative-editorial-lockdown-re-frame?rq=Three%20horizons%20. Transition Towns' Rob Hopkins describes this as moving from What Is to What If and then to What's Next?

225 The paper I wrote for the Barrow Cadbury Trust was part of an anthology called *Islam, Race and Being British*. Madeleine Bunting (Ed.). (2005) *The Guardian* in association with the Barrow Cadbury Trust.

226 The Big Society: in 2014, instead of increasing support for civil society, over £18 billion of government support was wiped from charities: www.ncvo.org.uk/about-us/media-centre/press-releases/621-over-1billion-government-income-wiped-from-charities

227 The Elephant is a growing list of systems actors we perceive to be working on the socio-economic-political system. They included people as diverse as: Uffe Elbæk, founder of Alternativet; Amisha Ghadiali, founder of The Future is Beautiful; Skeena Rathor, Labour councillor and one of the founders of Extinction Rebellion alongside Scilla Elworthy, thrice nominated Nobel Peace Laureate and founder of the Business Plan for Peace; Richard Bartlett, founder of Enspiral Networks; famous improv artist Pippa Evans; Jay Tompt, Director of the REconomy Project and co-founder of Regenerate Devon;

Jamie Bristow, Director of the Mindfulness Initiative whose work in the Westminster Parliament had introduced 200 MPs to this practice; David Wood, one of the inventors of mobile phone tech and author of *The Abolition of Aging*. YouTube featured the participants: www.youtube.com/channel/UC0gQQemO4-7sMSydUC6aBEg

228 Organisational and relational systems coaching ORSC: www.crrglobal.com/orsc.html

229 Systemic constellations are a way of working on issues within human systems. Developed by German psychotherapist Bert Hellinger, they originally focused on family systems to disclose the deeper forces that unknowingly influence our thoughts, behaviours and emotional experiences through the generations.

230 More on the fourth sector from the hosts of our conference: www.fourthsector.org/what-is-the-fourth-sector

231 Real Ideas Organisation arose from social arts networks taking over heritage buildings for community development. It is driving social enterprise all over the South West in the UK, but particularly in Plymouth, paying special attention to the future for young people: https://realideas.org/

232 Pop Plymouth is one of the first citizens' action networks we collaborated with in 2018; CEO Matt Bell is a trailblazer in the field: www.plymouthoctopus.org

233 Benefit corporations are those that include positive impact on society, workers, the community and the environment in addition to profit as its legally defined goals, in that the definition of 'best interest of the corporation' is specified to include those impacts.

234 SDG Transformations Forum: https://transformationsforum.net

235 Althorp in Northants, UK, is the burial place of Princess Diana. Her brother Charles Spencer and his wife Karen, were hosts for this gathering organised by Jeroo Billimoria.

236 Furlough – leave of absence, in this case with 80 per cent of your wages covered by the UK government.

237 Before&Now app available at: https://beforeandnow.glideapp.io

238 #buildbackbetter – a call to take advantage of the waking up during Covid to improve our socio-economic system: www.buildbackbetteruk.org

239 Circular economy: www.ellenmacarthurfoundation.org/circular-economy/concept

240 Well-being economy: https://wellbeingeconomy.org

241 Regenerative economy: -https://capitalinstitute.org/8-principles-regenerative-economy/

242 Doughnut economy: www.kateraworth.com/doughnut/

243 *Thrivability: Breaking Through to a World that Works* is a concept and book, by Jean Russell (Triarchy Press, 2013). Also see: https://wiki.p2pfoundation.net/Thrivability

244 Buen Vivir economy: www.tni.org/files/download/beyonddevelopment_buenvivir.pdf; www.theguardian.com/sustainable-business/blog/buen-vivir-philosophy-south-america-eduardo-gudynas

245 Regenerate Costa Rica: http://fieldguide.capitalinstitute.org/eduard-muller-biodiversity-extinction.html

246 Humanity Rising Days began offering daily broadcasts on the solutions available to our multiple crises from 22 May 2020. Days 114–118 were dedicated to Bouncing Beyond To A Regenerative World Day: www.youtube.com/results?search_query=Humanity+Rising+Bouncing+Beyond. Since that important move, our close colleague Karen Downes, founder of The Flourishing Initiative (co-founder of FemmeQ project with Scilla Elworthy), has co-curated a global FemmeQ gathering in Costa Rica 2021, bringing together local indigenous wisdom with global feminism across the generations.

247 Red Wedge, founded by singer Billy Bragg in 1985, was a pop music collective hoping to engage young people in politics, particularly the Labour Party, in the run-up to the 1987

general election. The Alternative UK co-Initiator Pat Kane was an active member as lead singer of Hue and Cry, as was SGI Buddhist Sandie Shaw.

248 The World Transformed is the title given to a series of events around the Labour Party conferences. They include more creative and grassroots approaches to change: however, they tend to stay on the fringe of Labour Party policymaking, not core to it.

249 A few examples of lifestyle change festivals include: Noisily, Buddhafield, Boomtown, Awaken, Shambala.

250 Local farmers' markets are good places to germinate CANs – Frome market was an early community binder that gave the town a sense of itself and later made Flatpack Democracy possible.

251 Campfire Convention, a busy socio-political network arose directly from – and is still fuelled by – Pete Lawrence's Big Chill Festivals and Cooking Vinyl Record label. What brings them together is a 'passion for life and a quest for social change': www.thealternative.org.uk/dailyalternative/2017/4/29/campfire-convention?rq=CAMPFIRE per cent20CONVENTION

252 Football prides itself on its soft power role: in an interview I conducted with Richard Scudamore CBE, then Executive Chairman of the English Premier League 2014–18, he credited Football against Racism with improving the image of Britain abroad. Most football clubs also have community functions, including learning clubs – Arsenal in the Community offers sports, social and educational programmes to 5,000 people every week, including language classes for refugees and computer programming for youth and elderly.

253 Burning Man: annual event in the Nevada desert where over 10,000 people gather to build Black Rock City, 'a temporary metropolis dedicated to community art, self-expression and self-reliance'. At the end of the gathering they dismantle it and leave the desert without a trace of their activity. Burning Man has a legacy of transformative communities around the globe intent on planetary stewardship.

254 'Microsolidarities' describes groups of people who want to explore social change through personal development together. Think reflexive friendship networks that become fractals of system change. See: www.microsolidarity.cc

255 Enspiral Networks: when microsolidarities become social enterprises with the ambition of changing the culture of collaboration globally: https://enspiral.com

256 Noisily Festival sees itself as actively integrating I, We and World. While it began as a music festival for eco-spiritual-political actors of all kinds, it is slowly becoming a change network of practitioners for personal, social and global change: www.thealternative.org.uk/dailyalternative/2019/5/11/alter-natives-lachie-festivals?rq=noisily

257 Green Heart of Kenya's vision is 'to provide an example for East Africa and the world for how development can have a positive impact on natural ecosystems and local communities, while also supporting the economy and driving profit. To achieve this, our mission is to develop the sustainable infrastructure, utilities and services required to host and support profitable, low-carbon and inclusive businesses across real estate and nature-based solutions': www.greenheartofkenya.com

258 Fun Palaces are an annual event supporting communities to co-create cultural events, sharing and celebrating the genius in everyone. Says founder Stella Duffy, 'Everyone is an artist, everyone is a scientist': https://funpalaces.co.uk/about-fun-palaces/

259 Chickenshed Theatre, founded in a chicken shed in 1974, became an international network of inclusive theatre projects – meaning no one excluded – stretching to China. *GlobalEyes* remains one of my favourite I–We–World pieces of theatre ever: www.youtube.com/watch?v=U2tN8Rxi8zE

260 Roberto Unger, former Culture Minister for Brazil and a great inspiration to many

politicians reaching for that magic factor – a new political life force: www.thealternative. org.uk/search?q=roberto+unger

261 Universal Basic Income would give everyone a small amount of money, guaranteed every month, simply for being a registered citizen. This saves the government all the resources used to set criteria and control receipt of welfare. The benefits to both employed and unemployed citizens are many. UBI trials are taking place all over the world but there is not enough conclusive evidence yet for any country to take it up permanently.

262 Perspectiva, Emerge and the Ekskäret Foundation (EF) are all actively bringing the bildung concept into the present day. Tomas Bjorkman, founder of EF, describes bildung as 'providing the cultural roots, a deep sense of identity, a moral compass, and places to go for spiritual and emotional nourishment which everyone needs in order to become a rounded, confident, autonomous, socially capable, mature, and comfortable adult who is at peace with oneself and one's path in life': www.nordicsecret.org/the-authors/

263 See: www.enrolyourself.com/

264 Digital Ego is an exciting exploration into the future of what it means to be free, to grow and flourish in the digital age, insisting upon the connections of Systems, Souls and Society. As part of Perspectiva, initiators Tom Chatfield and Dan Nixon are hoping to develop a meta-ethical framework for the digital era: https://systems-souls-society.com/ realisation/digital-ego-project/

265 Despite being contested by Senator Mitch McConnell, Senate Majority Leader in the Trump administration, Obama's pandemic plan of action can be found at: https://assets. documentcloud.org/documents/6819268/Pandemic-Playbook.pdf

266 NHS app fails to offer stay at home payments fairly: www.bbc.co.uk/news/ technology-54660237-

267 Sky News report: https://news.sky.com/story/coronavirus-only-9-of-britons-want-life-to-return-to-normal-once-lockdow-n-is-over-11974459

268 For many more of these stories, go to our 'coronavirus' tag on The Daily Alternative: www.thealternative.org.uk/dailyalternative/tag/coronavirus

269 Gladwell, M. (2000) *The Tipping Point*. New York: Little Brown.

270 Alasdair Gray, *The Scottish Review of Books*, 2013: www.scottishreviewofbooks. org/2013/03/early-days-of-a-better-nation/

271 Finger on the button is a reference to the fact that in every country that has nuclear weapons, the elected political leader is given the capability of launching them. To do so would cause the horrific death of innocent citizens in the country targeted and quite likely cause the horrific death of innumerable citizens in the home country as reprisals are triggered. Nuclear weapons are the pinnacle of a broken political system.

272 After Senosoenoto passed away in 1993 I gradually lost touch with Nichiren Shoshu Indonesia and now cannot trace those early pioneers. I only remembered Bhaktiar's name recently: I wonder if he is reading this?

273 While President Barack Obama was recognised as one of the first presidential candidates to successfully activate the grassroots in his campaign, he could not keep them connected and aligned after he was elected. It is often described as the biggest failure of his presidency, as the disconnect between the White House and the communities caused an alienation the Republican Party was able to exploit easily through Donald Trump's populist rhetoric: https://newrepublic.com/article/140245/obamas-lost-army-inside-fall-grassroots-machine

Acknowledgements

THIS BOOK has been a long time coming and covers the ground of my life to date. For that reason there are many, many people to thank, including some who have passed.

Thanks first to my son Connor for giving me a reason to push on and make a plan for the future. His own idealism and integrity – and skill in setting up the Nawtystep channel – shape my work and is a source of great confidence for me.

Thank you to my partner and co-initiator of The Alternative, Pat Kane, who has edited my writing for over a decade with love and grit, helping me to find a voice in the overly male political public space. Pat's own work as a singer and writer will always inspire me to go deeper and reach higher for the work of art: poiesis. Thanks too for bringing Grace and Ellie into our life as constant sources of joy.

Thanks to good friend and esteemed colleague Jonathan Rowson for inviting me to be part of the Perspectiva/Emerge playlist, as well as team. Not least for matching me with my editor, social innovator Minna Salami, who saw right through to my intentions and helped me deliver this book. To Tomas Bjorkman for his long-term encouragement and support. And to Ivo Juriaan Mensch who keeps the whole ship steady.

Thank you to my long-time mentors, starting with my Buddhist teachers (in order of encounter) Senosoenoto, Iwan Sastrowardojo, Daisaku Ikeda, Richard Causton and Kazuo Fujii, who taught me the daily arts of the impossible. Thank you to the 'father of peace studies' Johan Galtung for shifting me into meta-perspectives with conflict transformation and peace journalism. To my Uncle, UN University Rector, Soedjatmoko for keeping me global, and to Joseph Nye who helped me understand the subtleties of soft power. To Jo Griffin and Ivan Tyrell for teaching me about emotional needs and capacity and why we dream. To Ken Wilber who gave me new language for the connectedness of our inner and outer worlds. Many thanks to advertising guru Sir Frank Lowe and all at Capital City Academy where I spent five rewarding years as school governor with Chair, Garth Crooks. And finally Uffe Elbæk founder of Kaospilot and co-founder of Danish political parties Alternativet and Independent Greens. I may never match Uffe's daring-do, but I'll keep trying. All men, calling for the women to stand strong. Encouraging me to be what they cannot be, that the world needs now.

Thank you fellow travellers on the Alternative path: those who know we have to stand outside the dominant system as attractors for the future. I've mentioned many in this book but do so again now for their comradeship, longevity, fun and moving times. Firstly, extra special thanks to Maria Dorthea Skov, without whom there would be no Alternative UK.

Then alphabetically: Ada Colau, Adah Parris, Andrea Harding, Andrew Morrice, Ali Fisher, Alex Evans, Alistair Langer, Alvin Carpio, Amisha Ghadiali, Anairda, Andy Goldring, Andy Paice, Annabelle Macfadyen,

Annabelle McGoldrick, Anna Katharina Schaffner, Anthea Lawson, Anton Chernikov, Antonio Pisano, Ash Ghadiali, Beck Slama, Bettina Geiken, Birgitta Jonsdottir, Brian Frandsen, Brett Warshawsky, Carolina De Oliveira, Carsten Berg, Cat Tully, Dan Nixon, Daniel Görtz, Danii Evans, David Heinemann, Dave Carey, David Wood, Deepa Patel, Ed Saperia, Ed Whitelaw, Eduard Muller, Elizabeth Slade, Elke Esders, Elke Fein, Emil Ejner Friis, Erica Cerri, Eva Schonfeld, Fanny Norlin, Frances Foley, Greg Frey, Hannah Close, Hanno Burmester, Harald Schellander, Hilary Cottam, Hilary Kolinsky, Ian Kendrick, Ido Aharoni, Ilana Butler, Immy Kaur, Indy Johar, Isabel Carlisle, Ivan March, Jake Lynch, Jamie Bristow, Jamie Kelsey-Fry, Jasper Kenter, Jay Tompt, Jeremy Lent, Jonny Will Chambers, Julia Purcell, Julianne Muller, Justin Kenrick, Kai Brand-Jacobsen, Karen Downes, Karen O'Brien, Katherine Trebeck, Kim Gould, Klara Sucher, Klina Jordan, Kyle Reeves, Lachie Gordon, Lesley Adams, Liam Kavanagh, Liz Barry, Liz Ferguson, Luke Robert Mason, Lynne Franks, Madeleine Bunting, Marc Winn, Mark Brayne, Margaret Rose-Goddard, Mark Hessullund-Beanland, Mags Mulowska, Mary Valiakis, Matt Bell, Matthew Green, Matthew Kalman, Meenaskhi Gupta, Melissa Benn, Michael Brookes, Michael Matania, Michael Wernstedt, Mike Riddell, Mike Thomas, Monica Sharma, Nathaniel Whitestone, Neal Lawson, Niko Grunfeld, Oliver Riel, Oli Sylvester Bradley, Pam Barrett, Patrick Chalmers, Paul Thistlewaite, Pete Barden, Peter Jones, Peter Jenkinson, Pete Lawrence, Peter Macfadyen, Phil Teer, Phoebe Tickell, Pippa Evans, Priscilla Moura, Rasmus Nordqvist, Rachel Cottam, Richard Cauldrey, Richard Bartlett, Rob Hopkins, Romy Kramer, Ronan Harrington, Rosamonde Birch, Rosa Zubizarreta, Rosie Bell, Sam Weller, Sandra Waddock, Sanna Radelius, Sara Zaltash, Scilla Elworthy, Shelagh Wright, Skeena Rathor, Simon Anholt, Steffen Stauber, Stephane Kolinsky, Stephen Reid, Steve Waddell, Tarn Rodgers, Terry Patten, Tess Wilmot, Titilola McDowell, Toby Chaudhuri, Tom Atlee, Tom Chatfield, Vinay Gupta, Violeta Bulc, Will Franks, Zoe Svendsen.

Thanks to my close friends who do the 'human revolution' and believe with me that a beautiful future is possible: you know who you are. Special mention to Iain Whitmore for being my first husband, beautiful Father to Connor and for bringing Chris, Riley and Joni into our lives. To my warrior family Sabra, Yogi, Teohna, Sunil, Faynia, Kai and all the Tanna-

Williams. To my long-haul interlocutors Ali Gibson, Chantal Vouillemin, Eddy Canfor-Dumas, Tony Morris, Marina Cantacuzino MBE, Jamie Cresswell, Shona Main, Michelle and Michel Alkhouri-Carlile, Ian Pearce, Maria Onoufriou, Corinne Simcock, Jenny Demitri, Marco Magrini, Andreas Terhoeven and Johan Nordqvist. To Sue Rae for teaching me to hold my nerve over the years.

To Liz Kovar, Clare Manuel, Ruth Worontzak (and your beautiful families) for being inspirational women while growing our boys together.

Finally and fundamentally, Thank You to my Father, Raden Thomas Adnan and Mother, Mieke Verhoef, whose remarkable lives have never stopped pushing me onwards. To my Dutch family who birthed me and my Indonesian family – especially Tante Loekie – who took care of me during my steepest development curves. To my deceased brother Jaap, whose early death propelled me into a life of existential creativity. To my sisters Annetje Craig, Michelle Lowe, Maerisna, and also John Hole, unwitting guardian angels, who shaped my early self and continue to challenge me every step of the way to be more than I believe I can be.

I hope you all like this book – I wrote it through you.

Index

2 per cent 6, 19, 37, 83, 140, 189
15-M movement 117, 220. *See also Barcelona; Podemos*
  municipalism 160, 164, 202, 226
#MeToo 121

A

Ada 1–3, 18, 38, 122, 170, 197–9, 201–2, 204, 207
Ada Colau 104, 214. *See also feminisation of politics; Barcelona*
addiction 15, 61–2, 93, 98, 106, 218. *See also consumerism*
Adidas 26. *See also soft power*
advertising 15, 35–6, 60, 98, 218. *See also creativity; Mad Men*
agency 4, 10–11, 14, 18, 20, 33, 38–9, 41–2, 44, 47, 49, 57, 65, 68–9, 74–5, 80,
        82, 84, 90, 100, 110, 115, 119, 123–4, 126–8, 133, 135, 140, 142–3,
        148–51, 154, 168–70, 172–4, 177, 179, 181, 186–8, 192–3, 197–204, 223
  collective agency 83, 105, 126, 173, 201, 203

human agency 4, 14, 38, 69, 135
individual agency 124
personal agency 201
Alter Ego 16, 77, 215, 219
Alternativet 5–6, 18, 88, 130, 135, 137–41, 143, 163, 174, 224, 227. *See also Uffe Elbæk*
  Denmark 5–6, 18, 88, 135, 137–9, 143, 224
Alternative UK, The 5, 17, 40, 53–4, 126, 130, 139, 140, 142, 152, 172, 175, 192, 215–16, 219–21, 223
  Daily Alternative, The 19, 54, 75, 140, 169, 173, 175, 190, 193, 216, 218, 223, 225, 230
American Dream 13, 22, 92, 115, 134. *See also Hollywood; narrative; soft power; storytelling*
anarchism 158
  buddhist anarchist 199
  Havel, Václav 162–3, 226
  Ross, Carne 158
Anholt, Simon 18, 215
Anthropocene 112
AQAL (all quadrants all levels) 66. *See also Ken Wilber; Spiral Dynamics; Integral Philosophy*
Arab Spring 25, 88
architecture 7, 20, 32, 116, 122–3, 134
Ardern, Jacinda 112, 192
artificial intelligence 43, 95
Ashoka, Skoll Foundation 175
attention 2, 9–13, 25, 27, 29, 35, 37, 49, 50, 54, 57–60, 75, 90, 92, 97, 106–7, 109–11, 120, 138, 140, 143, 156, 165, 175, 184, 193, 197, 206, 218, 224, 228
attraction 13, 34, 48, 87, 98, 110, 153. *See also soft power*
autonomy 10, 17, 38, 44, 57–8, 71, 77, 82, 102, 114, 121, 128, 143, 151–2, 158–60, 166, 199. *See also emotional need; freedom*
Avaaz 26, 119, 222. *See also governance, petition*
ayahuasca (plant medecine) 75

B

BAME (Black, Asian and Minority Ethnic) 27
Barcelona 77, 104, 164, 214, 223
Barrett, Pam 144
Bartlett, Richard 182, 227
Bauwens, Michel 223. *See also P2P*
B-corps 77, 147, 174. *See also Fourth sector*
Beck, Don 64–6. *See also Spiral Dynamics*
becoming 4, 6, 8, 13, 25, 28, 43, 60, 71–2, 74, 82, 84–5, 105–6, 110, 119, 126, 129, 177, 194, 196, 200–1, 209, 229
Before&Now app 31, 228

behaviour 10, 13, 15, 25, 28, 34, 36, 56, 64, 68, 71, 77, 86, 93, 128–9, 133, 138, 166, 194. *See also nudge*
  behavioural science 53, 108
belief 48, 56, 71–2, 93, 124, 198–9
  belief system 71–72, 93, 124, 198–9
  self-belief 93, 199
Bellagio 174
belonging 15, 44, 60, 63, 71, 82, 143, 149, 156, 206
Big Society 171, 179, 227
Bildung 189, 203, 230. *See also Perspectiva*
bio-psycho-social-spiritual 16, 34, 86, 100, 131, 149
Bioregional Learning Centre 179
Birmingham 143, 154, 200
Bjorkman, Tomas 215, 230
Black Lives Matter 23, 30, 87, 206
Blair, Tony 12
  New Labour 12, 171
Bodhisattvas 51, 72, 145. *See also Buddhism*
boiling frogs 199
Bollier, David 224
Bounce Beyond 176–7, 179
boundaries 123, 177, 181
Bradbrook, Gail 75, 219, 226
Brexit 37–8, 58, 87, 121, 125, 140, 143, 159, 167, 200, 227
  Brexit Referendum 6, 36, 139
  Leave campaign 6, 36–7, 58, 87, 159, 168
  referendum 5, 58
Bristow, Jamie 219, 228
Buckfastleigh 144
Buckminster Fuller 42, 140, 149
Buddhism 2, 4, 49, 50, 71–2, 129, 217. *See also bodhisattva; Nichiren Shoshu Indonesia; Soka Gakkai International*
  Buddhahood 51
  Socially engaged 50
Build Back Better (#buildbackbetter) 176
Burning Man 76–7, 182, 219, 229
  Burners 76
  existential challenge of 76

C

Cambridge Analytica 36
Cameron, David 171
CANs (Citizen Action Networks) 19, 20, 40, 42–3, 127, 140–1, 145–9, 152–4, 161, 163–4, 182, 194, 198, 200, 203–5, 210, 225, 227, 229. *See also Transition Towns*
  Community Agency Networks 19, 140, 203

Carlisle, Isabel 179

Catalyst 2030 175

Causton, Richard 7, 214

chanting 3, 199, 202

Chickenshed Theatre 18, 183, 214, 229

circular 86, 206, 215
  circular economy 176, 228

citizen(s) 5, 16, 33, 40, 42–3, 60, 75, 83, 100–1, 104, 119–20, 124–5, 127, 133, 135, 142, 150, 152, 157–8, 160–1, 163, 169, 189, 192, 200, 204–5, 216–17, 220, 223, 225–6, 228, 230

Citizen Action Networks. *See CANs*

Citizens' Assembly 163, 225–6

Civic Square 154, 225

class 25, 32, 37, 68, 144, 166

Cleveland 39, 113, 200, 216
  community wealth building 39, 40, 200, 216

collaboration 19, 45, 128, 132, 145, 166, 174, 203, 229
  Co-labs 145, 152
  collaboratory 145, 148, 200

colonialism 84

commons 19, 39, 43, 85, 120, 172, 189, 203, 215–16, 223
  Commons model 40
  global commons 19, 43, 120

Compass 5–6, 16, 135, 213

Conflict and Peace Forums 8, 12, 72

conflict transformation 8, 14, 16

connection 6, 18, 24, 59, 60, 72, 75, 77–8, 83, 102, 110, 128, 133, 165, 169, 197, 202

consciousness 30, 50, 65, 81, 115

constitutes 91, 127, 133, 142, 150, 163

consumer(s) 22, 36, 60, 75, 98, 100, 102, 162
  consumerism 6, 15, 86, 99, 168, 218. *See also CANs*

container 84, 141–2, 146, 182, 199, 226

control 6, 10–11, 15, 20, 28, 32, 36, 38, 47, 57–8, 72, 75, 82, 85, 116, 124–5, 129, 142, 158–9, 165, 186–7, 189, 216, 222, 230
  losing control 129
  take back control 36, 58, 90, 152

Corbett, Sarah 183

Corbyn, Jeremy 16

cosmolocal 5, 19, 39, 43, 45, 116, 120, 133, 141, 145, 151, 154, 164, 190, 223, 225, 227
  Cosmolocalism 167, 172, 223

Costa Rica 169, 178–9, 227–8

Cottam, Hilary 73, 101–11, 132, 221–2. *See also relational welfare*
  Participle 101, 111

CounterCoin 146, 169, 225, 227

Covid 4, 22, 26, 28, 30, 37, 39, 42, 78, 100, 102, 112, 132–3, 153, 175–6, 190, 202, 206, 216–17, 219, 221–2, 225, 228
  pandemic 22, 28, 29, 78, 102, 114, 123, 132, 140, 153, 175, 190–1, 193, 201–2, 216, 230
Cox, Jo 5, 6, 139
Craftivism 183
  Corbett, Sarah 183
creativity 5, 9, 18, 120, 126–7, 131, 137, 153, 165, 169, 181, 190, 227
crisis 4, 18, 22, 29, 30, 37, 47, 56, 75, 78, 105, 112, 123, 131–2, 138, 140, 177, 188, 191, 215, 223
  climate crisis 22, 140, 188, 215
  triple crises 47, 190
cryptocurrency 217
culture 6, 12, 34, 38, 42–43, 48, 54, 64, 66, 72, 77, 80–81, 83, 87–88, 106–8, 125, 129, 136, 138–9, 143, 146–7, 150–2, 154, 157, 161, 165, 168, 170–1, 174, 179, 189, 202, 214, 216, 223, 225, 229
Cummings, Dominic 58, 218

D

Daily Alternative. *See Alternative UK*
Davis, Erik 74, 76, 86, 218–19
  techgnosis 76
  the S word 74
death 22, 29, 30, 70–1, 175, 191, 196, 216, 230
democracy 13, 20, 30, 32, 43, 58, 88, 134, 139, 146, 157, 160–1, 164, 169, 183, 198, 204, 217, 220, 223
  Democracy movements 16, 18, 40, 101, 118, 127, 157–8, 161, 229
  democratic 43, 139, 158, 164, 173, 204, 224–5
design 12, 17, 40, 54, 56, 59, 86–7, 102, 111, 120, 131, 153, 164, 176, 179, 223
desire 15, 18, 38–9, 45, 58, 76, 86, 151, 159, 182, 201
development 9, 16, 38, 44, 50, 64–5, 67–9, 76, 84, 86, 99, 104, 106, 110–11, 118, 121–2, 129, 142, 149, 151, 153, 160, 163, 169–70, 175, 178, 188–90, 199, 203, 228–9
  developmental literacy 69
Devon 154, 179, 225, 227
  Plymouth 144, 154, 174, 200, 225, 228
  South Devon 179
digital 13, 34, 43, 60, 88, 95, 165, 169, 173, 189, 192, 202, 217, 227, 230
diversity 12, 69, 80–2, 115, 134, 152, 160, 202, 224–5
division 42, 52, 75, 77, 83, 98, 152, 156, 167–8, 170
Dodd, Philip 73
Doughnut Economics 164. *See also Kate Raworth*
  Doughnut economy 177, 228
Downes, Karen 179, 228
Downing Street Project 12, 214
dreaming 14, 59, 117, 202, 218. *See also imagination; soft power*

dreaming brain 14, 59, 218
Duffy, Stella 183, 229. *See also Fun Palaces*

E

earth 45, 49, 84, 98, 114–16, 119, 127–8, 217, 224
economy 19, 24, 26, 33, 36–40, 53, 57, 60, 75, 84, 98–101, 107–8, 111, 116, 125,
      132, 147, 167–70, 174–8, 182, 188, 203–4, 215, 217, 220, 227–9. *See
      also Doughnut Economics*
  growth economy 26, 36, 53, 56, 60, 84, 98, 100, 168, 188
  next economies 165, 167, 176–8, 205
  well-being economy 40, 132, 176, 228
Elbæk, Uffe 5, 18, 135, 147, 174, 224, 227
electoral system 83
elephant, blind men and the 52, 172, 177
emotions 15, 50, 59, 82, 87, 91, 120–1, 142, 196, 199, 220
  emotional labour 52, 103, 108, 111
  emotional literacy 11, 69, 110
  emotional needs 57
Enspiral Networks 182, 227, 229
entrepreneur(s) 5, 48, 215
  social entrepreneurs/entrepreneurship 150, 153, 159, 169
environmental breakdown 22, 124
Europe 33, 87–8, 125, 135, 159, 189, 191
  European Union 5, 36, 121
Evans, Danii 18
existential 48, 75–7, 120, 131, 173
Extinction Rebellion (XR) 23, 27, 56, 75, 87, 153, 161, 215, 219, 226–7
  Future Democracy Hub 127, 161

F

Facebook 13, 34–6, 58, 60, 127, 134, 142, 165, 198, 216, 224
failure 14, 56, 79, 124, 141, 188, 191, 222, 226, 230
Farage, Nigel 38, 87, 220
feel 20, 40, 41, 48, 52, 55, 65, 68, 73, 79, 91, 124, 131, 143, 148, 150, 154–5,
      172–3, 179–80, 195–6. *See also ontologies*
  feeling 55, 57, 65, 75, 77–8, 80, 82, 91, 106, 122, 138, 141, 196
  sensibility 76, 84, 110, 150, 179, 194
feminine 11, 16, 105–12, 150, 179, 204, 209, 221–2
  conscious feminine 106–12
  female 7, 107–8, 191
  feminisation 12, 103–4, 152, 214, 221
  feminist 11, 25, 106, 139, 183
feminisation of politics 12, 104, 214, 221
festival(s) 5, 17–18, 76, 126, 133, 147, 151, 181–2, 203, 229
first past the post 6, 32, 83
Flatpack Democracy 16, 18, 40, 101, 118, 127, 157–8, 161, 217, 223, 229

flourishing 9, 17, 22, 40, 44, 49, 107, 110, 132, 134, 149, 152, 176, 189, 202–3, 205
Floyd, George 29, 30, 70
Foley, Frances 213
fourth sector 147, 174, 204, 228
fractal 18, 41, 42, 44, 117–9, 122, 127–9, 149, 154, 163, 174, 179, 184, 194, 203–4, 217
  fractal growth 119
fragmentation 36–7, 179
freedom 13, 32, 56, 58, 62, 70, 105, 121, 155–6, 158–9, 176, 218
Frei Grønne (Independent Greens) 139, 141, 224
friendly 44, 100, 150, 152, 158
  Friendly, The 145, 148
Fun Palaces 183, 229
Future Leeds 20
futurism 44, 173

G

Galtung, Johan 8, 9, 150, 214
gaming 25, 34–5
Gandhi 186–7
gender 11–12, 69, 104, 109, 166, 221, 225
geopolitics 116
  geopolitical 14, 87
Germany 29, 32–3, 112, 191, 224
Gladwell, Malcolm 193, 230
global 4–5, 7–9, 11, 16, 19, 22–32, 37, 39, 43, 47, 50, 56, 60, 70, 76, 84, 88, 94, 98, 104, 109, 115, 117, 119–21, 123–4, 126–8, 132–4, 136, 146, 149, 151, 169, 170, 172, 174–6, 178, 189, 190, 201–7, 215–16, 219, 222–3, 227–9
GlobalEyes 183, 229
globe 23, 27–8, 93–4, 114–5, 117, 119–21, 123, 125, 127, 148, 169, 174, 176, 202, 216, 229
glocal 39, 116. *See also cosmolocal*
Good Country Index, The 16, 215
  good country 18
Goodwin, Brian 73
Goonj 169. *See also social entrepreneur*
Gordon, Lachie 182
governance 19, 32, 43–4, 66, 125–6, 128, 133–4, 146–7, 149, 151, 158, 160, 163, 178, 197, 205, 216, 223, 226
  global governance 19, 126, 128, 146, 205
green 3, 37, 65, 75, 81–2, 88, 135, 137, 139, 162, 169, 176. *See also Spiral Dynamics*
Green Heart of Kenya 182, 229
Green Party 135, 137, 140
Griffin, Joe 57, 59, 218
growth economy 26, 36, 53, 56, 60, 84, 98, 100, 168, 188

relentless growth 75

H

hack(s) 101, 114
hard power 24, 77, 87, 93, 108–9, 115, 134, 165, 202
Harrington, Ronan 215
Hennig, Brett 158
hierarchy 57, 63, 65, 81, 93
hijack 6, 134, 164, 220
Hollywood 13, 93, 95, 115. *See also soft power*
homo economicus 16, 53, 64, 100
Hong Kong 118, 125, 151
Hopkins, Rob 116, 222, 227. *See also Transition Towns*
  From What Is to What If 116
Human Givens 14, 15, 57, 59, 62–3, 90, 158, 218. *See also emotional needs; Ivan Tyrell; Joe Griffin*
  Williams, Pat 90, 220
humanity 30, 49, 110, 179, 197, 202, 216, 228
human revolution 7, 20, 50, 207
hunter-gatherer 108

I

illusion 47, 56, 98, 134, 159
imagination 38, 59, 87, 110, 116, 124, 131, 161, 173, 185–6, 203. *See also dreaming brain, Human Givens, Rob Hopkins*
immersion 4, 151
immune 90, 98, 139
independence 65, 68, 77, 158–60
Independence parties 7, 37–8, 160
independent 39, 40, 111, 139, 150, 159–60, 181, 193, 204, 219, 223, 224–5, 227
India 32, 121, 154, 164, 169, 201, 225, 227
individual(s) 16, 33, 38, 44, 47, 49, 66, 68, 75, 82, 88, 91–2, 100, 104, 115–16, 124, 126, 156, 159–60, 165, 190, 192–3, 199,, 204 218, 221–2
  Individualists 49
Indonesia 1–4, 13, 72, 199, 213, 230
Instagram 35, 58, 60
Institute of Contemporary Arts (ICA) 73–4, 76
instrumentalisation 52, 144
Integral 10, 64, 66–7, 104, 214, 219, 221. *See also AQAL; Ken Wilber; Spiral Dynamics*
integrity 27, 41, 56, 59, 67, 73, 94, 163, 187
internal 7, 13, 16, 43, 48, 52, 56, 64, 66, 69, 74–5, 91, 99, 105, 128, 166, 179, 197, 201, 224
International Futures Forum 170. *See also Three Horizons*
internet 5–6, 13, 24–6, 33, 35–6, 76, 85–6, 94, 109, 114–7, 165, 190, 197
intimacy/intimate 57, 78, 105, 110, 181, 183. *See also emotional needs; social media; Zoom*

IPCC (UN Intergovernmental Panel on Climate Change) 33, 88, 101, 215
'Is the Party Over?' 6, 135
I–We–World 5, 16–17, 49, 52, 54, 95, 114, 122, 149, 165, 169, 201, 224

J

Johar, Indy 18, 215
Johnson, Boris 100, 221, 223, 226
Jonsdottir, Birgitta 220

K

Kalman, Matthew 10. *See also Mezey-Kalman*
Kane, Pat 5, 7, 18, 53, 214, 218, 229. *See also The Alternative UK; The Play Ethic;*
        Scottish Independence
  Hue and Cry 17, 229
Kaospilot 135–6, 224
Kolinsky, Stephan 173. *See also relational systems*
Korzybski, Alfred 67

L

Laloux, Frederik 68, 222
Lawson, Neal 16, 213–14
learning clubs 42, 146, 151, 189, 204, 229
Left, The 6, 7, 36–7, 44, 58, 80, 138, 155–6, 158, 209
  Left versus Right 6
legacy 52, 60, 139, 229
lenses 50, 66
LGBT 136
literacy 11, 69, 85, 110
  developmental literacy 69
  emotional literacy 11, 69, 110
livelihood 164
local 1, 7, 18–20, 24, 29, 39–40, 42–44, 50, 81, 88, 102, 108, 111, 114, 116–21,
        127, 142–3, 145, 149–51, 153, 157, 161, 167–71, 178–9, 182, 190, 192,
        204–5, 216–17, 221–3, 225–9. *See also glocal; cosmolocalism*
  localism 120, 160, 223
London Integral Circle 10, 67

M

Macfadyen, Peter and Annabelle 18, 157, 217
Mad Men 60, 218
magic/magical 3, 5, 13, 20, 108, 112, 134, 148, 198, 230
manipulation 15, 20, 36, 120, 143. *See also nudge; technology*
map 15–16, 65, 67–8, 127, 168, 219. *See also territory*
Martin, Trayvon 30
masculine 11, 106–10, 112, 150, 209
  bringing up a boy 11

male 7, 81, 93, 104, 109, 222
masculinity 11, 108, 215
Maslow, Abraham 57, 63, 64
  hierarchy of needs 57, 63
material 24, 34, 50, 63–4, 68, 73, 77, 92, 100, 106, 120, 127, 159, 170, 177, 183,
      188. *See also homo economicus; Maslow's hierarchy of needs*
  non-material 51, 75
McDonald's 26
meaning and purpose 15, 57, 60, 87, 169, 214. *See also Human Givens*
mental health 18, 22, 64, 132, 175. *See also masculine; suicide*
meta-
  meta-ethical 230
  meta-gatherings 125
  meta-modern 215
  meta-story 90
Mezey-Kalman, Matthew 67. *See also Matthew Kalman*
microsolidarities 182, 204, 229
Miliband, David 16
military complex 84
mindfulness 74–5, 202, 219, 228
mobilisations 125
Momentum 16
Monbiot, George 89, 220
mother 11, 29, 70–1, 105, 183, 197
  bringing up a boy 11
movement(s) 4, 7, 9–11, 16, 18, 23, 25–7, 30–1, 33, 37–9, 50, 72, 74, 77, 88–9,
      104, 106, 117, 119, 121, 124–7, 132, 136, 141, 153–4, 160–2, 165, 199,
      206, 214, 217, 220, 223, 225–6. *See also Occupy; Momentum; Transition Towns;
      Trust the People*
Muller, Eduard 178, 179. *See also Bounce Beyond; Costa Rica*
  biodiversity 29, 128, 169, 178, 202, 224
multicultural(ism) 81–2, 125
mutual 9, 32, 42, 60, 65, 81, 101, 102, 111, 192, 221, 227
  mutual aid 42, 102, 192,153, 217, 221, 225
  mutual credit 169, 227
  mutual tolerance 81
myth(s)/mythical 28, 92, 96

N

narrative(s) 6, 13, 27, 47, 87, 92–3, 101, 105, 115, 117, 121, 140, 152, 154, 164–5,
      170, 200–1, 215, 218
NATO 14, 214
Neighborocracy 121, 154, 164, 200, 223, 225. *See also CANs; India*
neighbourhood(s) 7, 42, 102, 192, 203–4 210, 221, 223, 225
neoliberal 86
NESTA (National Endowment for Media, Technology and the Arts) 17, 73

network(s) 8, 12–13, 16–17, 19–20, 24, 31–2, 35, 38, 40, 42–3, 49, 64, 94, 102,
110, 116–7, 121, 125–8, 133, 140, 145–9, 151, 153, 161, 175, 182, 192,
194, 203, 210, 215–6, 221, 223, 225, 227–9
neurological 91
New Zealand 29, 112, 192
NGO(s) 124, 147, 174
Nichiren Shoshu Indonesia 3, 213, 230. *See also Buddhism*
Noisily Festival 182, 229
non-state actor(s) 87, 94
nudge 10, 53, 194
Nye, Joe 13–14, 87, 93–4, 220

O

O'Brien, Professor Karen (*You Matter More Than You Think*) 41, 51, 194, 217
Occupy 26, 88, 93, 117, 161, 220, 226
ontology(ies)/ontological 68–9, 77, 122, 138, 141, 150, 204, 225
operating system(s) 16, 54, 64
Ostrom, Elinor 40, 152, 217

P

P2P (peer-to-peer) 38, 149, 216, 223. *See also commons; cosmolocal; Michel Bauwens;
David Bollier*
parallel polis/parallel power 162–3
participation 5, 8, 16, 33, 38, 44, 104, 127, 151–2, 161, 169, 204, 214, 217, 220,
224
  participatory 40, 101, 157, 171, 205, 225
  participatory budgeting 40, 157, 171
Participatory Cities 39, 152, 153, 217
patterns 12, 40–1, 44, 91–2, 117–19, 121, 128–9, 150, 170, 177, 194, 196, 217
  pattern matches 170
  pattern of relationships 18, 40, 127–8, 174
Peace Journalism 8, 72
people power 78, 87, 93, 141, 154, 162–3, 193, 202
People's Assemblies 40, 88, 161, 220, 226
People's Parliament 44, 164–5
Permaculture 38, 41, 216–17
personal 4, 11, 22, 31–2, 37, 42, 49, 52, 56, 58, 68, 74–5, 77, 97, 111, 115–16,
123–4, 126, 129, 160, 165–6, 169, 171, 188–90, 192–3, 201–3, 215, 229
Perspectiva 16, 18, 74, 215, 219, 230
petition 26, 119, 126, 133
planet 4–5, 15, 17–18, 23, 26–7, 39, 40–1, 43–5, 49, 53–4, 75, 77, 82, 88, 109–10,
112–16, 123, 125–8, 134, 137, 150, 152, 169, 176–7, 186, 192–3, 197,
202, 205, 208–9, 223–25
platform(s) 5–6, 13, 18, 34, 39, 44–5, 119, 126, 142, 146–7, 174, 179, 181, 204,
215–16, 219, 227
Play Ethic, The 17–18, 218

Plymouth 144, 154, 174, 200, 225, 228
poiesis 12
pol.is 43, 146, 164. *See also Pirate Party; Audrey Tang*
political parties
  Alternativet 5, 6, 18, 88, 130, 135, 137–41, 143, 163, 174, 224, 227
  Conservative Party 87, 157
  Five Star 88, 117, 163
  Labour Party 5, 12, 19, 58, 157, 171, 215, 227–9
  Pirate Party 88, 117, 220
  Podemos 88, 117, 163, 220
  UKIP (UK Independence Party) 38, 87
politics 4–6, 10, 12–13, 16–18, 20, 28, 32, 37–8, 42, 44–6, 49, 52–3, 58, 62–4,
        67–9, 75, 81, 83–4, 86, 93, 104, 106, 110, 114, 117, 119, 131, 133–5, 138,
        140, 143, 145, 148, 152, 154–6, 163–6, 170, 172, 180–1, 184, 188, 198,
        204, 214, 218–19, 221, 226, 228
populism 120, 198, 205
power 2, 4, 6–7, 12–18, 20, 23–4, 27, 32–3, 35–6, 44, 46–8, 52, 56, 67, 69–70,
        77–8, 81, 83, 85–90, 92–4, 105, 107–10, 114–19, 121, 124–5, 131, 134,
        137–8, 140–1, 147, 150–1, 153–4, 160–5, 170, 180, 186–7, 189, 192–3,
        195–6, 198, 202, 204, 206, 213, 217, 221, 225–6, 229. *See also hard power;
        people power; soft power*
  powerless/powerlessness 18, 23, 47, 54, 68, 120, 123, 131,154, 162, 169, 189,
        197
Preston Model 39–40, 216
proportional 32, 39, 137–8, 205, 213
  PR (proportional representation) 138
protest 125, 141, 161, 214, 220. *See also Extinction Rebellion; Occupy*
psyche 159
psychology 15, 52, 60, 160
  cognitive psychology 14, 36, 68, 75
psycho-social therapy 14, 57
public space 30, 38, 52, 75, 104–5, 107–12, 124, 133, 138, 165, 175, 179, 183,
        204, 221
purpose 15, 38, 44–5, 56–7, 60, 72, 82, 87, 142, 148, 160, 169, 214

Q

quantum 41, 51, 150, 193, 194, 209, 217
  quantum social change 193–4

R

radical animals 53
Radical Help 111
Raworth, Kate 164, 177. *See also Doughnut Economics*
Real Ideas Organisation 174, 228
rebel 97
reclamation of the mind 75

reconnection 5, 176
referendum 5–6, 36, 58, 139, 163
  Referendum 6
RegenA 115, 208, 222. *See also Greta Thunberg; School Strikes*
regenerative 12, 75, 98, 178, 206
  Regenerative economy 177, 228
reimagining 4, 8, 14, 64, 217
  Reimagining Social Work 64
relational 27, 42–4, 101, 110–11, 128, 132, 145, 150, 154, 173, 182, 202, 221, 228
  relational structures 110
  relational systems 173, 228
  relational welfare 42, 101, 111, 132
relationship(s) 7, 9, 12–15, 18–19, 31, 39–40, 42, 48, 51, 64, 68, 72, 74–7, 83,
        86–7, 97–8, 101, 105–7, 111, 115, 117, 120–2, 127–9, 134, 140–2, 146,
        149–51, 153, 157–8, 163, 169–72, 174, 177, 186–7, 190, 192, 194, 198–9,
        201–5, 217–18, 222, 224
resilience 16, 39, 86, 102, 204
response-ability 9, 40, 61, 75, 83, 188–9, 207
revolution 4, 7, 17, 20, 50, 88, 95, 117–18, 133, 136, 162, 207, 217, 220–1
  human revolution 7, 20, 50, 207
  personal revolution 4
  social revolution 4
Riddell, Mike 225, 227
Right, The 6, 36–7, 47, 81, 138, 155–6, 158, 180, 209
Rojava 158
Ross, Carne 158. *See also anarchism*
Roth, Laura 104
Rowson, Jonathan 18, 74, 215
Russian doll 62, 65, 82

S

sabotage(d) 86, 89, 132, 205
Sastrowardojo, Iwan 71
satyagraha 187. *See also Gandhi*
scaffolding 126
scaling 116–17, 127–8. *See also fractal growth*
School Strikes 23, 87. *See also Greta Thunberg*
science fiction 95
  Black Panther 95, 221
Scottish Independence 37
second tier 67, 81. *See also Spiral Dynamics*
self-conscious 30
self-destruction 55, 61, 109, 124, 176
Senosoenoto 2, 71, 199, 230
serendipity 119
  George Harrison plagiarism 118

integral leadership 119
radio, inventing 118, 222
Shea-Bird, Kate 104
SIMPOL 126, 223
singularity 76
social 2–5, 7, 14, 16, 22–3, 25–7, 31–8, 41–2, 47, 51, 57–60, 63–4, 75, 77, 82, 84,
    86, 90, 94, 97–8, 100–2, 108, 110–11, 116, 119, 121, 123, 125–6, 128,
    131, 133, 135–6, 143, 145, 147, 149–53, 159, 162, 166, 169, 172, 174–7,
    182–3, 188–90, 193–4, 200–5, 213–15, 217–18, 221, 223, 225–9
  social brains 59
  Socialist(s) 49, 80, 84, 162, 224
social enterprise(s) 116, 151, 174, 200, 228
social media 25–7, 31, 34, 58, 63, 86, 90, 94, 110, 119, 126, 133, 176, 189, 202,
    223. See also Facebook; Instagram; Twitter
sociocracy 164
socio-politics(al) 16, 19, 26, 32, 36, 44, 67, 75–6, 143–4, 150, 155, 162–3, 165,
    170, 182–3, 198, 204, 214, 218, 229
soft power 4, 13–6, 27, 87, 93, 94, 110, 115, 119, 134, 153, 165, 202, 229
  Soft Power Network 14
Soka Gakkai International (SGI) 7, 72, 213. See also Buddhism
solutions-based journalism 16
son 11, 14, 16, 113
sonder 20
sovereignty 43, 75, 182, 193
Spiral Dynamics 64, 66, 162, 219. See also AQAL; Don Beck; Integral Philosophy; Ken
    Wilber
  first tier 80, 83, 115
  second tier 67, 81
  teal 10, 81, 82, 163
spirituality 51, 71–4, 183, 218
status 11, 15, 57–8, 90, 98, 108. See also addiction; consumer; Human Givens
Stoke 154, 169, 200, 227. See also CounterCoin; Mike Riddell
story(ies) 2–5, 11, 13–14, 19–20, 22–3, 26, 32, 38, 41, 47–50, 55, 57, 79, 84,
    87–95, 97, 101, 109, 116, 119, 120, 130, 134, 147, 150, 154, 165, 170,
    172, 176, 179, 187–8, 193, 197, 199, 200, 202–3, 205–8, 215, 220, 230.
    See also George Monbiot; narrative; soft power; Pat Williams
  storytelling 3, 13, 94, 115, 133, 220
structure 6, 7, 65, 121, 126, 138, 146–7, 171–2, 226
suicide 106, 109, 125. See also masculine; mental health
system(s) 6–7, 9, 15–20, 26–8, 32–3, 37, 39, 41–2, 44–5, 47, 52–4, 56, 59, 64,
    71–2, 74–7, 82–6, 88, 92–3, 95, 100–1, 111, 114, 118, 120–2, 124–9,
    132–4, 136—40, 146–7, 149–52, 154, 161–5, 169,–70, 172–9, 182–4,
    187, 190, 192, 194, 197–200, 203–5, 216, 218, 222, 225–30

T

take back control 36, 58, 90, 152. See also Brexit, Leave campaign; reclamation of the mind

Tang, Audrey 43, 217
  pol.is 43, 146, 164
  Taiwan 43, 88, 112, 125, 169, 192, 217
teal 10, 81–2, 163. *See also Integral; Frederik Laloux; Spiral Dynamics*
technology 17, 24, 42, 48, 76, 86, 121, 146, 165, 173, 189, 192, 197–8, 201–2,
        205, 210. *See also digital; internal, artificial intelligence; techgnosis*
  automation 95, 184
Telawa 1–3, 5–7, 13, 20, 38, 45, 48, 134, 198, 200
territory 22, 57–8, 67–8, 78, 88, 130, 178, 219
tharn 83, 220
Three Horizons (3H) 170, 172, 177, 179, 227
three realms 201. *See also Buddhism; consciousness; I–We–World*
Thunberg, Greta 27, 56, 61, 87, 94, 187–8, 215
tolerance 82. *See also multiculturalism; mutual tolerance*
Tompt, Jay 169, 227
traction 138, 141, 143, 206, 226
transformation 2, 8, 14, 16, 32, 68, 77, 88, 106, 119, 150, 159, 165, 176–7, 186,
        206, 216, 225, 228
Transformations Forum 175–6, 228
Transition Towns 16, 18, 40, 75, 101, 116, 126, 143, 147, 215, 217, 223, 227. *See
        also CANs*
  rapid transition 120
trauma 14, 84, 204
Trebeck, Katherine 176
tribes 80, 92, 95, 115, 190
Trust the People 20, 154, 161, 225
truth-force 187
Tsai, Ing-wen 112, 192
Twin Towers 100, 119
Twitter 34, 58
Tyrell, Ivan 57, 59, 218

U

Unger, Roberto 184, 218, 229
United Nations (UN) 126, 175, 188, 215, 225
Universal Basic Income (UBI) 139, 189, 230
upgrading 42, 203. *See also Bildung*
US Presidents
  Clinton, Bill 13, 219
  Obama, Barack 191, 200, 230
  Trump, Donald 167, 191, 200, 205, 223, 230

V

values 9, 18, 24, 40–1, 66, 87, 95, 105–10, 112, 115–16, 119, 143, 145, 149, 153,
        156, 182, 202, 218, 224
  Alternativet six values 18, 137

virtual self 78

volunteer(s) 172, 174, 192

vulnerability 50, 85, 94, 132, 135, 217

W

Waddell, Steve 175–6. *See also Bounce Beyond; Transformations Forum*

waking up 3, 6, 15, 23–4, 28, 30–3, 102, 123, 125, 129, 133, 141, 152, 179, 199, 204, 228

well-being 37, 40, 47–8, 77, 91, 132–3, 140, 152–3, 158, 160, 217, 224. *See also mental health*

  Wellbeing Alliance (WEAll) 132

  well-being economy 40, 132

Westminster 37, 135, 140, 149, 171, 192, 228

  Westminster bubble 140

wholism 109

Widodo, Joko 200

Wilber, Ken 10, 66–8, 81–2, 214, 219. *See also AQAL; Integral Philosophy; Spiral Dynamics*

woke/wokeness 30, 45, 81, 82, 134, 205

women 11–12, 52, 60, 67–8, 84, 95, 103–10, 112, 121, 150, 161, 171, 176, 179, 185, 199, 204, 210, 214, 217, 221–2

Wood, David 18, 215, 228

world 3, 5, 7, 10–17, 20, 22, 24–5, 27–8, 32, 39–40, 46, 49–54, 59–61, 65–6, 70–1, 83, 85, 88, 94–5, 105–6, 108, 113–17, 119–25, 127–8, 132–3, 136,–7, 143, 149, 152, 159, 164–5, 167–9, 176–81, 183, 185, 187–90, 192, 194, 197–8, 201–5, 207, 209, 218–19, 223–4, 228–30

World Economic Forum 188

World Wide Web 13, 24–5, 124

X

XR 27–8, 75, 102, 127, 226. *See also Extinction Rebellion*

Y

young people 1, 3, 5, 25, 132, 135,–6, 160, 190, 228

Z

Zoom 29, 78, 80, 148, 219

Indra Adnan is co-initiator of The Alternative UK political platform which publishes The Daily Alternative, convenes new system actors and builds cosmolocal community agency networks (CANs). Indra is concurrently a psychosocial therapist, journalist and author. Through her work on international relations and soft power she has consulted to the World Economic Forum, the Indian and Danish governments, NATO, the Scottish Executive and the Institute of Contemporary Arts amongst others.

www.indraadnan.global
www.thealternative.org.uk

CPSIA information can be obtained
at www.ICGtesting.com
Printed in the USA
LVHW012105270222
712155LV00004B/263